RECONCILIATION

THE UBUNTU THEOLOGY OF DESMOND TUTU

MICHAEL BATTLE

THE PILGRIM PRESS
Cleveland, Ohio

The Pilgrim Press, Cleveland, Ohio 44115
© 1997 by Michael Battle

Biblical quotations are from the New Revised Standard Version of the Bible, ©
1989 by the Division of Christian Education of the National Council of the
Churches of Christ in the U.S.A., and are used by permission

Printed in the United States of America on acid-free paper

02   5   4   3   2

Library of Congress Cataloging-in-Publication Data

Battle, Michael Jesse, 1963–
     Reconciliation : the Ubuntu theology of Desmond Tutu / Michael Jesse
Battle.
        p.   cm.
     Includes bibliographical references and index.
     ISBN 0-8298-1158-3 (alk. paper)
     1. Tutu, Desmond—Contributions in Christian doctrine
reconciliation.   2. Reconciliation—Religious aspects—Christianity—
History of doctrines—20th century.   I. Title.
     BX5700.6.Z8T872   1997   97-8407
     230'.3'092—dc21   CIP

Unlike Westerners, Africans have a synthesizing mind set, as opposed to the occidental analytical one. That doesn't mean Africans are better or worse; it just says God is smart. Westerners have analysis. We have synthesis. Westerners have a very strong sense of individualism. We have a strong sense of community. Because Westerners have a strong sense of the value of the individual, they are able to take personal initiatives. It's not so easy, when you are a community-minded person, to go against the stream. . . . This feel for religious and spiritual realities has made it difficult for atheistic and materialistic ideologies, such as communism, to attract many African adherents.

—Desmond Tutu, "Where Is Now Thy God?"

CONTENTS

FOREWORD

Over the years of my Archbishopric I have had a number of young people at Bishopscourt. They came to share our journey alongside us in the diocese as we have tried to be true to the gospel of our Lord Jesus Christ through the pain and triumphs of our struggle against apartheid. They all proved to be splendid young men and women and I have welcomed their willingness to enter into our situation.

Michael was one such. I am glad that his experience was not only enriching to him but he in return has enriched us in delivering a treatise that some may find useful.

I hope Michael's interest in South Africa and particularly the role of the Church of the Province of Southern Africa within our situation will remain. God has blessed him with a fine mind, and I believe he will make a significant contribution in the years to come not only to the Episcopal Church but to the Anglican Communion.

ARCHBISHOP DESMOND TUTU

PREFACE

This book is not a systematic theology of Archbishop Desmond Tutu, but rather a meditation upon his theological convictions, his churchly and cultural contexts, and his deeply Christian spirituality. Some will no doubt ask how I, an African American scholar, can arrive at such a personal investigation of another society and culture—indeed, of Tutu.

Having spent over a year in residence with Tutu at Bishopscourt, I experienced his theology firsthand, participating with him in a spectrum of activities. These included daily offices; celebrating the Eucharist; attending church engagements, diocesan events, dignitary functions, and speaking engagements; traveling; visiting hospitalized persons, widows, and troubled priests; attending the Chris Hani memorial march in April 1993 and the World Council of Churches central committee meeting in Johannesburg in January 1994; listening to life-threatening phone calls for Tutu; inspecting the St. James Massacre and the Mitchell's Plain serial killings; making quarterly visits to the University of the Western Cape, where Tutu was chancellor; meeting Nelson Mandela, seeing Tutu cast his first ballot, and attending Nelson Mandela's inauguration as president of South Africa on May 10, 1994. In addition to these official activities, I participated with the archbishop in more personal communal activities including rugby matches, walking, and meals, and sometimes I served as his driver. The paramount experience for me, however, was being ordained a priest by Archbishop Tutu at St. George's Cathedral on my birthday, December 12, 1993. In light of all of this, I have a deeply personal investment in this subject.

In contrast, some might criticize me for being too close to my subject. I have tried to take special precautions to maintain a critical distance. This personal and professional proximity to Tutu allowed me to research original materials, including previously unpublished handwritten manuscripts and other documents not readily accessible to the general public. My goal in this book is not to dissect Tutu's life and work, but to present a spiritual engagement. Nevertheless, I leave to others the task of assessing how effective is this method of probing the thought and life of a person who continues to effect changes in his church and nation.

The reason for my method and modest claims regarding this book is straightforward. Despite the great volume and scope of Tutu's writings, he does not have a corpus of writing suited for Western claims of systematic theology. I have relied, therefore, on my access to Tutu and his work to identify the living tissues of his theology. What I refer to as Tutu's theology of ubuntu does not pretend to be a formal theology in the Western sense; it is concrete rather than systematic. Throughout this book, Tutu's theology will be presented in relation to its context. Indeed, I believe that Tutu is significant precisely *because* one cannot distinguish his theory from his praxis.

The bibliography lists many speeches, addresses, and sermons, which are the primary sources for this work. Unfortunately, some references are undated, leaving only a general chronological context for the remarks. The bibliography also contains a comprehensive list of Tutu's published work. Many of his essays and reflections are in the form of compilations, and editors have used these to identify and contrast Tutu's voice in relation to others. In many cases, these collections show that Tutu offers an interesting contrast to more radical views of speaking against apartheid. Consistently, his voice carries a conciliatory tone as he attacks racist ideology.

A significant aspect of Tutu's thought is set forth in "Some African Insights and the Old Testament," in which he explains his affinity for the Old Testament, arguing that to "claim that there were no religious truths or values in Africa before the Christian era is in effect to say that only in this continent did God remain utterly unknown."[1] Tutu proceeds from this premise to conclude that the biblical world was more congenial for the African worldview than for its Western counterpart.[2]

Tutu's distinctive African claim in regard to the Old Testament remains conciliatory because of his inclusion of ubuntu, an understanding of community unique to South Africa. He is aware, however, of the potential abuses of this concept. "Of course this strong group feeling [ubuntu] has the weaknesses of all communalism; it encourages conservation and conformity. It needs to be corrected by the teaching about [each individual's] inalienable uniqueness. . . . We need both aspects to balance each other."[3]

Tutu's most explicit account of black theology is in "Black Theology/African Theology—Soul Mates or Antagonists?" In this work Tutu concludes that both African and black theologies react against unacceptable conditions. African theology emerged from Christianity in its Western garb, and black theology excavated the entrenched ideology in the universal theology of the North Atlantic world.[4] Again, Tutu is conciliatory as he concludes, "It is only when African theology is true to itself that it will go on to speak relevantly to the contemporary African—surely its primary task—and also, incidentally, make its valuable contribution to the rich Christian heritage which belongs to all of us."[5]

Three of Tutu's longer works expand upon his theological appeal to move beyond racial definition. The first of these, *Crying in the Wilderness*, is a collection of sermons, speeches, articles, and press statements dating from Tutu's tenure as general secretary of the South African Council of Churches (SACC) and his encounter with the Eloff Commission (1978–1981). The work is most informative in regard to Tutu's thought concurrent with the rapid changes in South Africa at that time. Trevor Huddleston writes, in the foreword to this collection, "The most remarkable quality of these writings is their heart-breaking charity towards those who persecute and attempt to destroy the very best people in South Africa."[6]

Tutu's second major work is *Hope and Suffering*, also a collection of sermons and speeches, covering the period between May 6, 1976, and October 28, 1983. On May 6, 1976, Tutu wrote to Prime Minister John Vorster that "we may soon reach a point of no return, when events will generate a momentum of their own, when nothing will stop their reaching a bloody dénouement which is 'too ghastly to contemplate,' to quote your words, Sir."[7] Tragically, his warning came true on June 16 of that year when about six hundred people, most of them youths and students, were killed in the Soweto uprising.

The most conclusive work to date is Tutu's *The Rainbow People of God*,[8] edited by his media secretary, John Allen. Allen used the Soweto student uprising as the watershed event for understanding Tutu's context. Allen's deeper knowledge of Tutu, however, allowed him to show Tutu's work against apartheid more clearly. His arrangement of Tutu's work is also more extensive historically since it covers "the release of Nelson Mandela from prison in 1990, and the last sections chart the confusion and violence of the ensuing transition to democracy."[9]

A word about Tutu's political identity is also in order, for his theology is inseparable from his political life.[10] Because my objective is theologically oriented, I only sketch the political context in order to enter the painful identities of the groups involved—Africans, Afrikaners, British, Indians, Asians, and colored (persons of mixed race) peoples. South Africa's context is too large and complex to do otherwise.

Thus, the limit and scope of this work is largely defined by the powerful and entrenched Afrikaner theology of separation, the mediation theology of Anglicanism, and the persistent and explosive theology of African liberation. These three theologies provide a context for understanding the reason that Tutu adheres to ubuntu, which appeals to the peaceful cohabitation of African, British, and Afrikaner identities. Indeed, one might conceive of chapters 2 and 3 as focusing largely on the African liberation and theological resources, chapter 4 on the British-Anglican resources, and chapter 5 on a spirituality in direct opposition to the Afrikaner one. Yet the careful reader will see elements from all three sources in each chapter.

African identity is particularly charged from the outset: One necessarily confronts whether to accept the imposed identity given by Europeans—an identity caught in the ambiguity of legitimate or illegitimate political systems. To counter this ambiguity, I posit that no concept of either African or Afrikaner nationalism can be developed that does not take into account each of their histories of political oppression. This is a necessary motif in Tutu's thought in that the life-giving symbiosis of ubuntu can form correct political responses within the integrity of Christian commitments. This forms the basis for chapter 1. Throughout, I carefully document Tutu's statements in order to pinpoint his actions and deeds in relation to the theological model I present. Such documentation cannot be done without a large dose of Tutu's humor, as he himself explains:

> In October 1985, a few days after police had hidden in crates on a lorry to decoy youths to stone their vehicle and had succeeded in their awful plan, killing at least two youngsters, I went to Cape Town to speak at a protest meeting. The venue was close to Pollsmoor prison, where Nelson Mandela and others are now jailed.
>
> There had been understandable anger in the community, but, remarkably, the audience—a very mixed one indeed—had a wonderful capacity to laugh. Their funny bones were exposed, and it took very little to tickle them. It seemed extraordinary, this gift of laughter in the midst of so much anguish. Perhaps, as has sometimes been remarked, we laugh only because if we did not, we would cry and cry.[11]

Perhaps Tutu's humor might help us learn not to take the isolated self as seriously as the self in relation to others.

CHAPTER ONE

INTRODUCTION
Holding Back a Tide of Violence

Many observers believe that this irrepressible imp of a man
who describes himself as a teddy bear is the only figure
holding back a tide of black violence against the state. One
day white South Africa will realise, he believes, that he and
other [clergy], thrust to the fore by the imprisonment or
exile of black political leaders, have stood between South
Africa and catastrophe.
> —Peter Godwin, *The Sunday Times*

Tutu tirelessly denied that the color of one's skin can be an
index of one's value as a human being. Indeed, his ubuntu
theology can be understood in its entirety as a Christian re-
buttal to such a claim. The occasion for his theology was the
Christian faith as taught in his South African context; it pro-
mulgated specific racial identities and hierarchies as from God.

Indeed, Tutu's moral persuasion is rooted in the same Christian narrative claimed by those who espouse apartheid. Therefore, he had to convince his society that God's creation of humanity does not pivot around the Afrikaner's election as the
elite race or around a retaliatory African theology.[1] One test of
his theology is how he negotiates a Christian response in a
South African societal dependence on "apartheid" when the
very term is defined in a theological narrative.

Tutu experienced this white racial theology firsthand as
a child. "We played quite happily and often with white chil-

dren and as easily fought them as we taunted one another with racist insults. . . . The obsession of apartheid to separate the races was not yet so virulent."[2] When Tutu took up boxing "to face up to bullies,"[3] he encountered a group of white boys who called him *pik-swart*. Thinking that the epithet was the Afrikaans word for a garden tool, Tutu yelled back, "You *graaf* [shovel]!" It was during this exchange that Tutu realized the double meaning of *pik-swart*—not just "pitch fork" but also "pitch-black."[4] Black was not just the absence of light in South Africa, but the absence of identity.

Tutu locates his baptism into the political arena in 1976, when he was dean of the University of Johannesburg. He wrote a prophetic letter to Prime Minister Vorster urging that unless political change was inaugurated soon, a bloodbath would ensue.[5] The Soweto uprising occurred later that year. Tutu emerged as an African leader in the political realm at a time (between 1960 and 1992) when African political organizations were banned and many leaders jailed. Tutu's church leadership filled the void. Beyers Naudé observed in 1978, two years after the Soweto uprising, that Tutu scared State President P. W. Botha's government by being articulate and self-confident. Tutu is more than the "ultimate 'cheeky kaffir' [derogatory term for black person]—he represents a threat to their basic concepts about race upon which they have built their whole life and ideology."[6]

The complexity of competing Christian and political voices did not surprise Tutu, who stated, "Perhaps a community that had to meet secretly and was always in danger of being betrayed needed to be reminded that a man's enemies would often be those of his own household."[7] "Many people find it strange," Tutu said another time, "that Christians should speak of their persecution in South Africa when the South African Government is at pains to proclaim its Christianity."[8] To explain further the problem of competitive Christian voices, Tutu concluded: "Blacks are deeply distressed that they are the victims of a vicious and oppressive system that is perpetrated not by pagans but by those who claim that they too are Christian. Blacks ask, 'Do whites read the same Bible as we? Do they really worship the same God as we do? If they do then why can they treat us as they do now?'"[9]

THE CONTEXT OF APARTHEID

For Tutu, the racial put-downs from his youth as well as the political–racial distinctions between 1948 when apartheid was inaugurated formally, and 1990, when it was removed legally—these were not simply misguided, they were sin and the perpetual seeds of oppression. "The oppressed could become tomorrow's oppressor because sin is an ever-present possibility,"[10] Tutu declared, and because "periods of transition are by definition unstable."[11]

The argument that race is the most pertinent factor by which to judge human worth[12] presupposes that race defines not just the color of skin but the character of the person. Therefore, one who claims to determine another's race becomes the other's oppressor. Rowan Williams, an Anglican bishop in Wales, points out that "white domination has been built on the assumption that whites may say what they are independently of the needs and reality of other groups, who are built into white self-definition."[13]

South Africa, even after legalized racism was deposed in 1990, remains a deeply fragmented and polarized society. Who and where one is largely determines what she or he sees: Where a white sees a terrorist, a black sees a freedom fighter. But in South Africa, many influential people acted brutally out of what they saw. For example, Tutu once observed that P. W. Botha "was a member of a pro-nazi organisation, the *Ossewabrandwag*, which carried out acts of sabotage against the war effort. He claims he left it when it began to do that. Be that as it may, was that terrorism or not?"[14]

This need of the oppressor to define human beings racially gave rise to a theory called *physiognomy*, in which character was thought to be determined by physical characteristics. Because people of different races are different, declared Prime Minister Hendrik Verwoerd, they should develop separately.[15] For economic and ideological reasons, then, patterns were developed for how so-called superior racial identities should relate to so-called lesser ones. Apartheid is one example, as it upholds "a phalanx of iniquitous laws, such as the Population Registration Act, which decrees that all South Africans must be classified ethnically, and duly registered according to these race categories."[16]

The South African political scene and legal system had not allowed all people to appeal for equality. In such a context, Tutu's theological impact was all the more vital as he became an interim political voice when so many political leaders were banned. Still, although Tutu is seen in a political role, he maintained the struggle of liberation against apartheid through his Christian convictions. Central to Tutu's thought, life, and work of reconciliation has been his theological conviction that the new democratic South Africa could only succeed by "proving to themselves, to the world, and to white people that race is an irrelevance apart from an understanding of Ubuntu. We hope that in very short time, people will ask: 'Why were we so stupid for so long?'"[17]

UBUNTU THEOLOGY

This book proposes that Tutu's theological convictions undergird his strategy of addressing apartheid's theological and political classification of race. Ubuntu, the African concept of community embraced by Tutu, provides a corrective hermeneutic for Western salvation theology that focuses on the individual. Herein lies the best of Tutu's theological model—namely, an emphasis on the integrity of creation and the habitual recalling of our image of God (*imago Dei*) in the midst of human conflict.

Tutu's theological model seeks to restore the oppressor's humanity by releasing and enabling the oppressed to see their oppressors as peers under God. In this can be a mutual understanding, as Jesus teaches, through friendship (John 15:15). For Tutu, ubuntu expresses this mutuality. The relationship of oppressor and oppressed and the resulting definition of humanity through racial classification are broken through ubuntu, an alternative way of being in a hostile world.

Tutu's ubuntu theology begins with the account of God's creation, in which human identity is defined in the image of God. Tutu believes that God created humans as finite creatures made for the infinite. Thus, nothing less than God could ever hope to satisfy deep human longings. Secular prosperity seduces us into judging others as if value were dependent on the production of goods.[18] It is from this materialist understanding of human identity—an understanding prevalent in the West—that a society can only see racial difference as a threat and become become possessed by apartheid. According to Tutu, apartheid "makes no theological sense [because] it denies that human beings are created in the image of God."[19] This imago Dei theology better determines humanity because racial ideology inevitably leads to the use of power, and "the oppressor makes the claim to tell you who you are."[20]

To think beyond racial conflict, Tutu's theology must be viewed through the lens of ubuntu, because "we can be human only in . . . in community, in koinonia, in peace."[21] That is, the only way to make another person's determination of who one is make sense and remain properly intelligible to the two persons is to appeal to that which is beyond both of them.

African Christian Concept of God

For Tutu, only God "knows [suffering] from the inside and has overcome it not by waving a magic wand, but by going through the annihilation, the destruction, the pain, the anguish of a death as excruciating as the crucifixion. That seems to be the pattern of true greatness—that we have to undergo to be truly creative."[22]

Tutu believes that "through Jesus we know that God is and that God is for us, both cosmically and particularly. This all embracing love underlies, overreaches, interpenetrates and lies ahead of everything that is and, therefore, is not to be privatized. Yet, at the same time, that love supports the development of all individuals who are persons, privately, personally, relationally and socially."[23]

The Centrality of Worship Life

Tutu believes that "religion is what you do with suffering, yours and that of others."[24] Faith in the Christian God who entered suffering takes all human life seriously, including the resurrection of the body. The church practices this claim through ordinary, mundane, material things such as bread, water, wine, and oil in order that the material universe may not be "recalcitrant and alien to the spiritual, and that it will all be transfigured to share in the glory of the kingdom, where all things will have been made new, including human relationships, chief among them the socio-political and economic arrangements for our life together."[25]

This God, revealed in Jesus, helps persons determine their identity apart from being strangers and oppressors and helps them see God's reality in their individual encounters. In so doing, personhood is discovered. By recognizing the image of God in others, one comes to appreciate how God creates by relating to difference. Tutu defines the importance of difference in religion as he explains further how one participates in God's activity of creation:

> If religion is seeking to worship and praise God, then it is trying to be present, in awe, wanting to remain in a wordless, imageless experience. . . . It is to let God empty us of ourselves and to fill us with God's fullness, so that we become more and more Godlike, more and more Christlike, that we should live and, yet, it should not be we who live but Christ living in us. Then we shall be holy even as . . . God is holy, a holiness that is not static or to do with ritual purity, but a holiness that must express itself in ethical, political, economic and social responsibility for our neighbor, for the widow, for the orphan and the alien in our midst.[26]

Tutu sees all realms of life in relation to God. "I could not survive at all if I did not worship, if I did not meditate, if I did not try to have those moments of quiet to be with [God]."[27] He does not see his impact in South Africa as political, but spiritual. "It is because of my faith that I know apartheid to be totally evil" because, he continues, "apartheid says that human beings are fundamentally irreconcilable."[28]

AFRICAN CHRISTIAN SPIRITUALITY

Instead of the primacy of race, Tutu makes the spiritual central to life. The spiritual transforms all human realms, including the political, removing the justification to manipulate persons on the basis of their race. Here is the significance of Tutu's influence on South Africa and beyond. As the level of racial conflict rose, however, race again became the primary determiner of identity. As one commentator speculated on Tutu's influence and the resulting escalation of racial violence in South

Africa, "Somewhere there is a point beyond which [Tutu] may cease to have meaningful influence over the activists. If he passes that point, there is no national figure outside the jail cells who could replace him."[29] Peter Godwin came to a similar conclusion:

> Many observers believe that this irrepressible imp of a man who describes himself as a teddy bear is the only figure holding back a tide of black violence against the state. One day white South Africa will realise, he believes, that he and other [clergy], thrust to the fore by the imprisonment or exile of black political leaders, have stood between South Africa and catastrophe.[30]

Theological arguments for apartheid base persons' value on their political and biological attributes. Tutu believes that "if your value depends on something like the color of your skin, it means that not everybody can have the same value. That is contrary—totally contrary—to the Scriptures, which say our value is because we are created in the image of God."[31] Thus, Tutu includes in the spiritual all realms of life, including the political.

For Tutu, South African racism constituted an opportunity for the church to regain integrity and to promote the cause of justice and peace in a manner that had not been done since the beginning of the African independence process. Yet Tutu and many others were aware that such an opportunity can be dangerous. Citing the example of Archbishop Janani Luwan, who was murdered for criticizing the atrocities of Idi Amin, Tutu concluded, "This might be the awful price that the church in Africa might be required to pay to regain its integrity."[32] By being the church in the world, Tutu declares, "we bear witness more by what we are than by what we say and even do. . . . If we were being persecuted for being Christians, would there be enough evidence to convict me, to convict you?"[33]

Ubuntu as life in relation to God and neighbor, nourished by worship, manifests the church's integrity to show a hostile society a better way to determine identity than through an implicit cosmology of violence. The church in its public, spiritual witness must be active in the world in such a way as to expose any power alien to seeking God's image in the other.

> Christianity can never be a personal matter. It has public consequences and we must make public choices. Many people think Christians should be neutral or that the Church must be neutral. But in a situation of injustice and oppression such as we have in South Africa, not to choose to oppose is in fact to have chosen to side with the powerful, with the exploiter, with the oppressor.[34]

Indeed Tutu, when in the United States, warned the nation that "I think it is far easier to be a Christian, a person of belief and faith, in South Africa than it is here. For the issues in South Africa are so obviously clear; you are either for apartheid or against it."[35] Tutu seeks to be engaged in the transformation of the world so that the conditions of life for all are, as nearly as possible, the Christian ideal of God's dominion.[36] For him, democracy comes closest to this ideal:

> All human systems are bound to fall short in varying degrees of the absolute standards of the Gospel, so persons of faith will want to support that political system or proposal which in their view most approximates those standards on the nature of human community. . . . Consequently their involvement in socio-political and economic affairs will be dictated by the constraints of the Gospel, and not by political, or other, ideologies.[37]

Through the same constraints, racial ideology proved inconsistent with Tutu's model of theological ethics, namely his concept of ubuntu in light of imago Dei. Tutu describes himself "as an ordinary Christian leader. I am motivated by no political ideology or otherwise. What I do or say are determined by what I understand to be the imperatives of the gospel of . . . Jesus Christ. I believe I stand in the mainline of biblical and Christian tradition in my understanding of how the Christian faith impinges on our everyday life."[38]

CHAPTER TWO

A MILK-AND-HONEY LAND OF OPPRESSION

I speak out of a full heart for I am about to speak about a land which I love deeply and passionately, a beautiful land of rolling hills and gurgling streams, of clear starlit skies, of singing birds . . . a land God has richly endowed with the good things of the earth. . . . We would expect that such a land veritably flowing with milk and honey should be a land where peace and harmony and contentment reigned supreme. Alas, the opposite is the case.

—Desmond Tutu (1984–1985)

God did not make a mistake in creating us black. We are not carbon copies. We are glorious originals made in the image of God. But in South Africa, black is not just a skin colour, for we know blacks who have joined the ranks of our oppressors. Black is also a condition, a condition of being the victim of racial oppression, injustice and exploitation or one who, whatever their actual skin colour, have thrown in their lot and identified in solidarity with blacks.

—Desmond Tutu, "Koinonia II"

Had Archbishop Desmond Tutu been a politician dressed in religious garb, he might have sought a safer course of *realpolitik* than the one that he took: constructing an ubuntu theology that combined African, liberationist, and traditional Christian elements. Many, to be sure, saw Tutu as a politician, and he could even speak of his political role. For example, when Nelson Mandela was released in 1990 after twenty-seven years of imprisonment, he spent his first night of freedom in Tutu's residence in Bishopscourt. "The next morning as I bade farewell to him, I thought that now the moment had come for me to take the advice of my spiritual director . . . to become more contemplative. I would now have more time for meditation, more time to be with people who are hurting, more time to visit so-called squatter camps or informal settlements, to minister to the spiritual and material needs of people."[1]

Indeed, Tutu had hoped to leave what he called "the limelight of political work" to persons such as Mandela, but they had difficulty in making real progress—"the poor were still suffering, and the country was engulfed in violence," said Tutu. His goal was to ensure that any economic reconstruction benefited the poor, knowing that the unrealistic expectations of some people could not be realized. What needed to be realized—and Tutu saw that the church had to insist on this—was that "people experience a qualitative difference between life under apartheid and life under a democratic government."[2]

Tutu worked in the context of the oppressive system of legalized racism called apartheid, in which one so-called higher white tier (*bosskap*) dominated so-called lower colored (mixed races) and black tiers (*kaffir*). In their thirty-five years of rule, Tutu writes, "the Nationalists have found their own solution to the vexed question of political power and white–black coexistence in this part of the continent. They have decided that they will keep power firmly in their grasp and that coexistence will only be on terms dictated by them."[3]

This oppressive posture filtered down to how white officials viewed blacks. For example, Trevor Huddleston relates a conversation he had with a white, English-speaking police officer. The officer observed that "70 percent of the people in this place are criminals." In response, Huddleston stated that if this were the official attitude of the police, they would not easily win the trust and confidence of blacks. "It was, to me at least, an interesting comment on the whole, sad situation. Just one more indication of the same basic mental attitude. The native is the *problem* . . . never a person."[4]

This posture undergirded how blacks were treated by bureaucrats who carried out the inhuman and dehumanizing legislation of apartheid—personhood was lost in the shuffle of paper and power. "It was difficult to see that bewildered man cowering before you, hardly understanding the shouted order that merely adds to his confusion as he is shunted from one queue to the other, from one office to the next to get the prized stamp which will allow him to work."[5] What the bureaucracy did not see—indeed, could not recognize—was that this man might be the head of a family, the husband of some beloved wife, the doting father of children.

This posture created a two-track educational system. For most of South African history, certain persons were condemned by law to stunted physical, emotional, and intellectual growth. They were victims of a deliberately inferior education designed to prepare them for perpetual serfdom.

Finally, this posture justified a policy of uprooting black people from their ancestral homes only to dump them on the least desirable pieces of property. Tutu exclaims, "You don't dump people, you dump rubbish. You dump things. But our people are dumped in arid, poverty-stricken Bantustan homelands."[6] A reasonable person might then ask how such an oppressive system arose in this bountiful land.

A EUROPEAN HISTORY OF SOUTH AFRICA

South African written history has traditionally begun with Jan Van Riebeeck's so-called discovery of South Africa in

1652. In that year, European colonists arrived in southern Africa using guns and disease to conquer indigenous societies, such as the San and Khoi Khoi, and to take possession of the land.[7] More accurately, then, colonial South Africa began with seizure, oppression, and slavery.[8]

Although most black South Africans were not slaves, at least by North American definition, they became products of "habits of an established colonial power," which, according to Francis Wilson and Mamphela Ramphele, was

> soon calling for slaves (or for some "industrious Chinese") to meet their labour needs. In 1658, only six years after Van Riebeeck's arrival, the first shipment of slaves for private ownership landed at the Cape. Some came from the coast of Guinea; others from Angola. Within sixty years of the establishment of the European colony, there were more slaves than free burgers [citizens] in the western Cape. They were brought from West Africa, from Madagascar, and from southeast Asia.[9]

This exploitation of South Africa was a long process, punctuated in 1760 by requiring slaves to carry passes when they moved between rural and urban areas and in the Land Act of 1913, under which "no African was allowed to purchase land outside the reserves, those 'scheduled' and 'released' areas which eventually added up to a little less than 14 percent of the total country."[10] By 1948, Europeans (that is, Portuguese, British, Dutch, and French) perpetuated racism in its most insidious fashion, namely, apartheid laws.[11]

Through this colonial history, the economically developed European learned to name a new identity—African. In South Africa, the minority defined the majority, and this afflicting narrative haunts Africans continually in their encounters with Europeans. But something emerged that was even more hideous than this oppression of defining a people—religiously based racism.

Afrikaners and the British

Most of the first white settlers in what is now South Africa were robust pioneers, seeking to avoid being social and economic outcasts in the competitive society of seventeenth-century Holland. In southern Africa, they could form their own nation. Unlike the New England Puritans, this group of Afrikaners were a mixture of "diverse nationalities, adventurers who had volunteered their services in the hope of more certain reward than could be obtained elsewhere, . . . coarsened by the conditions under which they had lived ashore and on the sea, with their vices redeemed by the one great virtue they had, physical courage."[12] Gradually these European settlers cut their ties with Europe and evolved into a group known as Afrikaners, new white Africans who became distinct from their homelands as well as from Africa's indigenous peoples.[13]

A scramble for Africa began with the British occupation of the Cape in 1806. In order to exist in southern Africa, Afrikaners fought on the frontiers of Africa to establish themselves as white. (The British doubted for a long time that they were white.)

From 1806 until the execution of J. Fourie in December 1914, a "period of revelation" emerged that resulted in the Afrikaner's "sacred saga."[14] This people's theology showed "amazing similarity" to a liberation theology on behalf of the poor and oppressed because it developed as a theology in response to suffering.[15] This theology was manifested in the Kaffir War of 1834, a war that "signaled the dénouement of slavery and the increasing insecurity of the Afrikaner peoples whose property diminished 'under the flag of a [British] government which openly elected to uphold wrong.'"[16] Similar to the Israelites in the desert, the Afrikaner people in 1836 began their wilderness experience on a great trek. By this time the Afrikaners had assumed a racial superiority over the indigenous peoples, whom they named kaffirs, a derogatory term like "nigger" (although different in the sense that kaffir originally connoted a pagan or heathen).

For the Israelites, the Exodus experience led to gracious treatment for foreigners and wayfarers. But not so for Afrikaners, as Tutu states:

> We are daily amazed that Afrikaners with such a history, leaving the Cape because they were feeling oppressed by the British and braving the unknown dangers of the "dark interior" to seek and find liberation and freedom and even to fight for it. That people with such a history and such a tradition should be incapable of appreciating just how blacks feel. That people with such a history and tradition should be incapable of realising a major lesson of history that once a people are determined to become free then nothing will stop them becoming free. So it is with blacks—there is no question that we will be free.[17]

When speaking at the centenary of the Battle of Blood River, in 1938, Prime Minister D. F. Malan stated:

> The Trekkers received their task from God's hand. They gave their answer. They made their sacrifices. There is still a white race. There is a new volk. A decade later that nation had come to power. . . . Separate development under the leadership of God's chosen instrument—the Afrikaner people—was the divine plan of South Africa. The segregated nature of the Reformed churches epitomized this mindset: in addition to the white churches, there was the Sending Kerk (Mission

Church) for "coloureds" [excluded even though they were closely related by culture, language and blood to white Afrikaners], the Kerk van Africa for Africans and a small Indian Reformed Church. These so-called "Daughter Churches" were essentially subservient to the "Mother Church," dominated by predikants (pastors) who were seconded by the major white church, the Nederduitse Gereformeerde Kerk (NGK), and financially dependent. While the white DRC [Dutch Reformed Church] had listened to the cry of poor whites, serving the needs of vulnerable, urbanizing Afrikaners in earlier decades, they were now deaf to the voices of repressed and exploited blacks.[18]

The Influence of Calvinism

Many Afrikaners think of themselves as descendants of those seventeenth-century Calvinist rebels who fled religious persecution in Europe. For them, God created the Afrikaner people with a unique language, philosophy of life, history, and tradition. Afrikaner theology did not view their suffering as God's chastisement but rather as a sign that God would not fail them and their task was to remain faithful.[19] In this regard, Dunbar Moodie quotes John Calvin: "How much can it do to soften all the bitterness of the cross, that the more we are afflicted with adversities, the more surely our fellowship with Christ is conformed . . . to suffer persecution for righteousness' sake is a singular comfort. For it ought to occur to us how much honor God bestows upon us in thus furnishing us with the special badge of his soldiery."[20] Much of Afrikaner theology is based on Calvin's emphasis on God's sovereignty and providence. These foci are interpreted, however, as theological justifications for a police state, even for the creation of so-called special forces composed of mentally and physically disabled people.[21]

John Calvin's complex perception of civil authority lent itself to various interpretations. As a result, one Reformed Christian ethic was an affirmation of the absolute sovereignty of God and the covenantal relationship between God and God's people. Calvin taught that obedience to superiors is restricted by the prior obligation of obedience to God and insisted that civil authorities are divinely commissioned to meet the needs of the people.[22] Under this view, notions of the orders of creation, purity of race, ethnic identity, or any other rival authority were rendered insignificant.

Calvin's original understanding of divine sovereignty was as a doctrine of covenant that incorporated the people of God into God's redemptive work. Calvin imparted to the church, as an agent of God, a responsibility to engage in transforming the social, political, and economic structures of life. For Calvin, law was an instrument of social justice. Under this view, the church as a collective and in its individual members could only resist the claims of an apartheid state.

But Afrikaner theology appropriated this heritage in a different way, by understanding God's sovereignty as rendering justice according to racial groups. Therefore, apartheid laws evoked divine obedience consistent with an articulation of natural or universal rights. This theory of divine obedience, which has served the particular needs of societies at different periods of history, allows itself to be shaped and manipulated by dominant cultures of each successive age.[23]

To be sure, Afrikaner and African alike appropriated Calvin's system for their own ends. The sovereign God, in covenant with the people of God, shaped their political existence. According to Barth, this can only be the God "against the lofty and on behalf of the lowly; against those who already enjoy right and privilege and on behalf of those who are denied it and deprived of it."[24]

In fact, Afrikaners could and did use this description of God's favor to elevate their claims over the Africans and the British. Now claiming to be a chosen people, Afrikanerdom had to justify its economic and social power. One of these justifications was the divine legitimization of a white government to determine and control what was best for its citizens and natives—a religiously based racism. This legitimation rested upon a second foundation, namely European Enlightenment philosophy.

EUROPEAN ENLIGHTENMENT'S RACIAL LOGIC

The European Enlightenment's oppressive philosophy of race did not so much depart from the Christian Scriptures as it served to entrench the primacy of the thinking European subject.[25] The assertion was that order in the universe flowed from the great chain of being in which the moral and physical order of the world was rooted. God had placed within everything this order.

Humanity, through its reason, was able to understand this order as it witnessed the divine mind in creation. All things had a place, and one could see order through recognition of self in that order. All dominant forms of ideological discourse flowed from the European subject into constructed themes of what constitutes mature human identity.

From this intellectual climate, the fundamental distinction could be made that Africans were of a different race than Europeans and were not deserving of European standards. Thus, when a growing capitalist market sent traders and adventurers all over the world, a key commodity was discovered—unspoiled land—along with a lesser human species.[26] As V. Y. Mudimbe states, "The development of anthropology, which up to the very end of the eighteenth century was sought within travelers' narratives, now takes a radical turn. From now on it will develop into a clearly visible power–knowledge political system."[27]

This power–knowledge system classified Africans as *monstrum*—that is, "disorder." Non-Europeans were thought to be abnormal and yet somehow part of the will of God. Africans were monsters. The presence of apes as particular to Africa only increased this notion that Africans were not quite human.[28] This European view of blacks existed for centuries; as Tutu explains, "They used to have road signs that read 'Drive carefully, Natives cross here.'"[29]

Enlightenment Europeans commonly assumed that the origin of humanity and its differences were recorded in the Bible, especially in Noah's curse of Ham's son, Canaan. "When Noah awoke from his wine and knew what his youngest son had done to him [looking upon his nakedness], he said, 'Cursed be Canaan; lowest of slaves shall he be to his brothers.' He also said, 'Blessed by . . . God be Shem; and let Canaan be his slave" (Gen. 9:24–27). This became the central passage by which Europeans both interpreted dark skin as a curse and justified the economic market of slavery.[30] Tutu states:

> It is salutary and humbling to realize that slavery continued to be practiced right up to the 19th century. For those many centuries, while the Church preached the equality of human beings, people owned fellow human beings and treated them as their property, bought and sold over the market as so many cattle, admired for their strength and their breeding prowess. Slave families were separated as callously and heartlessly as horses and cattle were separated from their sires and dams and with about as much feeling, and at times less. And what is so shattering is to realize that almost all the slave owners and others engaged in this demeaning trade in fellow human beings were Christians, who graciously permitted their slaves to be evangelized as long as it meant teaching them to accept

docilely their station in life and not to become too "uppity." They were "Bible-thumping" and upright Christians, deeply religious, who saw nothing contrary to their faith in what they were doing.[31]

This Enlightenment Christianity developed a particular biblical interpretation of race and election. Race became a biblical and theological concept, in the sense that "you are a chosen race"(1 Pet. 2:9). The Greek word interpreted as "race" is *genos*—"a group, kind, or nation of peoples who come into being solely by the will of God." This coming into being proceeds from Israel's chosen status as a "treasured possession out of all the peoples" (Exod. 19:5).

These designations of race and election of peoples were carried over into the South African context to justify a moral scheme by which people should be separated. Whites may not have been able to state the philosophy, but they could draw out its implications and quote its presumed biblical underpinnings. For example, Schalk Vorster, an Afrikaner farmer, comments, "You must be committed to the concept of race. . . . If you read the Bible you will see that people were created with differences."[32]

Yet, as Hannah Arendt explains, it was the economic opportunity that made application of the Enlightment philosophy so attractive:

It is highly probable that the thinking in terms of race would have disappeared in due time together with other irresponsible opinions of the nineteenth century, if the "scramble for Africa" and the new era of imperialism had not exposed Western humanity to new and shocking experiences. Imperialism would have necessitated the invention of racism as the only possible "explanation" and excuse for its deeds, even if no race-thinking had ever existed in the civilized world.[33]

THE WHITE AFRIKANER–BRITISH APARTHEID

The British were a key impetus for the importation of the Enlightenment philosophy, and they operated from a religious model similar to the Afrikaner model: Religion coincides with and undergirds the aims of the state. The process of conquest and acquisition of the indigenous peoples of southern Africa yielded a modern, industrial South Africa.

True, a different kind of slavery existed before Europeans arrived in Africa.[34] But African slavery, while it could be just as violent as the European form, permitted an individual to adopt the new language and customs, thereby conforming to existing indigenous or nomadic identities.[35] In the European Enlightenment, however, a new kind of slavery, based on racial classification to which Africans could not conform due to fundamental philosophical and biological differences, was instituted.[36] Even when slaves were no longer kept, white domination continued.

Once the white domination of Africans by the Afrikaners and the British was secure, the demand for black, low-cost workers grew tremendously, especially for such industries as mining. In order to ensure white control over all aspects of African movement, various pass-and-permit laws were enacted to "expel all 'surplus' urban residents."[37] In effect, Africans were viewed as commodities that the government had the right to control.

South Africa is unique among world states in that racial classification was legal as the primary principle of its political and social order.[38] In an economic market in which liberty, rights, and freedom were ideals, a new material product could be acquired. This new market was the acquisition of a lower grade of peoples. Along with this new economic market came the justification for racism through the mechanism of apartheid—a religious and legal concept.

Apartheid, according to Michael Worsnip, is an Afrikaans word constructed to name the theological doctrine and practice of separation of complete groups of peoples. In Malan's National Party Commission Report of 1947, the word appears over forty times. Written to formulate the revived character of the National Party, the report resembled both a manifesto and a confession of faith. Apartheid then came into popular use as a 1948 campaign slogan of the National Party.[39]

The Malan administration fully adopted the tenets of apartheid. This legal separation of the races ensured both a constant supply of cheap, black labor and complete control over land rights by whites. This was done through a parliamentary procedure available to white voters only, a political process that slowly eliminated black participation in a centralized government. In 1956, *colored* (black and white, or mixed-race persons, along with Chinese immigrants) voters in the Cape Province could only elect *white* representatives to parliament. Four years later, the evolution of Africans' lack of political control culminated in the elimination of parliamentary seats for the white representatives of both black and colored voters.

One cannot understand theological discourse in South Africa apart from the history of apartheid. Apartheid brought together criteria by which white citizens would know how to behave morally in relation to African peoples. It was described as a policy based on Christian principles of justice, which would maintain and protect the white race as a distinctive group. Daniel F. Malan voices the sentiment of his people:

> Our history is the greatest masterpiece of the centuries. We hold this nationhood as our due for it was given us by the Architect of the universe. [God's] aim was the formation of a

new nation among the nations of the world. . . . The last hundred years have witnessed a miracle behind which must lie a divine plan. Indeed, the history of the Afrikaner reveals a will and a determination which makes one feel that Afrikanerdom is not the work of [human beings] but the creation of God.[40]

This kind of so-called just separation of races would be guaranteed for all pure racial groups. It elevated the Afrikaner people to the superior status of *bosskap* (supreme whites) and declared that Africans were *swart gevaar* (black danger). For the Afrikaner, this was a pedagogical method to teach how all races and cultures evolved toward a discovery of national self-respect and pride in race. President W. A. de Klerk states:

> Justice is therefore no cowardly surrender of one's own strivings, rights and claims. Justice is obedience. Justice is to live according to the rule or law of the Creator. To act according to the law for your own life is to express your own pure character and identity. Your own particular character is therefore your "law of life" and the obedience to it is justice. Therefore we say that autogenous development is the best exercise of justice. Justice is plurality. . . . Whoever deserts his own post and endangers his future, who by virtue of a misconception of love or justice, undertakes to fulfill the task of someone else is not exercising justice but is disloyal to his own calling and law of life.[41]

According to this logic, apartheid would also lead to greater mutual respect among the races in that the white race was placed in a position of "guardianship" and "trusteeship" over developing peoples, and the idea of separation would take place on a "natural basis."[42]

Being Black in South Africa

Tutu summarized in two principles the box into which apartheid placed blacks. "In South Africa you could say a generalisation with substantial validity is that we have a deeply polarised society as between black and white. . . . You could become an instant expert on South Africa by repeating yet another generalisation with the validity of a Euclidean theorem and it is this—what pleases most whites will almost certainly displease most blacks and vice versa."[43] Being black in such a context means that psychologically, all standards of achievement, status, and worth are imposed or inherited from the dominant society. Tutu explains the consequences of this predicament:

> You end up interiorising the definition others have given you. . . . I realised the power of this pernicious thing, this conditioning once when I visited Nigeria and was in the seventh heaven of delight when I noticed that both the captain and the co-pilot of the flight I had taken were black. But as we were preparing to land I discovered that I had a nagging worry about whether we were in fact going to make it. Could these blacks really fly this plane? I had been worried at the absence of a white person at the controls. I sighed with considerable relief when we did make it. Isn't that incredible—but that is what racial injustice and oppression can actually do. So you keep needing agents of exorcisms who will keep proving that blacks can indeed do it in all kinds of ways.[44]

Having whites define blackness puts black persons outside the dominant standards of intelligence, beauty, and worth. At the same time, whiteness assumes the proper control and manifestation of these standards in a protected normality. Tutu explains, "Recently we had a State of Emergency, but it is certain that if you had asked most whites what it meant, they would probably have said 'What State of Emergency?' because for them things were as normal as they have always been."[45]

Blackness prompted a state of emergency because it threatens to spill into or seduce white superiority. Again farmer Schalk Vorster remarks, "You must be committed to the concept of race. It's an ugly word as used by some people. But what is the opposite of racism? Communism? Or is it the [white] man who marries a black maid? It's important to me that people stand by their racial identity, otherwise you get bastardization."[46] Whatever bastardization might mean to whites, it means to blacks that they are foreigners or aliens. Tutu explains:

> Apart from the deep hurts that the apartheid policy daily inflicts on all its victims such as the assaults on their human dignity when adults are addressed as "boy" or "girl" or when any black over 16 years can be accosted in the street to produce a document proving their right to be there effectively restricting their freedom of movement, when a black cannot expect the common courtesies as a right, when shop assistants look at them with dead eyes which light up as they address a white person with a smile—what those who are not at the receiving end call the pinpricks of petty apartheid—there is the agony of grand apartheid, the Bantustan policy which means to turn blacks into aliens in their own mother-country, so that there will be no black South Africans.[47]

One response to such alienation was for blacks to relinquish African traditional ways in favor of a more so-called correct European lifestyle. That is, black self-esteem became bound to the successful acquisition of white culture, "in every aspect from material possessions and occupational skills through forms of etiquette and leisure pastimes."[48] This response, however, attempted to remove blackness, a doomed approach.

A second response was to embrace blackness. While Tutu found this helpful, his assessment of it was that it had not—and perhaps could not of its own—achieve the desired results of racial harmony:

> I am now convinced that the black consciousness movement did not accomplish its work completely. Too many of us still have a sense of self-loathing to the extent of our being capable of doing things that no self-respecting African would be capable of. This self-loathing is then projected on to other people. . . . We don't respect ourselves and we show it by being disrespectful to other people and often cow-towing to white people. . . . We must address all the causes of violence if we are to bring it to an end, but we in the black community must resolve to recapture the sense of dignity and community which we displayed during the apartheid era. . . . Intimidation is an acknowledgment of the weakness of your point of view.[49]

How, in light of this history and state of affairs, could black Christian theologians go about working for reconciliation?

RELIGIOUS RESISTANCE IN SOUTH AFRICA

Because the dominant, white group viewed Africans with such contempt as inferior beings, more than a few influential African thinkers also espoused ontological theories of racial constitution, namely, that one's race or skin color defined one's being.[50] Such assumptions only fed white superiority, whose proponents saw in Africa a frontier for shaping this superior identity in a new space.[51]

To counter this oppressive order, other thinkers both black and white employed Christian moral tenets to demand an end to racial discrimination. This Christian opposition contained at its core a struggle against secular identity. For example, the use of the color bar—the legal segretation of the races established in 1910 at the foundation of the Union of South Africa so that each race could develop along its own lines—was held up to the British authorities as offending the dignity and the religious values of creation.[52] Even so, a complex relationship and then alliance between the British and the Afrikaners developed. Once these two groups more or less acknowledged each other as superiors to blacks, the process of conquest and acquisition of the indigenous peoples of southern Africa flourished. It yielded a modern, industrial South Africa.

When black political opposition became a threat, black leaders were imprisoned. Desmond Tutu, as a religious objector to apartheid, had little foundation, other than Christian tenets, by which to argue against the vicious forces seeking to turn God's children "into non-persons living a twilight existence."[53] Tutu's moral persuasion could only have been rooted in a Christian narrative through which he had to convince white Christianity that God's creation does not imply a relative goodness of racial categories.

Although Tutu was not the only religious objector, it may be difficult for many outside the South African context to envision fully his situation. Even African Christian churches tolerated and transmitted the racist two-tier level of being— with whites as the dominators and blacks as the dominated— to the extent that these churches were willing to abide by the dominant group's definition of Africans as inferior. Perhaps because of the theological and political dictates of apartheid, these congregations perceived little opportunity to resist racial segregation.[54] Perhaps they held out hope that their compliance would produce greater sensitivity on the part of Afrikaners.

One might be amazed, as Tutu was, that the Afrikaners, having themselves been oppressed by the British, did not have more empathy for blacks who were also oppressed. But if the Afrikaners had missed this lesson, then surely they should have perceived from their own history that "once a people are determined to become free, then nothing will stop them [from] becoming free. So it is with blacks," Tutu stated; "there is no question that we will be free."[55]

The great obstacle to be overcome, then, was the general European assumption that Africans did not have enough human consciousness (that is, were not full human beings) to become citizens of a sovereign state. Indeed the Immorality Act prohibited interracial marriage and sexual intercourse. Denial of citizenship, even of peership—these were thought by Europeans to be the ways that civilized persons lived with beasts.

A second obstacle was the logical inconsistency being applied to the so-called civilized and noncivilized. As Tutu noted, it is fairly plausible to acknowledge racial groups, even racial minorities, as long as the composition of these groups is determined in a consistent manner. As Tutu pointed out, however, the sorting mechanism was utterly inconsistent. On the one hand, various groups of whites (English, Afrikaners, Germans, French) were said to cohere to make up one nation. On the other hand, blacks were asserted to be separate, forming distinct nations such as Xhosa, Zulu, and Tswana. He comments ironically:

> We then asked by what tour de force, by what alchemy was it possible for whites to be so disparate to cohere into one group; whereas, this failed so dismally with the blacks? And remarkably encountered was the extraordinary phenomenon

that the Xhosas did not form one nation—they actually split up into two nations, Siskeian Xhosa and Transkeian Xhosa. . . . All this was certainly too subtle for us, not surprisingly given that we were congenitally "slow thinkers."[56]

The basis for this inconsistent determination of racial nations was again theological. On one hand, South Africa was largely defined politically by the Nederduits Gereformeerde Kerk (NGK) or Dutch Reformed Church's interpretation of Calvinism. This interpretation reappropriates the Afrikaner as the central identity in South African society. Dunbar Moodie reveals more about the "Lord of Afrikanerdom," who is

> sovereign and intensely active, busy at every turning point in the affairs of nations and men. Like Assyria in the Book of Isaiah, the British empire was not only the incarnation of evil; it was ultimately the foil against which God revealed [God's] magnitude and glory to [the] Afrikaner people. In similar fashion, although the Zulu army symbolized the black African threat to the Afrikaner's racial identity, in theological terms the Zulus became God's agents for uniting [God's] people in holy covenant. . . . The civil theology is thus rooted in the belief that God has chosen the Afrikaner people for a special destiny.[57]

"Apartheid," observed Tutu in contrast, "supported by the NGK says human beings are made for separation, alienation, division and disunity. The Bible and Christianity say human beings are made for fellowship, communion and Koinonia."[58] In supporting this view, Tutu competed with another Christian narrative of election. As Dunbar Moodie describes, the Afrikaner civil religion becomes a doctrine for a New Israel.[59] This becomes a religious tradition emphasizing homogeneity as the necessary strategy for survival in a hostile world, divinely ordained to unite religious and civil society.[60]

Competing Theological Narratives

As both Africans and Afrikaners used Christianity to look forward to the achievement of an ideal society, they did so in competitive theologies. Tutu concludes that "none can be more intolerable than those who claim God to be on their side and think they have a monopoly on right and justice."[61] In the end, both African and Afrikaner nationalisms buttress their political claims on the basis of being a people chosen by God. African Christians, oppressed by both British and Afrikaner Christians, were especially aware of the way in which theology was used to subject and oppress, as Tutu joked bitterly: "When the white man first came here, he had the Bible and we had the land. Then the white man said to us, Come let us kneel and pray together. So we knelt and closed our eyes and prayed, and when we opened our eyes again, lo!—we had the Bible and he had the land."[62]

The problem of competitive Christian narratives and unequal identities grew as African Christians responded to the Afrikaner narrative. More particularly, Tutu answered that a narrative of violence cannot be used as the modus operandi for theological reflection. In Christian theology, everyone (i.e., Afrikaner, European, Indian, Asian, colored, and African) has the opportunity to discover "that they do indeed matter enormously to this God. They have infinite worth in God's sight. They were created in God's image. This news becomes subversive, explosive, revolutionary material in a situation of injustice and oppression."[63]

Afrikaners invoked their God, the champion of their cause, who led their trek into the interior of South Africa in what they saw as a repeat Exodus from Egypt. Like the Afrikaners, Africans—also an oppressed people—appealed to the Exodus motif as well and have considered themselves a chosen people. In these conflicting narratives, a destructive theological concept, such as apartheid, becomes kaleidoscopic in meaning. Apartheid may be defined as separate development, separate freedoms, and multinational democracy. In the end, however, racial classification is used by Afrikaner and Africans for their own ends, both evoking God's justification of racial violence. Tutu's theology of ubuntu needed to rise above such a face-off. Moreover, it needed to draw in—rather than alienate—nascent white resistance.

Some White Resistance

Even as the Afrikaner narrative softened somewhat, those Afrikaners who were in sympathy with the blacks convened periodically to examine the plight of Africans. Tutu, for example, describes just such a challenge by two Afrikaners, Frikkie Conradie and his wife, Marietjie:

> Can you imagine an Afrikaner, a [Dutch Reformed Church] dominie of all people, leaving his own community to identify himself so closely with the downtrodden, the poor and the suffering, a white man giving himself and his family to a black community to be their servant and to work for justice and reconciliation and to work under a black minister? It is unbelievable and yet we saw this miracle of God's grace working here in Alexandra Township, here in South Africa. ... Thank you God, thank you Marietjie for giving us hope of the new society God is building in South Africa. [God] will strengthen you and your son whom some people have called Vusumuzi—the one who raises up the house of Conradie.[64]

Not all Afrikaners are like Conradie. In fact, Conradie's mission belies a strong theological narrative within the Afrikaner community that may even claim itself as a liberation theology. The Conradies' criticisms, however, were still confined within the parameters of apartheid "and limited to ineffective handwringing about the destructive effects of migrant labor on African family life."[65]

Tutu's Theological Resistance

Not finding much support from outside the black community—and finding little courage within it—Tutu took a theological stance. But his resistance could be stated, as it often was, in clear, nontheological words. Tutu saw the predicament of race not as a contradiction but as a paradox in which each race defines the other, and the result is the beginning of reconciliation. This paradox is maintained, however, in light of Africa's oppressive colonial history.

Yet this colonial history at its core was theologically defined. As a corrective to such religious determination of identities, Tutu proposed:

> There must be a plurality of theologies, because we do not all apprehend or respond to the transcendent in exactly the same way, nor can we be expected to express our experience in the same way. And this is no cause for lament. Precisely the opposite—it is a reason for rejoicing because it makes mandatory our need for one another because our partial theologies will of necessity require to be corrected by other more or less partial theologies. It reinforces the motif of inter-dependence which is the inalienable characteristic of the body of Christ.[66]

Tutu's African-black theology, then, was a theology neither of special election of one race nor of retribution, but one that allowed whites and even secularists to embrace it. Indeed, this relational view of human identities encouraged the small victories by radical whites who were sympathetic to the plight of alienated blacks, as well as uncompromising blacks who achieved emancipation of slaves in South Africa.[67] Tutu's relational view, however, was further complicated by how the race predicament plays out in its form of colonization.

CHAPTER THREE

DELICATE NETWORKS OF INTERDEPENDENCE

A self-sufficient human being is subhuman. I have gifts that you do not have, so, consequently, I am unique—you have gifts that I do not have, so you are unique. God has made us so that we will need each other. We are made for a delicate network of interdependence. We see it on a macro level. Not even the most powerful nations in the world can be self-sufficient.

—Desmond Tutu, "God's Dream"(1992)

Ubuntu refers to the person who is welcoming, who is hospitable, who is warm and generous, who is affirming of others, who does not feel threatened that others are able and good for [this person] has a proper self-assurance that comes from knowing they belong in a greater whole, and know that they are diminished when another is humiliated, is diminished, is tortured, is oppressed, is treated as if they were less than who they are. What a wonderful world it can be, it will be, when we know that our destinies are locked inextricably into one another's. . . . We are being forced if not by prosperity then by impending disaster to realise that we are one another's brothers and sisters. To share the prosperity of affluent countries with indigent ones is not really altruism. It is ultimately the best kind of self-interest, for if the poor countries become prosperous in their turn,

then they provide vigourous markets for the consumer
goods produced elsewhere. The debt burden is a bomb that
could shatter the economy of the globe to smithereens. And
so a new and just economic world order would benefit both
rich and poor countries.

—Desmond Tutu, "The New World Order" (1992)

Apartheid, now no longer the legal institution of South Africa, established dominion over and domination of blacks
and coloreds by whites. Yet arguing for fairer or more hu-
mane treatment of blacks by whites was not a workable plan.
Behind this domination stood the clashing cultures of the
Western and African worlds. Because of their impasse, Tutu
sought to examine the bankrupt elements of Western culture
and the overly collectivist elements of African culture in order to fashion an ubuntu theology.

MATERIAL AND SPIRITUAL REALITIES

Humanism in the West recognizes truth as based on materialism. In the West's economic system, for example, people
find their basis in the "autonomy of market forces." Tutu
notes, "Is it not revealing how when we meet people for the
first time we soon ask, 'By the way, what do you do?' meaning what gives you value?"[1] In such a system, Tutu observes,
personhood is defined through the value of the product one
produces. These material forces, however, also result in athe-
ism and dehumanization because the spiritual is ignored and
even denigrated.

Such observations by Tutu are not novel. For example, Augustine Shutte, a white South African philosopher, describes
the materialism that characterizes contemporary European
philosophy and affects the understanding of personhood in
this way:

Each individual is rather like an atom, separate, autonomous and constrained only by alien forces imposed on it from without. Morality is seen as an essentially private matter. . . . In this view there is virtually no such thing as a common human nature. . . . The only thing we have in common is the capacity to originate action, the negative freedom to choose. As such we can of course be the subject of rights, but these rights are not derived from our common human nature. Rather they are produced by agreement of all interested parties.[2]

Such Western humanism, then, claims that truth is found in individuals' rational capacities.

In contrast, the African understanding seeks a balance between material and spiritual realities.[3] Yet this African view did not lead, Tutu concluded, to a ready-made solution of personhood, but to an African extreme of community. Three types of human groupings can be discerned: collectives, constituted human groups, and random collections of individuals. African social and philosophical understandings usually adopt the first human grouping, collectives. The Western understanding is more like the second category, constituted human groups. In an African understanding, human society is something constituted organically, whereas in Western egalitarian understandings, societies are more of an inorganic association of individuals.

These contrasting views of community also play out on the level of personhood. Many Western views of personhood center on the lone individual, whose essential characteristic is that of self-determination, whereas the African view of a person depicts the person's meaning or intelligibility only in the context of his or her environment. In the African concept of ubuntu, which Tutu appropriated for his own purposes, human community is vital for the individual's acquisition of personhood.

In African collectivism, freedom is the lack of constraint produced by cooperation in common life, the overcoming of all kinds of conflict. If the African collective organism is developed to its extreme, ethical choice may easily become the will of the powerful members of the community. Tutu saw in Western thought that laws exist to ensure that the will of the powerful expresses the will of the people; in African thought few conceptual restraints are available to guard against a tendency for a few to claim or exercise control over the many.

The crucial distinction between African and Western thought is that in the African view of humanity, "the community . . . defines the person as person, not some isolated static quality of rationality, will, or memory."[4] Yet both the Western and African conceptions of the human person (that is, inorganic and organic) are materialistic because they fail to recognize a dimension of persons that transcends the scope of scientific knowability.

In this clash of cultural thought, Tutu took something from each in order to form a new ubuntu theology. His inheritance of spirituality and African thought did not allow him to postulate individualism as an all-determining factor. In his theology, as we shall see, community is vital to self-identity. But Tutu did not merely adhere to African conceptualizations of community or to Western individualism, because these sometimes lacked sufficient notions of self-identity and restraint from domination. He went further to make theological claims about how community forms *individuals* as peers.

FOUR VECTORS IN UBUNTU THEOLOGY

White people, Tutu once observed, "laugh, they love, they cuddle babies, they weep, they eat, they sleep—they are human. But if they are human, why, oh why can't they see that we laugh too, we love too, we weep too, we cuddle babies too, we eat, we sleep—why can't they see that it is impossible for things to go on like this?"[5] Tutu's theology, formed in the context of apartheid and its clash of European and African cultures, is best understood by means of ubuntu.

Ubuntu is the plural form of the African word *Bantu*, coined by Wilhelm Bleek to identify a similar linguistic bond among African speakers.[6] *Ubuntu* means "humanity" and is related both to *umuntu*, which is the category of intelligent human force that includes spirits, the human dead, and the living,[7] and to *ntu*, which is God's being as metadynamic (active rather than metaphysical).[8]

Tutu is from the Xhosa people, and his sense of ubuntu derives from the proverbial Xhosa expression *"ubuntu ungamntu ngabanye abantu,"* which, translated roughly, means "each individual's humanity is ideally expressed in relationship with others" or "a person depends on other people to be a person."[9] Muendanyi Mahamba describes someone with ubuntu as someone who cares about the deepest needs of others and faithfully observes all social obligations. Such a person is conscious not only of personal rights but also of duties to her or his neighbor.

One of Tutu's first references to ubuntu is in his description of the African worldview:

In the African *Weltanschauung*, a person is not basically an independent solitary entity. A person is human precisely in being enveloped in the community of other human beings, in being caught up in the bundle of life. To be is to participate. The summum bonum here is not independence but sharing, interdependence. And what is true of the human person is surely true of human aggregations. Even in modern day Africa this understanding of human nature determines some government policies. After all the Arusha Declaration is counterbalanced by the concept of "ujamaa" in

Tanzania and "harambee" in Kenya. This is the reason I have spoken of a proper ambivalence towards [economic] viability—acknowledged its positive aspects while rejecting its negative ones and this in an explicit way. A dialectical tension exists here which must not be too easily resolved by opting for one or other of the alternatives.[10]

From this African worldview, ubuntu shaped Tutu's subsequent work as the center from which to make racial reconciliation comprehensible in the African culture. Tutu needed to communicate at this level because interdependence is necessary for persons to exercise, develop, and fulfill their potential to be both individuals and a community.[11] Only by means of absolute dependence on God and neighbor—including both blacks and whites—can true human identity be discovered. Indeed, such human interdependence is built into our very creation by our being created in God's image, our common *imago Dei*.

Four vectors of Tutu's ubuntu theology can be discerned. First, this theology builds up true, interdependent community. Second, it recognizes persons as distinctive in their identities. Third, it combines the best of European and African cultures to produce a new and distinctive theology. And fourth, it is strong enough to address—even overthrow—apartheid.

Ubuntu Theology Builds Interdependent Community

Ubuntu, for Tutu, is the environment of vulnerability that builds true community. This vulnerability begins when human divisions are set aside. "Apartheid," according to Tutu, "says people are created for separation, people are created for apartheid, people are created for alienation and division, disharmony and disunity; we say, the scripture says, people are made for togetherness, people are made for fellowship."[12] And we are made for fellowship because only in a vulnerable set of relationships are we able to recognize that our humanity is bound up in the humanity of others.

Perhaps what makes participation in the ubuntu community so different for many Westerners is that ubuntu theology excludes competitiveness.[13] Instead of being manipulative and self-seeking, the person is "more willing to make excuses for others"[14] and even discover new meaning in these others. Communal competition, in contrast, makes humans and their community into little more than a pack of animals. As Tutu points out, "If you throw a bone to a group of dogs, you won't hear them say: 'After you!'"[15]

From Tutu's perspective of ubuntu, human systems that encourage a high degree of competitiveness and selfishness demonstrate the greatest discrepancy—an "incommensurate difference"—from God's creation of interdependence.[16] This discrepancy can be illustrated by Tutu's interpretation of the creation narrative in which Adam needs Eve as a sign of our interdependency.

> You know that lovely story in the Bible. Adam is placed in the Garden of Eden and everything is honky-dory in the garden. Everything is very nice, they are all very friendly with each other. Did I say, everybody was happy? No, actually Adam was not entirely happy and God is solicitous for Adam and He looks on and says, "No, it is not good for man to be alone." So God says, "Adam, how about choosing a partner?" So God makes the animals pass one by one in front of Adam. And God says to Adam, "What about this one?" Adam says, "Not on your life."
>
> "What about this one?" "No."
>
> God says, "Ah, I got it." So God puts Adam to sleep and out of his rib he produces this delectable creature Eve and

when Adam awakes, he says "wow, this is just what the doctor ordered." But that is to say, you and I are made for interdependency.[17]

Yet Tutu's vulnerable community digs even deeper into
vulnerability than Adam did, because such a community lays
aside all racial distinctions as determinative of human identity. Ubuntu proclaims that people should rejoice in how God
has created persons differently—as Adam and Eve discovered—so that new meanings and identities are always possible. "No real human being," Tutu asserts, "can be absolutely self-sufficient. Such a person would be subhuman. We
belong therefore in a network of delicate relationships of interdependence. It is marvelous to know that one who has
been nurtured in a living, affirming, accepting family tends
to be loving, affirming and accepting of others in his or her
turn. We do need other people and they help to form us in a
profound way."[18]

The only way persons and communities can be free is together, despite racial classifications. Human categories and
effort will not ultimately achieve the goal of a flourishing
community. Therefore, an appeal to participate in that which
is greater—God—provides the theological impetus for
ubuntu.

In this, Tutu anticipates ubuntu's own problematic—namely,
the needs of the many outweighing those of the few. As we
shall see in more detail, Tutu stresses the Christian definition
of relationship, as opposed to other social forms of communalism, to define ubuntu. Influenced deeply by Anglican spirituality, Tutu is able to overcome African philosophy's tendency
to go to the opposite extreme of discounting individuals for
the sake of community. For him, being properly related in a
theological ubuntu does not denigrate individuality. Instead it
builds an interdependent community.

Ubuntu Theology Recognizes Persons as Distinctive

In light of Tutu's complex task of addressing both the white and the black communities, ubuntu theology may seem unrealistic. Throughout most of South African history, black-and-white relationships had disintegrated. Ubuntu theology needed to counter a long tradition of antagonistic and individualistic language.

Ubuntu theology asserts that persons are ends in themselves only through the discovery of who they are in others.[19] For example, one cannot recognize one's own physical beauty unless another person is present who can reveal or reflect that beauty. Or, again, if human beings were to grow up individually among wolves, then they would not know how to communicate as human beings. They would not know human ways of eating, sitting, and walking. Therefore, humans become persons only by living in an environment where there is the interaction of diverse personalities and cultures. If there is no such environment, personhood does not survive.

Yet the problem in human community is not so much that some lack knowledge of how to behave in company with others, but that they put themselves forward in ways meant to exhibit their superiority, rather than their distinctiveness. Tutu illustrates this with the following allegory:

> There was once a light bulb which shone and shone like no light bulb had shone before. It captured all the limelight and began to strut about arrogantly quite unmindful of how it was that it could shine so brilliantly, thinking that it was all due to its own merit and skill. Then one day someone disconnected the famous light bulb from the light socket and placed it on a table and try as hard as it could, the light bulb could bring forth no light and brilliance. It lay there looking so disconsolate and dark and cold—and useless. Yes, it had

never known that its light came from the power station and that it had been connected to the dynamo by little wires and flexes that lay hidden and unseen and totally unsung.[20]

The distinctiveness of each person depends upon her or his connection with other persons and a recognition of a more encompassing context. All humans are born with potential, according to ubuntu theology, but this potential can been understood only in the context of others and God.

Ubuntu, then, provides an alternative to vengeance because it provides an invaluable perspective in which white and black people may see themselves as other than racial rivals. "When you look at someone with eyes of love," Tutu believes, "you see a reality differently from that of someone who looks at the same person without love, with hatred or even just indifference."[21] Indifference to others is a product of apartheid.

In contrast to the system of apartheid, Tutu believes that in ubuntu theology, personhood is formed ultimately through the church as the church witnesses to the world that God is the one who loves human identities into being. That is, God's love is present before everything else, and God is the source of all power.

To gain the vision of ubuntu is to negotiate how to be in the world and to access the life of grace in God. As the light bulb allegory illustrates, any claim of control or power is delusory and foolish. Tutu notes how differently the community of God in Christ operates: "Jesus gave a new, a very important responsibility to Peter. He said, 'Feed my sheep.' It's almost like asking a thief to become your treasurer."[22]

Being recognized as a distinctive person, therefore, requires that one be transformed to a new identity. As the light bulb allegory illustrates, this new perspective fully encompasses the truth of connections to a power source. Tutu states, "God does not love us because we are lovable, but we are lovable precisely because God loves us. God's love is what gives us our worth. . . . So we are liberated from the desire to achieve, to impress. We are the children of the divine love and nothing can change that fundamental fact about us."[22]

Time and again, Tutu also finds the stories of Jesus' love and tremendous faith in people as offering this same transformation to become individuals. Jesus

> got them having faith in themselves with a proper kind of self-assurance, exorcising them from the horrible paralysing sense of inadequacy that plagues so many of us. After the resurrection, he met Peter and did not berate him for denying [Jesus] because [Jesus] helped him cancel it out through a three-fold positive assertion: "Yes, I love you." To this man who had denied him, Jesus gave not less but increased responsibility—Feed my sheep. Become—you vacillating old so and so—my chief apostle and pastor.[24]

Ubuntu Theology Integrates Cultures

Ubuntu, as we have noted, is the quality of interaction in which one's own humanness depends on recognizing it in the other. Such recognition comes out of each person's culture, but also transcends culture because of the human interaction.

Augustine Shutte provides one illustration of this from John Heron's research on the phenomenon of mutual gazing. In this case, the Zulu greeting *ndibona* ("I see you") is coupled with the Zulu response *sawubona* ("yes"). "In meeting your gaze," Shutte notes, "it is not the physical properties of your eyes that I fix on, as, say, an eye-specialist would. . . . In fact when I pick up your gaze my eyes actually either simply oscillate back and forth between your eyes, or else fixate on a point equidistant between them.

What I pick up is the gaze, and in the gaze the presence of a person actively present to me. And the same is simultaneously true of you."[25] The gaze is neither African nor European, but human. By recognizing one's identity in the other, Tutu's theology guards against the Western propensity for racial classifications. That is, Tutu's ubuntu seeks to show that persons are more than either black or white; they are human.

What is seen in the other when viewed through ubuntu is imago Dei, God's wonderfully distinctive creation in the other, the divine life of that person. Just as the Son and the Holy Spirit are defined by the Father, so is personhood defined in the other. One would not know the meaning of salvation or intelligence unless such meanings were made intelligible by the reference of someone else.

Tutu's ubuntu involves a system in which not only is each person unique, but so are the nations of the world. The world is to be international. Tutu explains:

> A self-sufficient human being is subhuman. I have gifts that you do not have, so, consequently, I am unique—you have gifts that I do not have, so you are unique. God has made us so that we will need each other. We are made for a delicate network of interdependence. We see it on a macro level. Not even the most powerful nations in the world can be self-sufficient.[26]

Therefore, ubuntu implies more than a nonracial, nonsexist, and nonexploitative society. Rather, it "is a touchstone by which the quality of a society has to be continually tested, no matter what ideology is reigning. It must be incorporated not only in the society of the future but also in the process of the struggle towards that future."[27] The concept of ubuntu demonstrates that persons are not defined by natural sets of properties but by the relationships between them and others. So also with cultures, in that these combine to form a distinctive society.

Ubuntu Theology Can Overthrow Apartheid

Tutu's definition of ubuntu and how his theological interpretation of it counters the narrative of apartheid both have to do with how the imago Dei is understood in South Africa as the locus of one's identity. "It is absolutely necessary for us to share certain values," Tutu noted on one occasion; "otherwise discourse between us would be impossible for we would be without common points of reference."[28]

The implicit power analysis of ubuntu became explicit as it faced off against apartheid. The first step as Tutu saw it—and in some ways the only step—was that ubuntu would humanize the oppressors in the eyes of blacks and that a sense of common humanity would form:

> We will grow in the knowledge that they [white people] too are God's children, even though they may be our oppressors, though they may be our enemies. Paradoxically, and more truly, they are really our sisters and our brothers, because we have dared, and have the privilege to call God "Abba," Our Father. Therefore, they belong together with us in the family of God, and their humanity is caught up in our humanity, as ours is caught up in theirs.[29]

This stance had so profound an effect on Tutu that one defining feature of his episcopate has been the conscious movement toward contemplative spirituality. His ability humanly to stare down apartheid was precisely through ubuntu as a theological spirituality rather than a political program:

We are each a God-carrier, a tabernacle of the Holy Spirit, indwelt by God the holy and most blessed Trinity. To treat one such as less than this is not just wrong. . . . It is to spit in the face of God. Consequently injustice, racism, exploitation, oppression are to be opposed not as a political task but as a response to a religious, a spiritual imperative. Not to oppose these manifestations of evil would be tantamount to disobeying God. God has created us for interdependence as God has created us in [the divine] image—the image of a divine fellowship of the holy and blessed Trinity. The self-sufficient human being is a contradiction in terms, is subhuman. God has created us to be different in order that we can realize our need of one another.[30]

Out of this spirituality, Tutu encouraged others to live in a confident manner:

So you say to that old lady walking the dusty streets of Soweto, whose African name her employer doesn't know because she says it's too difficult, so I'll call you by a name, even if it is not yours. You are Jane, Jane Annie. You say to her, "Mummy, mummy, as you walk the streets and they say who's that and you say, I am God's viceroy. You are someone very special to God and the divine image did not say it will indwell clever people. Whether you are clever or not so clever, whether you are beautiful or when people see you, they cover their faces, oh yes; whether you are tall or short, whether you are substantial or not so substantial [you are God's viceroys].[31]

And out of this confidence—of being God's viceroy—persons in the community of ubuntu are moved to care for others:

We do not need to be too clever. We must just be receptive, open, appreciative, to smell the fragrance of the flowers, to feel the cold splash of the rain, to catch the familiar odor of damp soil, to see the ragged mother dandling her malnourished baby in rags. And maybe to be moved to cry, to pray, to be silent, and to let the Spirit inside us pray with groanings that cannot be put into words. To marvel at the fact that poor, hungry people can laugh, can love, can be caring, can share, can nurture, can embrace, can cry, can whimper, can crawl over and die—that these tattered rags of humanity are Jesus Christ: "Inasmuch as you did it to the least of these my sisters and brothers." They are God's stand-ins, created in his image. They are precious, they have their names engraved on God's palms, the hairs of their heads are numbered, and God knows them, these nonentities, these anonymous ones who are killed and nobody seems to care.[32]

Indeed, Tutu returned to this point frequently in his speeches and sermons, in a variety of ways. For example, when Tutu described the radical point about Jesus' question to a lawyer who had asked about who is one's neighbor, he can take full advantage of a parable that describes the good Samaritan as coming from a lower racial class of his day yet giving aid to a wounded person of a higher racial class: "Who proved a neighbour to the man in need? You, gathered here, . . . are meant to be asking, 'To whom am I going to be a neighbour, who is in need and whose need must I meet as a neighbour with this privilege and this responsibility?' You and I are the ones who are to be judged for failing to be neighbour to those in need."[33]

The opposite of ubuntu with its concern for the neighbor is a fabricated society of competition, such as South Africa under apartheid. Such competitive societies are signs of the fall of creation. Instead, ubuntu theology is about the achievement of absolute dependence on God and neighbor in such a way that human identity is discovered therein.

Thus, Tutu's life and thought appealed to his society to move beyond racial distinctions as determinative of human identity. Ubuntu helped make sense of how South Africans should then proceed to operate on the basis of more than racial identity.

WHAT IS PROBLEMATIC IN UBUNTU?

Already made clear is that ubuntu has little to do with Western humanism, which locates truth in an individual's capacity for reason and self-determination. In contrast, the African concept of ubuntu emphasizes the community as defining the person. Indeed, a logical implication of ubuntu and African conceptualizations of community, especially for Westerners, would be that individuals have no existence apart from their relations with other persons. The question needs to be asked: If the individual self is defined by his or her relations with others, what are the relations? How does the community take on this definitional role?

African philosophers usually respond by employing an African concept of personality called *seriti* (plural, *diriti*), which identifies a life force that makes no distinction between body and soul. For example, Gabriel Setiloane, an African theologian, notes that the Sotho-Tswana culture, like the Hebrew culture, believes that humanity is irreducibly psychophysical—body-and-soul. In such a cultural understanding, to attack the body is to attack the soul and its culture.[34]

To cause bloodshed, then, is not only to injure a person's body-soul but also to damage the community's seriti, which results in a weakened society. Blood[35] and seriti are connected in such a way that human virtue is passed on from generation to generation. Therefore, African rituals need to be conducted to restore the constant damage done to persons' seriti so that injured individuals do not pass weakened seriti onto the whole community, which includes children, cattle, crops, and possessions.[36]

Ubuntu, then, names the individual's connectedness to her or his community; seriti names the life force by which a community of persons are connected to each other. Both concepts assume that a person is intelligible only by being connected to social and natural environments. In this constant mutual interchange of personhood and community, seriti becomes indistinguishable from ubuntu in that the unity of the life force depends on the individual's unity with the community. Setiloane explains: "It is as if each person were a magnet, creating together a complex field. Within that field, any change in the degree of magnetisation, any movement, of one affects the magnetisation of all."[37]

That the concepts of seriti and ubuntu need to be understood alongside one another seems clear. Otherwise a person's life force would have little enduring reality apart from that person's sense of community.[38] According to Shutte, however, there remains an inconsistent account of how the experience of reciprocity and mutuality identified in ubuntu fits with the metaphysical claims of life force found in the concept of seriti.[39] Moreover as K. Wiredu points out, the African idea of community is always in danger of undermining individual freedom, especially in the context of authoritarian political structures or superstitious beliefs relating to one's health.[40]

Both Shutte and Wiredu are helpful in that they seek to provide an account of ubuntu that need not be destructive of individual freedom.[41] Tutu has also been alert to this danger:

> I have to confess that to our shame in Africa, on the whole, we have not been able to accommodate differences of opinion. When you differ from someone, often that is taken to mean that you are an enemy. But that is actually not traditionally African, because in the traditional African community, the chief

was a good chief if he could work out a consensus, and a consensus occurs because people have different points of view. . . . In many parts of Africa we must acknowledge with a deep chagrin that the only change experienced by many ordinary people is in the complexion of their oppressors.[42]

When using an important cultural concept such as ubuntu, it is necessary to distinguish its beneficial effect from ways in which it may be abused. Tutu has incorporated two safeguards. The first is his explanation of how persons connect with and are dependent upon God (and we shall return to this later in more detail). The second is his insistence upon true consensus in building democratic forms:

The truly democratic state would let people celebrate their rich diversity. We are becoming increasingly pluralistic, and there is a danger, of course, that we become so diverse that we might find we share very little in common. But we must beware of a dull uniformity. Homogeneity should not be the enemy of heterogeneity. We must help cultivate tolerance which is the hallmark of the mature, of the secure or the self-confident who are not threatened by the autonomy of others and who don't have to assert themselves by an aggressive abrasiveness. There is often a conspiracy among government and powerful media to make us turn in on ourselves, to be concerned about belonging to like-minded, to be concerned only about our community, about our state, our nation. We forget we belong to the world and that we have sisters and brothers out there who share a common humanity.[43]

In short, ubuntu is not simply as another communitarian model. In any consideration of the political implementation, Tutu's ubuntu theology stresses that human means must be consistent with human ends. That is, the strong freedoms of individuality and community in African culture should remain indistinguishable. In this way, no one would suffer at the expense of the other. A profound lesson of South African history is that the racist means used to pursue political ends structured an oppressive community that was antithetical to the ideals of African culture.

CHAPTER FOUR

FILLED WITH THE FULLNESS OF GOD

God created this world because God loves and when things went wrong, because of sin, God redeemed it. God, in Christ, emptied God's being of divine glory and God paid the price for our sin. It is all mystery, ultimately, and we cannot hope to encapsulate it in words. Words become an obstacle and a barrier. Instead, we need silence in the presence of this God we worship and adore, to be emptied of ourselves and to be filled with God, and so to become more truly ourselves as we are filled with the fullness of God.

—Desmond Tutu (sermon)

Western preoccupation with power and dominance are closely associated with an imperial image of God. But the self-emptying, self-sacrificing God of the cross defies conventional political wisdom.

—Desmond Tutu, "Postscript: To Be Human
Is to Be Free" (1993)

The African concept of God, more particularly the Bantu God, is the Supreme Being who is the first cause of all *ntu* (beings). The transcendence of God is implied in God's two names, *Iya-mbere* ("One who is before everything") and *Iya-kare* ("One who is at the very beginning"). The concept of God's eternal existence is that of permanent habit; that is, "God is the habitual source of activity in beings." Multiple attributes of God often serve as doxological names for God. God is *Iya-mbere, Iya-kare, Rurema* ("Creator"), *Rugira* ("One who acts in the most excellent way"), *Rugabo* ("the Powerful"), *Rugaba* ("Omniscient distributor of goods"), *Rwagisha* ("One who blesses"), *Nyamurunga* ("One who synthesizes"), and so forth.[1]

A description of several Bantu characteristics of the Rwandan concept of God is helpful in seeing the African influence in Tutu's theology. D. A. Masolo concludes, through A. Kagame's model, that the concepts of God's absolute power and God's supremacy logically lead the Bantu of Rwanda to believe that all human activities are to be attributed to God only as analogies. Kagame concludes that although human beings are described as knowing, seeing, and acting, only God truly knows, sees, and acts.[2] Thus, a moral act is determined to be good or evil to the extent that the act conforms to its proper end, namely, the well-being of humanity and God.[3]

Tutu does not take African philosophical religion to its logical end of positing an anthropomorphic God. Instead, he believes:

> God depends on you and says, "Open yourself to be filled with the Holy Spirit and be still as you contemplate these images which will open your mind to God's truth, and open your eyes to God's world and . . . friends, the weak, the poor, the hungry, the homeless, the drug addict, the gay person, the down-and-out." And God will say to you, "Thank you for loving me in loving them." Isn't God wonderful? This omnipotent but weak God? This immortal but dying God? This God who waits on you and me to be . . . partners?[4]

Tutu's statement does, however, reflect two elements in the African concept of God. First, God is the transcendent external existent. That is, God is in another mode of existence and is not defined through movement, either acting or being acted upon. In contrast, both *umuntu* (human being or force with intelligence) and *ikintu* (a thing and other forces) either act or are acted upon.

Second, God is immanent. This creates an epistemological problem in the African concept of God that is similar to Middle Platonism, in which no existence of God is possible without God's eternal generation of creation. The African concept of nothingness is not absolute in Bantu philosophy, but is always conceived in relation to being. Nothingness is simply isolated existence.[5] Kagame states: "When essence (*ntu*) is perfected by the degree of existing, it becomes part of *the existing*. *The existing* cannot be used as a synonym of *being there*, since in Bantu languages, the verb *to be* cannot signify *to exist*. The opposite of the existing is *nothing*." Therefore, Kagame concludes that "the *nothing* exists" and that "it is the entity which is at the basis of the *multiple*. One being is distant from another, because there is the *nothing* between them."[6]

Although a pantheistic view of God might seem inevitable in African discourse, God can also be described as being outside created categories. However, such transcendence causes another problem in African philosophy. V. Y. Mudimbe explains, "Although God is the origin and meaning of *ntu*, [God] is beyond it to the point that, according to Kagame and Mulago, one cannot say that God is an essence."[7] Given the qualifications debated among African philosophers, how might this view of an African God influence Christian discourse?

John Mbiti presents an African Christian view of God that takes into account these conceptual problems. Considering many natural objects and phenomena attesting to God's involvement in creation, there is no space where, or time when, God is not contemporaneous with all things. For Mbiti, this is not pantheism, and there is no evidence that African people consider God to be everything in order to be God.[8] Tutu agrees through God's impetus to create on account of love:

> The Omnipotent and all knowing one who dwells in light inaccessible before whom the angels and archangels and the whole company of heaven veil their sight as they fall in worship ceaselessly day and night crying "Holy, Holy, Holy Lord God Almighty—Heaven and earth are full of thy Glory"—this God who is God from all eternity needing nothing to be God having all plenitude . . . It is such a God who created us, created us because [God] wanted us, out of the bounty of [God's] divine and overflowing love. And that invests each one of us with incredible worth, that we are each the consequence of the divine love created because we were wanted and not because we were needed, the object of a love that lacked nothing, that lacks nothing, that will lack nothing to be truly and fully God.[9]

Therefore, God is the origin and sustenance of all things in African discourse. God is older than the *zamani* (Swahili, "past") and can be properly considered outside and beyond creation. This solves the above problem of pantheism, because God is personally involved in creation in such a way that creation is not outside of relationship with God. God is thus simultaneously transcendent and immanent. A balanced understanding of these two extremes is necessary in order to understand African conceptions of God.[10] This African understanding explains Tutu's use of ubuntu as a balancing metaphor in which human participation in the divine life allows for common discourse among diverse identities. Tutu concludes: God "has chosen us to be . . . partners, therefore everything [God] does with us is theandric—both divine and human. God chooses to limit [the divine self] according to

our limitations, to [become] a weak God [whose] divine om-
nipotence is conditioned by our human weakness."[11]

The most common description of God among African
peoples is as Creator.[12] God creates the existence of *ntu*, en-
dowing beings also with properties of creation, namely, re-
production and activity. In African discourse, God's attributes derive from God's work of creation. God is called
the sun because God is like this celestial body that is able to
exert powerful force despite its tremendous distance from
the earth.[13] Relying on God's effect of creation, Africans encounter the nature of the spiritual world by means of visible and concrete phenomena and in terms of ordinary language and ordinary experience.[14] God conserves creation
and provides the providence by which the existence of the
ntu is regulated by God's wisdom.[15] God the Creator is the
most definitive African conception for Tutu's theology, as
he states:

> We are created in the image of God by a God who is creative,
> and so we should have opportunities to be creative, to dabble
> in music, in painting, in drawing, in being creative in differ-
> ent kinds of ways. What we do should often be its own re-
> ward; we should not value a thing because it was of prag-
> matic or commercial value. Of what pragmatic or money
> value is a glorious sunset, a Beethoven symphony, a beauti-
> ful rose dappled with dew sparkling in the morning sunshine?
> What money value do you attach to walking barefooted in
> the sea, washed by the sand of the beach, or to holding hands
> with your beloved as you crush the golden leaves rustling
> underfoot? It is impossible to assign any commercial value
> to these things, but lives, without those and similar things,
> we reckon to be horribly impoverished almost to the point of
> being dehumanized. The Bible does say "Man does not live
> by bread alone."[16]

God is the telos of creation, and in this way creatures can never lose their existence.[17] This faith statement is not just African; it is also the traditional Anglican emphasis on the incarnation. Here, influenced by both African emphasis on creation and Anglican emphasis on the incarnation, Tutu believes the staggering result of kenosis (Greek, "self-emptying" or "pouring out") is that creation is the outpouring of God's love. Wherever God's love is, there is creation. God creates by relating difference. The greatest example of this is the relation between infinite and finite found in Christ. Tutu explains:

> Western preoccupation with power and dominance are closely associated with an imperial image of God. But the self-emptying, self-sacrificing God of the cross defies conventional political wisdom.
>
> The kenotic nature of God is also revealed in the mystery of creation. Austin Farrer quotes at length from a Jewish story. "The Rabbi says: 'Now I tell you that the question, why God permits this or that natural evil, is among the questions allowing no answer. I will tell you why. The Holy One, blessed be he, filled all immensity before the world was and there was no place where He was not. So neither was there any place where a world could be for he was all, and in all. So what did he do? He drew back the skirts of his glory to make a little space where he was not and there he created a world. And so, where the world is, there he is not. And that is why we look in vain for his hand in the chances of nature. Nevertheless, blessed be he, he has visited us with this loving kindness.'" Farrer then comments: "Obviously, it takes you nowhere to speak of God's being present or absent in any plain way at one place or another. In one way, he is everywhere present, since whatever exists manifests his present will that it should exist."[18]

God *creates* because God *loves*. In God there is no difference between these two verbs—*love* and *create*. God's creation as an expression of God's love invites persons, created in God's image, into being for others. Human nature is to love in such a way that something new and alive is always created. As Tutu believes, "We and all creation are the creatures of love. We are made by love, we are marked by love and we are made for love."[19] This love becomes most intelligible for Tutu through the concept of kenosis, in which God's love redeems creation through the outpouring of the divine life made known in Christ. It is here that Tutu's doctrine of God is distinguished from other African doctrines of God.

From a Christian theological perspective, much of African philosophy seeks only to revitalize African traditional religions. In many works seeking to construct a bridge between African and European philosophical systems, philosophers such as Masolo express antipathy toward Christian theology. Masolo declares, "There is nothing, for example, which proves that the idea of unity is superior to that of multiplicity or pluralism, or that monotheism is superior to or develops from polytheism."[20] For Masolo, Christianity is the enemy of African thought. He concludes, "Combined with the suppressive measures taken against African religious beliefs and practices by the colonial and missionary forces, the vagueness of African traditional religions has contributed significantly to their rapid collapse and disappearance."[21]

Masolo believes that a Christian theology—such as that espoused by Tutu—hinders authentic conceptualization of African gods because African Christian theologians are too "eager to demonstrate African religious concepts" by means of Greek metaphysics.[22] Herein is the tension between African and European conceptualizations of God. For scholars like Masolo, God cannot be Christian because a Christian God represents the European God. Therefore, such scholars may never arrive at the source of Tutu's theology, the triune God.

Unlike Masolo's account of African philosophy, Tutu's Christian faith acknowledges a radical break between God and creation which makes God more transcendent in theology than in philosophy. For Tutu, God creates because God loves. In this sense, Tutu's theology is the mixture of an African emphasis on God as Creator and an Anglican emphasis on God's interaction with creation through Christ. Both emphases show that creation results from the providential will of God. Tutu cannot accept an African notion such as Masolo's that creation has existed coeternally with many gods. Tutu operates from the church's theology: God reveals God's self through three persons in one nature. Thus one may conclude that written within the limitation of human and theological language is this great mystery of personal transcendence.

Tutu's account of God offers an invitation to the divine life in which one may successfully encounter the revelation of God that occurs between silence and knowledge, between the earthly and heavenly. Christian theology suggests the possibility of speaking ineffably in space and time, an impossible task that the theologian knows can only be completed by a God-formed intelligence.

Tutu locates theology in a relationship of revelation of God in Christ in which the initiative belongs to God, while simultaneously implying a human response—the free response of faith and love. This ability to locate theology appropriately through relationship is also known to Tutu as ubuntu.

TUTU'S CHRISTIAN EPISTEMOLOGY

By seeking to acknowledge the deeper realities of God and community in relation to the Bantu worldview, Tutu gives African epistemology a voice to address the problematic of how ubuntu is individualized. Tutu's ubuntu acknowledges theological reflection that celebrates a person's way of knowing through dependence on African culture and on the church's tradition and history. Ubuntu is a way of knowing in which one's intellectual growth concerning God's dynamic moves in concert with who one becomes in God. That is, Tutu adheres to the Eastern church's notions of participation in the divine life as a way of solving Western dualisms. This is the way of deification or *theosis*, an Eastern church concept in which human salvation is participation in the life of God. Therefore, sin is not so much an occurrence that results in the fall of human beings, but is more akin to an Irenaean account of how human beings mature as they participate more deeply in the divine life. Tutu states:

> We believe that when our Lord, the second Person of the Trinity, assumed our humanity, he did so not as a temporary measure. He became a human being forever so that our flesh has been united permanently with divinity, meaning that we have the capacity to be deified. He became as we are, so said St. Irenaeus, so that we could become as he is. The first Epistle of John declares that we do not know what we shall be, but we know that when Christ is revealed we shall be as he is (1 John 3:2). That is why he can be the High Priest, who ever lives to make intercession for us, for only those who have been made like unto the children of Abraham, not angelic beings, can become High Priests. (Heb. 2:16–7; 5:1–2)[23]

Thus, Tutu's greater emphasis on the relational nature of God does not necessarily mean that his thought can be contrasted with African epistemological methodologies as some might suggest.

Tutu engages the problem of how ubuntu is individualized in the following manner. A person's identity manifests more clearly in encounter with both the deeper mystery of the unknowable God and the God known in Christ. If one truly participates in the claim of being made in the image of God, a transformation occurs in which an individual becomes a person or personality. Such a transformation results in a more profound understanding of self and community. Personhood is now understood in context of both the unknowable mystery of God and what is known in Christ. This is the terrifying process of losing one's identity in order to emerge a redeemed person with respect to God and to other selves. Tutu concludes, "What extraordinary creatures we are. Almost the ultimate paradox, but not quite. Here we are utterly finite and limited but made for the infinite. St. Augustine put it well when he said, 'Thou [God] has made us for thyself and our hearts are restless until they find their rest in thee.'"[24]

Tutu reminded his congregation during the Feast of St. Michael and All Angels that life has a depth that is beyond two dimensions:

> Jesus leads us into all truth through his Spirit, and therefore as a Christian I glory in the tremendous discoveries of science. I do not see science as a rival or enemy of religion. All truth is of God and can never be self-contradicting. We don't have a God who rules only over the areas of human ignorance [so that] as the frontiers of knowledge extend [God's] domain keeps diminishing.[25]

Tutu's epistemology claims that a person knows other deeper realities, such as God and community, only by acknowledging and participating in these realities through prayer, meditation, and worship. Tutu's appeal to the mystery of the divine life is not an appeal to ignorance, but more specifically to the mystery of persons who are in God and creation.

Tutu's theological epistemology is akin to that of a scientist who acknowledges varying forms of knowledge. A legitimate scientist has the humility to admit that there are other ways of knowing, and that although they are different, they are valid. A warranted science deals with the parameters within which it operates and where its pronouncements would be appropriate. Tutu concludes, "The physical scientist can quite legitimately and properly speculate about decibels of sound and vibrations and airwaves—that would be one way of describing what happened when a group of people gathered under the baton . . . but it would be woefully inadequate to be the only description of a Beethoven Symphony."[26] Erring scientists are the equivalent of Job's friends, who think they know everything and that everything can be described rationally, but they "would not know what it meant to repent in dust and ashes."[27]

Ubuntu theology is formed around the fact that so much about another person cannot be known and, especially, cannot be known responsibly by human beings. Tutu turns the concept of ubuntu into a theological concept in which human beings are called to be persons because we are made in the image of God. This image is at odds with the conceptualization that God's image in human beings creates a "radical unity of the human person."[28] It is also at odds with African discourse, especially the emphasis that community so defines a person that upon forgetting one's ancestors one ceases to exist. Instead Tutu states, "If it was only one person it would be all right. But it is glorious when it is a harmony, a harmony of different voices. Glorious. God is smart. God says, it is precisely our diversity that makes for our unity. It is precisely because you are you and I am me that [God] says, 'you hold on together.'"[29]

To reflect on the essence of being a person is to become aware of a necessary lack of definition. An individual may be wealthy in material goods but still lack ubuntu, for it is deeply spiritual and physical in form and not dependent on material possessions. Tutu states that in traditional African society, "You might have much of the world's riches, and you might hold a portion of authority, but if you have no 'ubuntu' you do not amount to much."[30]

In an address at Morehouse Medical School, Tutu described ubuntu as hospitality, as an open and welcoming attitude that is willing to share, to be generous and caring. Ubuntu is the development of a person who proves to be a neighbor to strangers and welcomes them as friends. Ubuntu rests on knowledge that human existence is inextricably bound up with God's creation and that a solitary human being is a contradiction in terms. "I need other persons," Tutu concluded, "to become a person myself."[31] Tutu then repeated his common refrain of ubuntu:

> We say a person is a person through other persons. We don't come fully formed into the world. We learn how to think, how to walk, how to speak, how to behave, indeed how to be human from other human beings. We need other human beings in order to be human. We are made for togetherness, we are made for family for fellowship, to exist in a tender network of interdependence. That is why apartheid and all racism are so fundamentally evil for they declare that we are made for separation, for enmity, for alienation, and for apartness. . . . This is how you have ubuntu—you care, you are hospitable, you're gentle, you're compassionate and concerned. Go forth as a new doctor, conscious that everybody is to be revered, reverenced as created in God's image whether inner-city, and rural areas; go forth to demonstrate your ubuntu, to care for them, to heal them especially those who are despised, marginalised. Go forth to make the world a better place for you can make a differ-

ence. The task is daunting, of course, but it is our necessary struggle.[32]

A human being is a "glorious original" created for existing in a delicate network of relationships. The fundamental law of our being is interdependence, and if this network is interrupted, the whole network breaks. Tutu asserts that we are made for "relationships not alienation: for laughter not anger, for love not fear, for peace not war." He continues:

> It is religion that enables us in a day-to-day living experience of learning, sharing and caring. Together we come to an understanding of our dependence upon God, and of our interdependence on each other as God's children. It is the recognition of the God in each of us that gives us the key to our future happiness. For if we are interdependent as the whole network of nature declares us to be, we destroy ourselves when we destroy each other.[33]

While governments spend an obscene amount of money on armaments of war, a tiny fraction of that amount would give God's children clean water and adequate housing.[34] A theological understanding of ubuntu would not allow governments to justify the uprooting of black people from their ancestral homes only to dump them on the least desirable pieces of property. Tutu explains, "You don't dump people, you dump rubbish. You dump things. But our people are dumped in arid, poverty-stricken Bantustan homelands."[35] It is in the face of such horrible disparities that Tutu's theological convictions appear with great vigor.

Specific to the apartheid context of South Africa, Tutu believed that black and white humanity was caught up in false survival schemes that did not take into account whether human beings are to survive at all, much less flourish. Survival can only occur through conversion of black and white freedoms and identities, which are inextricably linked together. Tutu offered the following story to illustrate "this fundamental principle of all life, not least of the spiritual life—our dependence on others":

> There was once a man who was a staunch churchgoer and a deeply committed Christian. He supported most of the activities of his local church. And then for no apparent reason he stopped attending church and became just a hanger on. His minister visited him one wintry evening. He found him sitting before a splendid fire with red glowing coals, radiating a lovely warmth round the room. The minister sat quietly with his former parishioner gazing into the fire. Then he stooped and with the tongs, removed one of those red glowing coals from the fire and put it on the pavement. The inevitable happened. That glowing coal gradually lost its heat, and turned in a while into a grey lump of cold ashes. The minister did not say a word. He got up and walked away. On the following Sunday, the old man turned up in church. A solitary Christian is a contradiction in terms.[36]

The only way persons and communities can be free is together, despite racial classifications. Human effort will not ultimately achieve the goal of a flourishing community. Therefore, an appeal to participate in that which is greater—God—provides the theological impetus for ubuntu.

> The only way we can be people is together, black and white. And so you say, 'Hey, how can you say, people are utterly, ultimately irreconcilable as apartheid says when it separates people.' We say: You know the central teaching of our faith is that God in Christ effected reconciliation. God in Christ broke down the middle wall of partition. God in Christ was recon-

ciling the world to himself and our Lord says, "If I be lifted up, I will draw all unto me." . . . Ephesians says, "Since it was God's intention to bring all things to a unity in Christ, for he is our peace, and we are given the glorious ministry of reconciliation."[37]

For Tutu, the biblical understanding of human beings derives from God's covenant with human communities. God created us, Tutu believes, to live in community with other human beings. We must work for reconciliation and peace among creation, because this is our covenant with God.

The evolution of the world is a great manifestation of God. As scientists understand more and more about the interdependence not only of living things but of rocks, rivers—the *whole* of the universe—I am left in awe that I, too, am a part of this tremendous miracle. Not only am I a part of this pulsating network, but I am an indispensable part. It is not only theology that teaches me this, but it is the truth that environmentalists shout from the rooftops. . . . All women and men participate in that reflected glory. We believe that we are in fact the image of our Creator. Our response must be to live up to that amazing potential—to give God glory by reflecting [God's] beauty and . . . love.[38]

Tutu believes that God's desire for all creation is depicted in the creation narrative. God put Adam in the garden and everything was wonderful. God created a primordial harmony that excluded bloodshed; it was a "paradisal existence with the lion gamboling with the frisky lamb."[39] We are meant to be interdependent, to live in fellowship, in *koinonia*. Tutu believes:

The Bible sees us living harmoniously with God, with our fellow human beings, and with the rest of God's creation—

and so, we must all be "green." We must be concerned about the environment, about pollution, about finding alternative sources of energy, about depleting irreplaceable resources, about the so-called hothouse effect, about damage to the ozone layer, about deforestation, about soil erosion, and the encroachment of the desert—for God has sent us in [God's] world to be stewards of [the divine] bounty. We are meant to rule over God's world as God would rule—gently, compassionately, graciously, caringly. We are meant to leave the world a safer and better place than we found it.[40]

Therefore, any artificial barriers to separate human beings on the basis of race, status, wealth, gender, or age, are contrary to God's will. Christians should oppose any enforced separation or discrimination.[41]

Tutu's theology is characterized by deep reflection on creation and the image of God. He appeals for his society to see that the triune God encompasses the greatest mystery of how diversity can be unity. Tutu states, "It is no use trying to avoid [God's creation] because we are face to face here not with a puzzle but with mystery. A puzzle in principle can be solved if you have enough data. A mystery can never be solved. It just deepens."[42] Because God's ineffable nature prevents ready definitions of how we as God's creation participate in God's image, we are completely dependent on the image of God revealed in Jesus Christ.

TUTU'S CHRISTOLOGY

Central to Tutu's appeal to move beyond basing identity primarily on race is Tutu's Christology, in which black and white Christians look to Jesus to see a different reality than that defined by apartheid. For Tutu, Jesus moves human attention away from finite perspectives of human identity. That is, who one understands Christ to be is determined by who the beholder is. This means that training in true worship of God (habitual recollection) and discipleship are necessary for persons to see Christ. As Tutu believes, a correct understanding of Christ "depends on who and where you are and what is going to be pertinent for you."[43]

Tutu's Christology depicts both the particularity of Jesus as a Jew among the monotheistic Israelites and the universality of Jesus as the Messiah of the Gentiles. Both views of a savior joined in Jesus form a new humanity (Eph. 2). By stripping Jesus of his Jewish identity, a tendency found in theologians and biblical scholars of the Enlightenment, one is denied an understanding of the particular as access to truth— that is, denying that Gentiles were saved through God's election of Israel. In this light, Tutu's Christology becomes an apologetic against theological accounts that seek to justify one racial identity over another.

Through the particularity of a Jewish Jesus, God takes away the sins of the world. Through this priestly act, every culture is affirmed as God's proper creation. Consequently, Christ commands his disciples to go out into the world in the priestly role of baptizing new identities. This was also the promise to Abraham, to make him a blessing to all the nations. Such discipleship can provide both affirmation and critique of cultural understandings. For example, Philip affirms the Ethiopian and yet Philip baptizes a new destiny for the Ethiopian (Acts 8:38). Peter translates a new identity for Cornelius as Peter is, in turn, converted to see: "You yourselves know that it is unlawful for a Jew to associate with or to visit a Gentile; but God has shown me that I should not call anyone profane or unclean" (Acts 10:28). The priestly nature of being a Christian is bound to an understanding of Christ's discipleship in that no one escapes God's judgment of Christ's obedience. All are called to acknowledge that we are made aware of the sinful propensity of all cultures through the life, death, and resurrection of Christ. Through Christ, interdependence is made most intelligible.

Although Christ reveals interdependent existence, the whole creation continues to travail in bondage, longing for its release as it looks for the revelation of the glorious liberty of God's children (Rom. 8:18–22). Through Jesus, God has intervened decisively on the side of humanity by being the unbound strongman who snatches back the ill-gotten booty of Beelzebub (Matt. 12:29–31). The church believes that only Christ has the authority to define the other because he alone is without sin and so truly can see who the other is. Any others, black or white, who think that they know the full identity of another person or community solely on the basis of racial classification fall into sin. Sinners view limited knowledge as though it were eternal, and in this self-deception, become slaves to sin, to death, to the devil (Rom. 6:5–13; John 8:30–35).

For Tutu, the truth about persons is made known only through our relationship with Christ Jesus, who sets us free from deception and sin, thereby making it really possible to know the other. Jesus is then depicted as the one who is setting God's children free. It is imperative for him to heal the woman who has been afflicted for eighteen years, even if it must happen on the Sabbath, because this daughter of Abraham has been kept a prisoner by Satan in her infirmity (Luke 13:10–17).[44]

The writers of Ephesians and Colossians delight in describing Christ as a conquering general who has routed the powers of evil and now, having restored humanity, is leading them in a public spectacle in his conquering hero's procession (Eph. 4:7f.; Col. 2:15). This biblical interpretation facilitates Tutu's appeal for his society to move beyond privileging certain racial identities. In this regard, Tutu believes that God restores humanity in such a way that persons no longer own themselves (1 Pet. 1:18; Acts 20:28). Instead, all persons have been made free to be a royal household, serving God as priests (Rev. 1:15f.).

Such service begins at the cross. Without this starting point, there is no discipleship toward renewed human identity. Jesus states, "Whoever does not take up the cross and follow me is not worthy of me. Those who find their life will lose it, and those who lose their life for my sake will find it" (Matt. 10:38–39). The crown of all this New Testament evidence of Christ's renewal of human identity occurs in Jesus' characterization of his ministry in the words of Isaiah:

> The Spirit of [God] is upon me
> for [God] has anointed me
> [God] has sent me to announce good news to the poor,
> to proclaim release for prisoners and recovery of sight for the blind;
> to let the broken victims go free
> to proclaim the acceptable year of [God]. (Isa. 61:1–3)

And that acceptable year was the year of Jubilee, the year for setting slaves free (Lev. 25).[45]

In his ministry Jesus aroused the wrath of the religious establishment by hobnobbing with those who were called sinners: prostitutes and tax collectors (Mark 2:15–17). In relation to the despised of society, Jesus declared, "Whoever has seen me has seen God" (John 14:9). He was revealing the selfsame God who was biased in favor of the poor, the oppressed, and the outcast, and Jesus ultimately died for being on that side.[46]

> Jesus' ministry was one of identification with the victims of oppression, thus exposing the reality of sin. Liberating them

from the power of sin and reconciling them with God and with one another, he restored them to the fullness of their humanity. Therefore the Church's mission is the realisation of the wholeness of the human person. . . . Our conviction is that theologians should have a fuller understanding of living in the streets, for this also means being committed to a lifestyle of solidarity with the poor and the oppressed and involvement in action with them. Theology is not neutral. In a sense all theology is committed, conditioned notably by the socio-cultural context in which it is developed. The Christian theological task in our countries is to be "self-critical of theologians" conditioned by the value system of their environment. It has to be seen in relation to the need to live and work with those who cannot help themselves and to be with them in their struggle for liberation.[47]

Jesus becomes a paradigm for dealing with race and culture. Through him, Tutu makes sense of how the many become one. Jesus ultimately invites all racial and cultural identities to live out the call given first to Israel to be the people of God. Therefore, the reality of ubuntu is bound up in Jesus, who creates new relationships in the world.

Jesus, as the Human One, is called to transcend cultural boundaries and conventions, to bring into view the power to redefine cultural constructs, and to establish a new identity. This vocation comes from the relationship of the immanent Trinity, which demonstrates through Jesus that biological identities can no longer identify the Christian (Matt. 12:46–49). A new cultural logic is produced through Jesus, who requires of humanity obedience to the transcendent identity of baptism.

Jesus is the mediator of a new identity of interdependent relationship which reorders the distorted ways in which identity is formed. He lives a life of metanoia (Greek, "complete change of mind"), fulfilling the church's identity of modeling interdependent relationships to the world. For example, Jesus overcomes temptation by utter dependence upon the Father, which provides an end to individualism (John 6:57). The human and divine dependence of Jesus assures the church of a new identity in which the individual and the community exist in dependence. Jesus causes a new cultural politic in which social and economic agendas are based on the life of the triune God and defined by relationships with new sisters and brothers. In short, Jesus makes the other more important than the self in order to understand self-identity.

Some two thousand years later, Jesus' comforting presence, the Holy Spirit, enables us to move through the bondage of oppressive identities into reconciled ones. The Holy Spirit continues to bring Pentecost and reorients Jesus' followers (the church) outward and against cultural boundaries, even the boundary of death (Matt. 28:16). It is the presence of the Spirit that makes possible moving out to other cultures. Through Jesus, the Holy Spirit makes possible the constant redefinition of human identity, but such identity must be willing to die for a new identity to live (John 14:15–21; Rom. 6:1–11). For the Christian, baptism is this act of dying to the old identity to be born again in Christ. From such a Christology Tutu makes sense of the ruptures between African philosophy and Christian theological discourse. It is from Tutu's Christology that one begins to understand his doctrine of God and to see how Tutu views his role as a spiritual leader in politics.

TUTU'S GOD OF KENOSIS

Influenced by both African and Western thought, Tutu has a familial view of God, which he explains thus:

It was providential for me as it must have been for so many of us that our parents were Christians, that we assimilated so many things relating to our faith unconsciously at our mother's knees. We caught glimpses of what God must be like. . . . We experienced the compassion and gentleness of God from our mothers (at least sometimes when they were not tanning our hides). And we learned to speak, however fitfully and haltingly, with God in our recited prayers as our mothers knelt with us by our bedsides.[48]

Tutu's familial view of God, however, does not imply a domesticated concept of God in which God is merely human shouted loudly or spelled with a capital *H*. Just as being is understood through relationship in African discourse, so too is Tutu's view of accessing the mysteries of the triune God. He observes:

What God is, is what God does. God's [care] is from all eternity in which there is a ceaseless movement of love, an outpouring, a giving, sacrifice at the heart of the divine life. God gives to God the Son all of [God's] being and empties [the divine self] in the [love] of the Son who is coequal, coeternal with God, light of light, very God of very God . . . all eternity returns the love and the life and the being that the Son receives and gives back to the Father in equal measure, emptying himself totally without remainder, always giving, always receiving, always giving without end and this movement of life, of love of being is God the Holy Spirit, who binds the Father and Son and we have the eternal, ineffable triangle of love.[49]

Tutu's familial view of God derives from his African and European background in which he holds God's transcendence and immanence together. This means that when dealing with God, persons do not relate to one another as abstract entities, but as visceral bodies and souls. That is, Tutu is not an assimilationist black who blindly follows a "white's religion," but a Christian leader who sees human beings as far more than their racial classifications.

The God Christians worship is a God who is wonderfully transcendent—other than all there is. The psalmist and the prophet alike speak of the wonder of God's ways and thoughts, acknowledging that they are beyond our ways and thoughts. This God is utterly unlike anyone or anything else; even to behold God's face is an impossibility for a human being, because to do so would result in the death of the beholder.

Because of the utter holiness and otherness of God, Israel is forbidden to make an image of this God. There is nothing that can be a fit image or symbol for such a Supreme Being. Thus, John is true to the whole biblical tradition when he sums it all up by saying, "God is Spirit." This is the God who dwells in light inaccessible, so that the very angels veil their eyes in the divine presence. God is utterly unknowable, except insofar as God makes God's self known.

Yet when this God wanted to intervene in the affairs of God's creatures, God did not do what would appear to have been the natural thing to do. God did not come as a spiritual being, not as an angel. No, this God came as a human being. God came in a really human and physical way. A woman became pregnant, and God was born as a helpless baby, depending on mother and father for protection, for feeding, for love, for teaching.[50]

Maggie Ross, a notable influence on Tutu's theology,[51] declares that the familial nature of God is so vulnerable that mercy is willing to enter and pour through creation, not only when it is at its best, but most of all, when it is at its worst. For Ross, this is kenosis, when God willingly limits God's power in the self-emptying of Christ as seen in the Philippian hymn (Phil. 2:5–9) in which God takes the form of a servant, being born in the likeness of a human being. Ross concludes, "And God incarnate in Jesus is willing to be made object by the creation in order to overcome the abyss between subject and object, and thus destroy death and the fear of death."[52] Ross's view of kenosis, in which God has been emptied into creation, provides the conceptualization for Tutu to proclaim that loving God is authenticated by loving neighbor.[53]

Tutu also illustrates God's kenosis through Adam and Eve. They were befriended by God in such a way that God made them in the divine image, so that they had space to be persons, free to love God or refuse to love God, and free to obey or not to obey God. To have been made in any other way would have denied "God's readiness to limit the power of God, so that creation and humanity could exist in freedom and integrity."[54] As Tutu explains, this shows the integrity of God through the concept of kenosis:

This God, God from all eternity, is a blazing furnace of holy love in which the Father pours forth all . . . being to the Son who, coequal and co-eternal with the Father, pours back in equal measure his entire being in an eternal self-emptying to be filled without ceasing—with the Holy Spirit, binding the Father and the Son together forever. This kenosis, this self-emptying, this self-giving is an abiding characteristic of our God. This utterly self-sufficient God created all there is because God loved it. God loves it now. And God will love it forever and ever, world without end. Human words are inadequate to comprehend and describe this divine mystery. In the end we can only be silent . . . God created this world because God loves and when things went wrong, because of sin, God redeemed it. God, in Christ, emptied God's being of divine glory and God paid the price for our sin. It is all mystery, ultimately, and we cannot hope to encapsulate it in words. Words become an obstacle and a barrier. Instead, we need silence in the presence of this God we worship and adore, to be emptied of ourselves and to be filled with God, and so to become more truly ourselves as we are filled with the fullness of God.[55]

Ross influenced Tutu toward a kenotic theology in which the sacrificial and relational means by which God is present to the world are crucial for how we may serve society as Christians. God is present to the world through suffering for others. The kenotic nature of God also becomes crucial for how Tutu envisions the church serving his particular context of South Africa.

Ross's account of kenosis demonstrates that to sin in the face of unalterable love is much more painful than to sin in the face of an implacable authority. A person's return to God, having sinned and having returned God's gaze, restores a loving exchange in which oppressive racial classifications can be broken down. Through kenosis, the effects of apartheid's heresy are transformed. Caught up in kenosis, human turning to God enables even fragmented identities to be made whole through creation and re-creation in the pure fire of self-emptying love.

Although kenosis is often confined to mystical discourse, Tutu's affinity for kenotic theology encourages him to conceive how identities of race caused by apartheid can be reconciled in God's relationship to the world. Kenotic spirituality, as articulated by Ross, enables Tutu to proclaim God's justice as the act of self-emptying in a corrupted order that sees itself as just and true. A view of a kenotic God allows for harmonizing the Christian narratives of the African and the Afrikaner, instead of furthering their competition. Tutu states, "We worship a God who is a weak God. We worship a God who is a dying God. And through that death life comes."[56]

The subversive force of Tutu's kenotic assertion extends not only to theological discourse but also to the derivative forms of social power justified in South African political structures. Clearly, when the discernment of God is challenged, the images that take public form are in deep jeopardy. The image of human persons as only black or white is scrambled. Thus, Tutu wants to be disruptive through kenosis, in which the image of God as participant in the human condition is provided.

> God is ready to jeopardise the success of [God's] enterprise by engaging as [God's] partners those such as ourselves, wayward or impotent as we know ourselves to be. The divine human partnership is termed theandric. We see it in the very composition of the Bible where God speaks in the inadequate human words of [God's] human partners—God's eternal Word spoken through time bound words; God is ready to be understood and misunderstood as [any] human partner can understand and misunderstand [God], God ever willing to be immersed in the human condition, the Human mess, not standing aloof on some inaccessible Olympian height to shout down useful advice, but God coming down ultimately identifying so fully with our condition that [God] had to become a real human being, thrust through with the excruciating agony of the sword of our alienation and fragmented life. God calls us to be co-workers, co-creators and co-redeemers.[57]

UBUNTU'S LIBERATION

In Tutu's hands, ubuntu represents the claim that human identities are uniquely made to be more cooperative than competitive. In our God-given differences, we are called to realize our need for one another. For Tutu, then, racial distinctions matter only insofar as they demonstrate God's phenomenal creation, in which there is the end result of interdependency. This means that instead of a theology of separation or election, God's creation is seen both through the lens of ubuntu, as an African influence, and of kenosis, as a Christian theological influence. Both help Tutu to think about how God's image encourages diversity in a hostile world. Tutu states:

> God loves those who do not love, not because they were good, but because [God] is that kind of God—just as light cannot help seeking to dispel darkness. . . . And so when God had formed the Israelite slaves into a people, [God's] peculiar people, . . . holy nation, . . . royal priesthood, God demanded that they reflect [God's] character. Be holy as God was holy—remarkably a holiness that had little to do with natural purity as if a static attribute, but it was dynamic having to do with how they ordered their socio-political, economic life and ultimately tested by how they treated the widow, the orphan and the alien. (Lev. 19)[58]

Tutu's model of ubuntu seeks to be a conduit of this holiness in the midst of a society's unholy alliance with apartheid. In the context of South Africa, ubuntu is a vital concept by which Tutu aims to move his society toward a paradigm of reconciliation in which racial and cultural differences are no longer placed in a hierarchy of power. His theological model exposes the fragility of human identity through the means of God's kenotic entry into creation. Like God, and in God's image, human beings are to be persons who no longer claim power or hierarchical identities. Instead, they move toward being born anew into a society capable of containing difference without such difference destroying the society.

Tutu's ubuntu means that racial identity, as defined by those in power, can no longer be the sole determinant for humanity. Instead, Tutu seeks a conciliatory solution through ecclesiology and ubuntu. In the process, Tutu forms a different kind of black theology.

Persons and governments cannot stipulate God's preference for some persons on the basis of race. Because of this premise, Tutu's theological model presents a particular spirituality of liberation in which black theology is a component. Tutu states:

> I am an exponent of black theology and the firm believer in black consciousness. Black theology merely incarnates the Christian faith for blacks, just as German, Scandinavian, and other types of theology incarnate the Christian faith for their various peoples. Black theology is firmly biblical. I am ready to demonstrate this to anyone who is willing to listen.
>
> Black consciousness is of God. [Jesus] said the two major laws are "Love God and thy neighbour as thyself." A proper self-love is an indispensable ingredient to love of others. Black consciousness seeks to awake in the black person an awareness of their worth as a child of God. Apartheid, oppression, injustice are blasphemous and evil because they have made God's children doubt that they are God's children.
>
> Black consciousness is deeply religious. It is not anti-white. It is pro-black and only if it succeeds will it be possible to have any reconciliation. Reconciliation happens only between persons not between persons and dehumanised half-persons. Why is black consciousness such a horrendous thing and Afrikaner consciousness so admirable?[59]

Instead of accepting apartheid's classifications of a lower tier (*kaffir*) and a higher tier (*bosskap*), Tutu uses the concept of ubuntu to affirm the practices of an indigenous theological vision to provide common discourse for those who call themselves South Africans. Although he speaks of ubuntu in the South African context, he does not develop it as definitively African.

Instead of perpetuating conflicting gospels between African and Afrikaner, Tutu's theological convictions of "nonracialism"[60] emerge from practices of the Christian life such as prayer, liturgy, and conversion. Tutu uses these practices to undermine a racist Christianity; he offers a mutual means of struggle for sympathetic Europeans to accept an African's humanity and for the African to forgive the hostile racist practices of Europeans. Tutu inherited these theological convictions from his church and African tradition, which facilitated his strong appeal for South Africa[61] (in all its diversity of peoples) to be faithful to the particular nature and work of Christ's redemption in the world. The beauty of this inheritance is that Tutu's ecclesiology and ubuntu lead him to model reconciliation (i.e., proper relatedness), even among those defined as enemies. By being so faithful, there is mutual dependence of white and black Christians in South Africa in their efforts to achieve liberation and justice. As Tutu concludes, "I will want to show that apartheid, separate development, parallel democracy or whatever this racist ideology is currently called is evil totally and without remainder. . . . [Apartheid] more shatteringly denies the central act of reconciliation which the New Testament declares was achieved by God in [God's] Son our Lord Jesus Christ."[62]

CHAPTER FIVE

INSPIRED BY WORSHIP
AND ADORATION OF GOD

I come as your Pastor of both black and white. I love you
all very deeply. I am concerned for the agony and anguish
of families where their sons are fighting on the border,
fighting an unnecessary war to defend something I
believe is utterly indefensible. The problem of our country
is not on the border. It is right here in our midst—it is
apartheid, it is injustice and oppression.

Inspired by our worship and adoration of God and so
made sensitive to discover Jesus Christ among the poor,
the hungry, the oppressed, I hope that you will speak out
against what causes suffering and anguish to God's
children just because they are black, and I am confident
that you will support your Bishop when he witnesses on
your behalf. . . . Let us talk together black and white.

—Desmond Tutu, "Enthronement Charge" (sermon, 1985)

That South Africa's system of apartheid competes with God
for loyalty and that the way out of the racial deadlock could
only be in recognizing humankind as created in the image of
God—these are the first two elements of Tutu's ubuntu theology of reconciliation. One might well wonder, then, how
the political application of this theology related to Tutu's role
as archbishop in the Anglican Church of the Province of
Southern Africa (CPSA). Was this church not the white European oppressor's institution? Upon what resources was

he able to call? To what extent did such activism place Tutu in tension with his own religious community?

ANGLICAN VIEW OF THE CHURCH IN SOUTH AFRICA

The contemporary catechism of the Anglican Church of the Province of South Africa seems rather straightforward in its definitions of the Christian church. The church "is the community of the new covenant," "described in the Bible as the body of which Jesus Christ is the head and of which all baptized persons are members." Its mission is "to restore all people to unity with God and each other in Christ," which it pursues "as it prays and worships, proclaims the gospel, and promotes justice, peace, and love" and "through the ministry of all the members."[1]

The Anglican Church in South Africa was established in 1870, and now has twenty-two dioceses in Lesotho, Mozambique, Namibia, South Africa, Swaziland, and the South Atlantic Island of St. Helena. Its membership comprises about three million people representing diverse languages, races, and cultures. It encompasses both catholic and evangelical traditions, including the charismatic renewal that seeks a creative tension of tolerance.[2] Despite the potential richness of its worship life, the Anglican Church in South Africa has not yet fully embraced the diversity of its members. Thus, one of its major challenges is to discern the good in each culture that it represents and to produce something authentically Southern African.[3]

The Anglican Communion

The Anglican Church of the Province of South Africa is related to the Church of England, but they are distinct churches. The Anglican Communion was developed in two stages. The first stage included colonialization in the United States, Australia, Canada, New Zealand, and South Africa at the beginning of the seventeenth century. The second involved missionary work, beginning in the eighteenth century, in Asia, Africa, and Latin America. The Anglican Church, in many of these regions, offers an alternative to the Church of England, which was frequently the object of rebellion when a particular territory was under colonial rule.

As defined in one of its major documents, the Anglican Communion is "a worldwide family of churches. There are more than 70 million Anglican Christians, in 29 autonomous churches spread across 160 countries in every continent."[4] Autonomous churches in the Anglican Communion are unified through their "history, their theology and their relationship to the Archbishop of Canterbury." The common theology "upholds and proclaims the Catholic and Apostolic faith, based on the creeds and scripture, interpreted in the light of Christian tradition, scholarship, and reason."[5] As archbishop of an autonomous church, Tutu had sufficient latitude to shape a contextual theological approach.

Not unlike other Christian traditions, the Anglican Communion is committed to the proclamation of the good news of the gospel to the whole creation by baptism, in the name of the triune God. Herein individual persons are made one with Christ and received into the church. This act of unity is made known in the rite of the Holy Eucharist, which is central to the act of worship for Anglicans. In this rite, the offering of prayer and praise recall the life, death, and resurrection of Christ as a proclamation of the Word and celebration of the sacrament.

A History of Protest

The Anglican witness is peculiar to South Africa because it precipitated the inception of the Anglican Communion. The first Lambeth conference was called largely to deal with the so-called Colenso controversy.[6] Bishop John William Colenso in the late 1800s dissented from England over the ill treatment of Africans. Since then, the Anglican Church has sought to describe its catholicity through the resulting Lambeth conferences.

Until recently, South African legislation, referred to as the "church clause," declared multiracial church gatherings illegal. An earlier Anglican archbishop in South Africa, Geoffrey Clayton, on behalf of the bishops, signed a letter on Ash Wednesday, March 6, 1957, to the prime minister, Dr. Hendrik Verwoerd. The bishops wanted him to know that if the government were to promulgate that law, they would advise their congregations to disobey it. Although the law was not abolished, it was rarely implemented.

In the Anglican Church in South Africa, others besides Clayton advocated the equality of Africans in South African society. For example, the Anglican bishop of Pretoria sent two resolutions from the diocesan and episcopal synods of the church of the Province of South Africa to the national convention in 1908. They expressed the hope that union would be established on the foundations of cooperation, trust, and justice towards all sections of the population.[7] This concern began to spread to other church bodies. Michael Worsnip, in his work on the Anglican Church in South Africa, describes the period between 1948 and 1957 as the time in which the Anglican Church wrestled with its identity as the church of the establishment.[8] During this time the Anglican Church challenged the government and refused to obey the demands of the proposed Native Laws Amendment Act. Worsnip's work is helpful in examining the attitudes, conditions, events, and perspectives that developed into an attitudinal divide in South African Anglicanism between activists and gradualists.

Today this divide can be described as between the activists, reconciliationalists, and territorialists. In part this is because, as Worsnip points out, the Anglican Church could not become the established church even if it wanted to do so. The presence of the Dutch Reformed Church and the politics of the British government have meant that since the Voluntary Bill of 1875, no established church has existed in South Africa.[9] With the provincial synod of 1870, the Anglican Church in South Africa became an autonomous body within the worldwide Anglican Communion, even though it could not exist legally in South Africa. Thus, a voluntary society that adhered to the faith, doctrine, and discipline of the Church of England was attempted, incurring a new set of problems in the African context.

Due to the seeming lack of commitment from more than a few in the Anglican Church, however, it is difficult to conclude that the Anglican Church was a forerunner in the fight for the African cause. What is clear is that the Anglican Church carried within itself the impulses for protest. Archbishop Desmond Tutu had as a resource this tradition of protest regarding ill treatment which he was able to turn outward on the national scene.

The Case of Cape Town

The diocese of Cape Town offers a perspective on how the Anglican Church in South Africa had to grow in relation to apartheid. This diocese witnessed the greatest upheaval of people under apartheid's Group Areas Act because it consists of urban parishes within a wide radius of Cape Town as well as large, rural parishes in towns and districts outside of Cape Town. Thousands of colored (mixed-race) and black persons were relocated to less desirable places in order to allow whites better access to land and property. Thus were established the vast housing estates of the Cape Flats. Despite the travel distance, some colored people (the largest ethnic group in the Cape) continued to worship in parishes in Cape Town proper, from which they were evicted.

The Group Areas Act forced black people to move to Cape Town in order to escape the poverty of the so-called Ciskei and Transkei homelands. Thus, they became migrant or contract workers who could not own property or legally bring their families to Cape Town. The result was the construction of the poverty-stricken areas of Crossroads and Khaylitsha. Black men lived in hostels and were legally restricted from living with their wives and children in the Cape. Many defied this legislation, becoming homeless in order to be with their families.

In the new South Africa, laws limiting the influx of black people into white areas have been repealed. Urbanization occurs at an overwhelming rate. This has rendered the material resources of local churches inadequate to respond to the overwhelming needs—apart from the resources of worship—of their congregants.

Elsewhere, in rural areas of the Cape defined mostly by fruit farms, people have struggled against paternalistic systems of land distribution and farm workers' rights. Their resistance against the laws of apartheid needed to be channeled constructively to create an alternative society to apartheid—a task that the church could (and with Tutu did) undertake.[10]

Tutu's Assessment of the Anglican Church

The question that addressed Archbishop Tutu was: How can the people be offered this vision of constructive change? For Tutu, it was through the liturgy of the Anglican Church, through recalling the presence of God in the midst of relationships, which should lead to the reality of grace and the ability to discern right action and being. Tutu states:

> For me, it would be impossible to engage in the kind of public life I have had if this was not undergirded by the spiritual life. Our tradition is one where we have, as far as possible, a daily Eucharist and an extended time of quiet in meditation, and mid-day we have (again, the Anglo-catholic thing) to pause for the Angelus. Particularly now, in South Africa, all religious people are being called to pause in the middle of the day to pray for peace in our country and to seek to be aware that whatever you are doing is within the context of serving God. . . .
>
>   I belong in the Church and know that, however feeble my own prayers are, I am sustained by the fervour and the prayers and intercessions of all these people around the world. There is this constant stream of worship and adoration and all I need to do is to jump into the stream and float and be carried by the current of the worship and adoration of far holier people than me.[11]

The South African context of apartheid illumines an interesting juxtaposition in the Anglican Church's liturgy. The liturgy seeks a common worship and life across the church. Instead of achieving an undergirding common theology, however, a confusion between what was Anglican and what was British created disparate views of the church. Tutu explains:

> We should so order the life of our churches so that others do not feel they are God's stepchildren and that God's home-language is English, and that the British parliamentary procedure is necessarily the best way of doing our business. . . . Our church structures should reflect the reality that blacks form 80 percent

of our church population. We are indigenised in the bad sense of being conformed to the ways of the world we inhabit. Our churches, whilst seeking to move away from the ways of the past, have been bastions of the very policies for which they have condemned the government.[12]

Africans, in particular, were made to lose or belittle their own uniqueness in forming a common church. Tutu states, "These poor creatures must be made to sing the white man's hymns hopelessly, badly translated, they had to worship in the white man's unemotional and individualistic way, they had to think and speak of God and all the wonderful Gospel truths in the white man's well proven terms."[13] In this, he counters those who think they know what the church is when, in fact, they are operating from an established, institutional perspective.

To compensate for the oppressive history of a colonial church—and to retrieve the Anglican Church's own sporadic protests regarding ill treatment—Tutu embraced the Anglican Church as the liturgical church that embodies the relentless fight against apartheid. Somehow this liturgical church is to represent both the white community, whose imperial power is just as strong at present as it was in the colonial era, and the black community, whose dream of full participation in South Africa is now being formed into reality. Tutu claims to do this through a church which "is the continuation of Christ's life on earth, teaching, healing, empowering." He continues:

It is the storehouse of the energy and power of good which must combat the power of evil to the end, and which as it triumphs over the dark power makes all things new. . . . To express the priesthood and the church in general you have to think of a double duty: to bring God to the world, and to bring the world to God. . . . The common priesthood is the priesthood of service. . . . And again the two things, work and worship, are mutually interactive: you make your worship complete when you make it a part of your work for the world; you make your work complete when you turn it into loving service for the world and so into worship of the Redeemer of the world.[14]

For Tutu, the liturgical church comprises a wide spectrum of people: from healers to murderers, from saints to scoundrels. He asks:

Is [the church] a cosy club for like-minded persons who can be persuaded once a week to disturb their normal routine to have their Christian prejudices confirmed whilst they are insulated against the harsh realities of life out there without being shaken out of a complacency as they are assured that God has sanctified their sacrosanct way of life? Or does it exist to be a kind of mystical ivory tower of some spiritual ghetto unconcerned about what goes on under the noses of its members whilst they claim to offer worship to God in the meantime as excuse for that neglect? Or does it exist to become involved in a mad rush of good works agitating its members into a frazzle as they rush from one good work to another leaving behind the so-called beneficiaries of all this wearing the haggard and woebegone expressions of those who have been done good by at all costs? . . . The Church is the fellowship whence adoration, worship and praise ascend to the heavenly throne."[15]

The miracle of the church is that everyone—the poor, the rich, the free, the slave, male, female, black, white—can find one identity in Christ. All can be organized into one, interdependent entity to carry on diverse functions for the good of the one body.

In the church, distinctions are not cause for disunity, but are necessary for the organic unity that is the Body of Christ. Such a church is essential where racial discrimination, repression, and injustice are sanctioned by law, because it is through the church that an alternative reality may be experienced. "And so it happened," Tutu recalls, "that certain churches took to putting up notices announcing what should surely be obvious, that this house is open to people of all races who would be welcome to all services. In the South African setting, this was not only odd but was often regarded as subversive of good order."[16]

As a result of this view of the church, Tutu stated, "I will want most diocesan meetings to begin with Eucharist. I want to stress the centrality of the spiritual, and I will hope we can help to develop in all parishes, daily Eucharist, Bible Study, and prayer groups, for our resources are ultimately spiritual."[17] Only by examining these spiritual resources from Tutu's perspective can his view of the church be fully appreciated. It is to the Sunday Eucharist that we now turn.

THE ANGLICAN ORDER OF WORSHIP

What is it, then, that Bishop Tutu found so influential and nourishing in the Anglican order of worship? Tutu's speeches, essays, and other sources are rich with reflections, appeals to his hearers, and anecdotes that all relate back to this worship order. A few of these connections are offered to illustrate how worship informed Tutu's worldview and actions in relation to his vision of the church.

"The Lord Be with You"

The greeting for the Holy Eucharist, "The Lord be with you," seeks to turn human attention to God. These words begin the integration of liturgy into the experiences of everyday life. The people respond, "And also with you," in recognition that God is not only with them but also with the priest.[18]

In order for God's presence to be meaningful in the context of the church, an openness to allowing God to restore relationship amidst warring identities needs to be present. In this regard Tutu asks: "What is our pastoral responsibility to our white membership who are scared of sharing political power who are holding on for dear life and making it more and more certain that there will be a violent denouement to the drama being played out here? And what do we do with the black community which is wracked by so much disunity?"[19] Instead of living in despair, separated from God, Tutu believes that the community's attention needs to be brought back to God and made aware that God is with them. God's presence creates new ways of being the church in South Africa that reaches beyond bourgeois realism and promotes an ethic beyond facile moral appeal.

In worship is a means to practice the presence of God in a way that continually expands the understanding of how persons are in relation. Expressed in Tutu's daily practice of prayer is the conviction that God's presence sustains life, even in the midst of the tragedies of South Africa.[20] All life belongs to God, including politics. If the church seeks to be uninvolved with the world, it worships a God other than the God found in Christ. Everyday life is meant to be a working out of a life of worship so that, as Simone Weil aptly articulates, our attention span for God is increased.[21] When such attention is achieved, even oppressors are transformed to see their identity as sinful and perverted.

Gloria in Excelsis

The ancient hymn "Glory to God in the highest and peace to God's people on earth" is expanded from the angels' praise of the baby Jesus in Luke 2:14. By reciting or singing this hymn, the church is reminded to praise Jesus, who is about to be encountered in the sacrament.

Tutu's ecclesiology forms around this encounter: "We worship and adore God because the chief purpose of being human is to glorify God and to enjoy God forever."[22] For Tutu, worship is the whole purpose of life (e.g., Rom. 12:1–2). In short, for Tutu, being human is to worship. He explains that in a "worshipful encounter with God we not only discover something of God's awesome majesty, but we also gain a whole new perspective on life. In the exhilaration of the discovery we exclaim, 'Hey, this is God! This is God's world and God is in charge of this world, whatever the appearances to the contrary might be.'"[23]

The difficulty is worshiping the true God. The church dare not compartmentalize life lest we become like the devil who negotiates the world through definitions of insatiable appetites, kingdoms, and risk. All of the world belongs to God. Therefore, the church must constantly live in the tension of opposite forces instead of operating from such false dichotomies as white versus black identities. Through worship God calls the church to serve Jesus by learning to be the kind of persons who naturally serve God in all of creation. Thus, a Christian identity without distinction between act and being is formed. For example, in Matthew 25:31–46 (the parable of great judgment), the Human One is pleased with those who are unaware of their good deeds. And most distinctively in this text, Tutu holds to the interpretation that when serving the least of society, one worships Jesus himself.[24]

The Collect for Purity

Similar to the greeting for the rite of Holy Eucharist, the Collect for Purity directs those who worship to concentrate their minds and hearts on God. Purity refers to this focused state of mind. The word "collect" may also originate from a custom in Rome where there was a prayer after the congregation (*collecta*) gathered together.[25] This collect acknowledges the dissonance between what we believe and what we do. Therefore, it provides a liturgical basis for introspection.

Through the church, Tutu believes that God created persons for a purpose, namely, to be reconciled ultimately in the person of Jesus Christ. But the presence of sin suggests that such reconciliation has not yet occurred. Whatever one's particular definition of sin, it only becomes intelligible through Christ's atonement, which restores the ruptures between persons and renews the beauty of human identities through sacrifice. The purity of Jesus attracted or "collected" the forces of evil and, as Gregory of Nyssa believed, sabotaged their reign in the world through the miracle of God's cross. Along with this restoration is the renewal of human access to God.

Tutu states, "Our people say Ubuntu. Ubuntu is something you say when someone has wronged you. What you long for is not revenge. What you long for is a healing of relationships."[26] Refusal to see related identities is Tutu's definition of sin, the converse of ubuntu.

Sin thus affects the way persons understand themselves to be and their relationship to creation. Therefore a confession of faith is closely tied to a confession of sin because the understanding of sin takes into account the need of the other. Sin is not merely individual but also communal, made up of all those who contribute to the breakage of communion. To know what to confess as sin depends on the Collect for Purity. For Tutu, if confession is more than a sentimental act, the confessor must be able to name more than sin as abstraction; he or she must be able to name the particular offense against the other. Otherwise, confession is a trivialized process.[27]

Lord Have Mercy

The Kyrie, "Lord, have mercy," is the cry of those who can name their offenses against others and want to be absolved of them. It is also the gathered cry to God for the sake of all. South Africa is a society in which harm has been done to others by people intent on protecting their own identities. Tutu states, "The Afrikaners say they won't easily forget what the British did to them in the concentration camps. They might forgive but forget, not easily. We won't forget easily what this government and white people have done and continue to do in their vicious policy of forced population removals."[28] In this context, questions of how persons become accountable to others seem insurmountable. How does the white person repay centuries of dehumanizing black people, especially in light of a premise that the guiding principle of life is survival of the fittest?

God's mercy cannot be left solely to those in government who rule based on what is perceived as progress for the common good. Instead, the church must witness to the world that the highest good is not defined only by evolutionary progress. Rather, the highest good is God, who is to be worshiped and adored so that human reason may transcend the logical ends of evolutionary progress. Otherwise, the logical end of human constructs of reality is "eat or be eaten." From this, we need the rescue of God's mercy.

Against the identity of human persons being the objectified means of another person's progress, the church intercedes on behalf of all creation so that our disposition to consume life may cease.

> Others have wanted to fragment and divide and alienate us from one another and separate us into hostile and warring factions estranged from one another. God sent Jesus Christ to be our peace, breaking down the middle wall of partition.

. . . Jesus Christ came to effect reconciliation between us and God and between us and our neighbours and to us has been committed this ministry of reconciliation, of love, of working for peace because we work for justice.[29]

The Word of God

The reading of the Scriptures and preaching are means by which the oppressed and the oppressor continue to learn of God's self-communication. One central implication of this Word of God is that it has spiritual repercussions in all matters of life; Tutu's favorite text is Ephesians 2:14: "For Jesus himself is our peace who has made the two, one, and has destroyed the barrier the dividing wall of hostility by abolishing in his flesh the law with his commandments and regulations."[30]

Perhaps the element of the Anglican rite most visible to the world has occurred precisely here in his preaching against apartheid. Tutu's sermons continually explore how the work of Christ reconciles humans. This excerpt from a sermon is one example:

Tonight we are reminded forcefully that we are the Body of Christ—The mystical body which receives the Sacramental body in order to become more fully the mystical body the Church. For tonight we commemorate the institution of the Holy Eucharist in the Sacrament of the Body and Blood of our Saviour Jesus Christ.

My brothers and sisters, we are the body of Jesus Christ who loved unto the end. We who are His Body are meant to reflect His characteristics. He Himself said that the outstanding mark of the church, that which would distinguish us in the world, was not wealth, was not influence, no—what would distinguish us was to be this: "A New Commandment I give to you that you love one another. As I have loved you so are you to love one another. If there is this love among you then all will know that you are my disciples" (John 13:34–35).

It was this love which drew the pagans into the early church as they remarked with wonder, "How these Christians love one another," they are like members of one family, brothers and sisters. Someone has said "relatives" aren't there to be liked, they are there to be relatives.[31]

The Nicene Creed

The Nicene Creed provides continued expression of the church's faith as agreed upon at the Council of Constantinople in 381 c.e., a decision that marked the end of the controversy concerning the divinity of Christ as the child of God. Central to this creed is Christology, which is the reason that the Eucharist—the rite of thanksgiving—becomes the whole act of worship revolving around Jesus and the salvation that he instilled in the world.

For Tutu, the creed is not simply a statement of what the church believes. It is also the church's deliberate commitment to worship God in the world as revealed in Christ. Tutu's model of the church demonstrates that every recital of the creed is the assertion that we belong to God through relational means of Trinity (i.e., the persons of Father, Son, and Holy Spirit). Following from the relational conceptualization of God as the Trinity, the church believes itself to be one, holy, catholic, and apostolic—descriptions that show the connection between the doctrine of God as relational and a commitment to a common life of the church.[32]

This connection helps to explain Tutu's model of the composition of the church. Tutu states:

It does not matter that the church is not full, that there are but one or two parishioners present. For you are never alone.

The whole church of God is present with you at every celebration because Christ the Lamb of God is present and where
Christ is, the Church is present also—the church quiescent of
those who are asleep in Christ, the church militant of those
working with Christ in His vineyard on earth and the church
triumphant of those in glory who behold God face to face.
The church is not empty for if our eyes could be opened we
should see it filled to overflowing with angels and archangels and the cloud of witnesses surrounding us.[33]

The Prayers of the People

Prayer is the offering of self through the practice of God's presence in the world. Western Christian spirituality is often criticized as being "navel-gazing," providing little recourse to social action because of its individualism. This is a perennial
problem for Christian theologians, especially moral theologians
who seek to rediscover their ascetic roots.[34] Tutu's ubuntu theology provides an alternative to the typical Western spirituality obsessed with the self. Tutu states:

> Life is meant to give us the opportunity to grow in intimacy
> with God through a deepening of our life of prayer. . . . Through
> prayer, Bible reading, meditation and the regular use of the
> sacraments and through retreats, . . . we must be growing in
> contemplation of the God who has created us for the divine
> life. That is all we can bring the world which is distinctively
> Christian, our prayers, our spiritual life. A church that does
> not pray is quite useless. Christians who do not pray are of no
> earthly worth. We must be marked by a heightened God con-
> sciousness. And then all kinds of things will happen.[35]

Ever since the early church, Christians have sought to influence societal matters by integrating the life of prayer with

the daily life of the individual and community. In prayer as the practice of the presence of God, the individual cannot help but pay attention to the needs of a community that believes it is different from the world. Christian intercession trains the individual to move beyond requests for individual benefit and into the dynamic of being properly related to God and neighbor.

Sharing the Peace

Sharing the Lord's Peace by greeting one's fellow congregants at a particular point in the worship service manifests God's reconciliation within the community. "How," asks Tutu, "could the world believe the Gospel of reconciliation delivered by an unreconciled Church?"[36] For him, the church is to be "God's agent of salvation to transfigure the world."[37]

The ideal of Tutu's ecclesiology is to further his theological model of divine and human relationship in which the continuity of the liturgy of the church flows back into the world through the sharing of the Peace. In this respect, Tutu's ecclesiology forms a relational theology[38] that seeks to describe how reconciliation of disparate identities may occur in an apartheid context.

In South Africa, the term *reconciliation* does not capture the magnitude of the task. When all African communities achieve full share in determining policies in South Africa, only then, thinks Tutu, will the possibility exist for reconciliation among all races and cultures. Therefore, through black liberation in South Africa, Tutu seeks the correct relational complement of black and white liberation: No one is a person in South Africa until blacks attain the freedom to open their God-given personhood and humanity. Reconciliation implies a prior relationship that was broken and that is being restored. But in South Africa, relationships have always been distorted by the presupposition of the superiority of the white male. For churches to foster repentance and reconciliation means that they must build a degree of mutual understanding and acceptance that will be entirely new to South Africa—and to the world. Therefore, Tutu places the onus for true reconciliation on whites.[39]

If reconciliation can be given any coherent meaning, perhaps it needs to be understood in terms of the task of each believer questioning at the heart of faith. This questioning is not our interrogation of the heart, but its interrogation of us. The intractable strangeness of the ground of belief needs constantly to be allowed to challenge the fixed assumptions of one's religiosity.

Tutu believes that reconciliation is a deeply personal affair among equals. It can happen only between persons of shared identity. Blacks need to claim their inheritance as children of God; whites need fully to realize that black persons are of infinite value as persons created in the image of the triune God. Only thus will they both be able to acknowledge the human personhood of each other, neither one superhuman, but human and frail together.

The Presentation of Gifts

The giving of money or gifts in the liturgy (*liturgia*, "work of the people") is intended to provide for the mission of the church and the needs of the poor. The church teaches the world to learn to love real people. The church facilitates the flourishing of human gifts in communal settings through prayer, singing, and the sharing of the body and blood of Christ. These sacramental acts facilitate the practice of shared human identities. Tutu observes: "Because we are a family, we will be characterised by our readiness to share, to share worship, to share pain and joy, to share equitably in the wealth of our country, in its resources, in its land, in its economic and social amenities, in political power. Those who don't share end up losing all."[40]

Tutu lives in the optimism of a new world as he states: "I believe in miracles and therefore I know that justice and righteousness will overcome evil and oppression, and we shall all be free, black and white together. I pray we are seeing the dawning of that day."[41] But this optimism comes at the price of being transformed: "No longer to be dependent upon the material crutches of security, possessions, and power, to which we cling, but [God] is asking us to throw down those crutches, stand upright, and to become truly ourselves"— that is, to be God's children in a way that leaves nothing for self, but God.[42]

The Taking of the Bread and Wine

The institution of the Eucharist begins with the events of the Last Supper, on the night in which Judas handed over Jesus to the authorities. The use of the imperfect tense, *paradidonai*, in Ephesians 5:2 and 25, conveys the meaning that Jesus *continues* giving himself over to the authorities. Present-day disciples may reflect on how they also are responsible in their daily lives for betraying Jesus.[43]

This portion of the rite explicates Tutu's view of prayer[44] as the true means by which Christ offered himself. For Tutu, prayer is the offering of self through the habitual practice of God's presence until God is one day experienced in full. Christ initiated this habit at the Last Supper, when, after offering the bread and wine, he informed the disciples that the offering would be transformed in the dominion of God (Mark 14:22–23). This view of prayer guards against both facile notions of access to God through one's "personal relationship with God" and notions that common prayer is static and perfunctory. Prayer as offering of self opens the sign of blessing for continual service to the world. Tutu explains that "the most important thing is that God is being worshipped and adored."[45]

The common practice of the Holy Eucharist begins when the bread and wine are brought to the altar from the congregation, continuing the early custom whereby worshipers provided what was needed for the Eucharist, to help them understand their involvement in the whole celebration. After taking the bread and the wine, the priest washes his or her hands. This is the *lavabo*, from the Latin of Psalm 26:6: "I wash my hands in innocence, and go about thy altar, O Lord." Following this ritual of being absolved from sin, the priest assumes the priestly role of offering the sacrifice of Christ.

The priest then adds water to wine, showing the humanity and divinity of Christ. The prayer, dating back to the fifth century, that is offered at this time is: "Almighty God who wonderfully created us in your own image and yet more wonderfully restored us, grant that as your Son our Lord Jesus Christ came to share in our humanity, so may we be brought to share in his divine life."[46] This prayer refers to God as "God of all creation," which reminds the church that despite the reality of the South African tragedy of a racial war, God still cares for the whole earth.

The Great Thanksgiving

The central act of praise and thanksgiving for God's work of salvation in Christ is said over the bread and wine. This is the climax of the whole act of worship, in which we make present the once-for-all offering of Christ on the cross and his resurrection. It is not simply a remembrance of God's presence in Christ; it is the liturgical way in which we recognize Christ as a present reality by which the life of the church and the world is continually renewed and sustained.[47]

The Eucharistic prayer is given in four forms, and a fifth is provided in an alternative order. In each case, the prayer should be seen as a unity, so that the same posture should be adopted by worshipers throughout. The Great Thanksgiving begins with the renewed assurance of God's presence among the people. Following a dialogue of praise to God between priest and people, Tutu's prayer in the Great Thanksgiving describes what God has done in and through Christ in creation and redemption and in making us God's people. The Great Thanksgiving displays the appreciation for "the mystery of faith" revealed in Christ.[48] Tutu illustrates:

> We are a family. That is wonderful. It is wonderful that the service of Inauguration is celebrated with the Eucharist, the Great Thanksgiving. I have already shown just how much we have to thank God and other people. . . . It is fitting that we are gathered at the Lord's Table. It is interesting that Jesus did not say we should build Him a statue. He did not write a book by which He would be remembered. He said He wanted to be remembered by something so homely, so ordinary as a meal—through the breaking of the bread and the drinking of the wine.
>
> What is most characteristic of a meal? Wouldn't you say it is *sharing*? In traditional African feasting people do not eat out of separate plates. They share out of one utensil. . . . In sophisticated places we still have vestiges of this way of eating out of one dish. One usually carves the one joint and shares it among those who will be eating. Vegetables are placed in one dish and the guests share out of that one dish. . . . Likewise, sharing one's heart is the great thing about the family context in which usually the youngest and those whom make very little contribution eat the most.[49]

The Great Thanksgiving translates into the lives of Christians in the following way. "As Christians," Tutu believes, "we are expected to be Eucharistic people—those who cannot cease saying 'Thank You' to God."[50] Tutu's thankfulness offers a great example of the sacramental model of the church through his emphasis on recalling the presence of Christ in the midst of tragedy and violence. For Tutu, to recall Christ's presence continually in the world is to comfort and strengthen, heal and pacify, and all this in order to facilitate unity in the midst of a bewildered and bleeding land. Through Tutu's Anglican tradition, a sacramental church, he is able to be thankful through the practices of the church that claim God is present in all contexts, even in tragedy.

The Sanctus

The Sanctus—"Holy, holy, holy Lord / God of power and might / heaven and earth are full of your glory"—is derived from Isaiah's vision (Isa. 6:3) and invites the whole congregation to join "with angels and archangels and with all the company of heaven" in praise and adoration. The Sanctus signifies the unity of holiness in which heaven interpenetrates earth.

Tutu offers an interesting perspective on how the holy God interpenetrates human personal relationships:

Human beings must not just by rights be respected but they must be held in awe and reverence. In our Anglican church tradition often we have what is called the "Reserved Sacrament" in a tabernacle on an altar and a light always burns to alert the faithful that the sacrament is reserved in that part of the church. When we pass in front of an altar we normally reverence the altar with a bow, but before the reserved sacrament we usually genuflect. It is not fanciful to say that if we took our theology seriously, we should genuflect to one another.[51]

Through this holy respect not only for God but also for one another, Tutu believes God's intention is to unite all that separates and divides the peoples of this world. The purpose of the church is to be the instrument of this intention; and, as Tutu concludes, "If we are faithful we will help to bring to pass that great vision of John the Divine—of people from every race, tribe, nation and language united in the praise and worship of Almighty God."[52] In the Sanctus, Tutu now enters this ceaseless paean of praise uttered by heaven and earth.

This holiness is not ethereal, however. For Tutu, if worship is to be an encounter with God as Ultimate Reality, it is this Reality that needs to shape the church's perceptions of social reality. The church cannot allow its goals and action to be shaped and determined by bourgeois notions of what is possible. The church is to be holy. This is the single most important service that the church can render to the world, as Tutu's understanding of church provides an alternative vision of what by God's grace is socially possible. It is the task of the church to infuse God's holiness into human reality. In the biblical tradition, holiness is not gnosis, but a way of living or acting in obedience to God's creative and redemptive participation in human history.

The Institution Narrative

"This is my body broken for you" is in the present tense; Christ is given to the communicant. The Eucharist is not simply a memorial of a past act in history, it encompasses past, present, and future: "This is my body which is given for you."[53] This conflation of time is evidenced in the Last Supper, which involves *anamnesis* ("remembrance"; cf. 1 Cor. 11:25) as a way of remembering Christ in an ongoing way. In the narrative of the Last Supper, the congregation express their understanding of the present reality of Christ in the world. The church's current reality is realized in the sacrament.

As the priest presides at this sacrament, the acclamation of Christ's broken body and poured blood for the sake of the world joins the priest with the whole congregation in the celebration of the Eucharist. From this point, the rite of the Holy Eucharist proceeds with the Eucharistic prayers, all of which end with a petition of the realization of the unity of Christ's church. The amen (Hebrew: "So let it be") indicates the people's assent to these prayers.

The *epiklesis* (Greek, "to send your Holy Spirit upon the offering of your holy Church") follows the words of institution. The transfigurative sign of the Holy Spirit is thanksgiving—the original meaning of *eucharist*. The belief that the words of institution themselves effected the consecration of the elements seems to have originated from Ambrose, a fourth-century C.E. bishop of Milan. This relationship between the Holy Spirit and the elements became a regular understanding of the Western church. This also was a common understanding in the Eastern church, in which Cyril of Jerusalem, also in the fourth century C.E., taught his catechumens that the consecration of the elements was effected by the epiklesis "that he may make the bread the body of Christ and wine the blood of Christ."

This discussion of epiklesis is important for Tutu's theology, which places a great deal of emphasis on transformation:

> The principle of transfiguration is actually central to the Christian faith. According to it, something is raised to another and

higher level of reality or becomes a channel for communicating that higher reality. In the Christian Church we see the principle of Transfiguration at work when for instance bread and wine are raised to another level of reality to become the body and blood of Jesus Christ or become the channels for communicating to the recipients the very divine life itself. . . . It is the transfiguration principle at work when an erstwhile persecutor of the Christians can be transformed into the chief of apostles as the apostle to the Gentles.[54]

Following the tradition of the early church theologians, Tutu believes that whatever the Holy Spirit lays hold of is sanctified and changed, even in the South African context. This view avoids seeing magical powers in doctrines of transubstantiation and ascribes new significance to the doctrine of *pneumatology* (Greek, "understanding of the spirit"). Therefore, the epiklesis can be seen as a prayer for the consecration of the people as well as of the elements of bread and wine.[55]

Epiklesis informs Tutu's view that transfiguration is at work not only through ordinary elements such as bread and wine, but also through the apparently recalcitrant matter of racial identity. He believes human identities are lifted to a higher order of being by becoming channels of the divine life. For Tutu, this transfiguration occurs through the broken bread and the poured cup, from which the church sees the body and blood of Christ continually present in the world.[56]

The Prayer Jesus Taught

The Prayer of Jesus follows and expresses the unity of the congregation and priest as they recognize that they are celebrating the Eucharist together. The petition "Give us today our daily bread" is also interpreted as the bread of the Eucharist, both a supernatural and a daily bread, nourishing both souls and bodies, spiritual and material needs.[57] Tutu places the onus on God to deliver us from temptation so as to bring about the redemption of the world. Tutu's model of the church is an instrument of transfiguration, reminding the world that it does not live by bread alone. God's mission, Tutu believes, is to bring all things to their fulfillment in God's dominion, "where His will obtains for the Good of all, to bring all things to a wholeness, to a shalom that has always been God's will for the entire creation."[58]

The Breaking of the Bread

Jesus' Prayer is followed by the Breaking of the Bread. Originally this expression described the practical function of distributing the bread among the congregants, but became meaningful in the sense that communicants could share in the body of Christ in a sacramental sense.

Tutu states in *The Road to Rustenburg* that the church responds to the divine and gracious call of God so that it may be true to its commission.[58] The church is called to act as Christ's body, which speaks, with a united voice, a word that will inspire God's people to give birth to the dominion of God in South Africa. Tutu asserts that among "those hard truths, uncomfortable words, are that we belong together in one body because Jesus has broken down the wall of partition since he is our peace. In this Koinonia there is neither Greek nor Jew, male nor female, free nor slave, but we are all one in him. We have a new identity which transcends our ethnic, racial, cultural identity."[59]

And as members of the church, a *koinonia* (Greek, "fellowship") forms: "The bread which we break, is it not a participation [i.e., koinonia] in the body of Christ?"[60] The unity signified by the Peace is now confirmed and exhibited by sharing in the single loaf. The practice today of distributing wafers obscures this symbolism, but perhaps the ceremonial breaking of a special wafer by the priest serves as a sufficient symbol of unity here. The second meaning of the Breaking of the Bread refers to the breaking of Christ's body on the cross (1 Cor. 11:24), even though as the true Passover lamb, not a bone of his body was broken (John 19:36).[61]

The Agnus Dei, "O Lamb of God that takes away the sins of the world, have mercy upon us," usually follows the breaking of the bread. Based on the words of John 1:29, the Agnus Dei is meant to be said while the bread is being broken for distribution to the entire congregation. This prayer refers to all that estranges us from God so that, in the end, Tutu yearns through this prayer, "fervently for the day when [both he and the Dutch Reformed Church] could celebrate the Holy Mysteries together."[62]

The Communion

The prayer of humble access—whose first words are "We do not presume to come to this your table, merciful Lord, trusting in our own righteousness, but in your manifold and great mercies"—is said before taking the elements so that the person may receive Christ in humility and grace. The invitation to communion calls people to feed on Christ in their hearts with faith and thanksgiving. The sacrament itself is the assurance of Christ's presence for the individual communicant, but the communicant also depends on the congregation's deliberate commitment to Christ in Christ's service to the world. Communion suggests a dramatic reorientation of human relationships with God and with one another in such a way that there is an expectation or anticipation of being situated differently in the world.

In short, communion with God places the church in unusual places in the world. Tutu illustrates:

> Last week, Wednesday, I celebrated my 25th anniversary as a priest and had the unusual privilege of celebrating the Eucharist on that morning in the women's section of a maximum prison in New York. I don't know what it says of me but when I telephoned my youngest daughter in Washington and told her I was calling from a prison she said, "Oh what have you done now?[63]

By being so placed, the church resists all that denies human access to a communion of identities. Tutu learns this from the Eucharist, in which the congregation drinks from one cup because life is meaningless unless it is understood in relationship to others. As Tutu is fond of saying, "We can be human only together," and this happens through the concept and practice of the church's communion. Without such communion, "peace and stability remain ever elusive."[64]

The Dismissal

After the communion, Tutu maintains a period of silence, and then a hymn follows. At this point, the remains of the sacramental bread and wine are consumed. Then Tutu declares, "Give thanks to the Lord for he is gracious." A thanksgiving prayer follows, referring to the holy mysteries that relate to the nuance of Christ's body now conjoined with the congregation. Then comes the prayer of dedication, offering the church to the service of God. The offering of the church is not something that it can add to the offering of Christ; its offering is instead conjoined in Christ. Indeed the church, now conjoined to Christ, interacts with the world on all levels, even the political.

Through the Holy Eucharist, Tutu offers himself to the service of God in his daily life. The Eucharistic prayers are not only descriptions of the unique sacrifice of Christ, but also the church's continuing offering of itself in Christ. Being in Christ constantly renews the church to serve the world in the Eucharist through the Holy Spirit. At the end of the Eucharist, Tutu's model of the church demonstrates action on behalf of the world through unity with Christ. In the end, it is from this resource of the Anglican rite of the Holy Eucharist that Tutu can be both bishop and politician as he lives out his life in the world, where true discipleship is to be displayed. Thus, one can see how Tutu's ecclesiology is shaped by worship, which gives him the categories for his politics of reconciliation of the races.

The final dismissal, "Go in peace, to love and serve the Lord," often pronounced by the deacon, is summons to service accepted by the congregation in their response "In the name of Christ. Amen." From this, Tutu determines, "Go forth to make South Africa more compassionate, more caring, more loving, more sharing. Go forth and recognise in someone of a different race your brother, your sister and treat them as such."[65]

CHURCH AS WORSHIP LIFE IN ACTION

In defining the role of the church, Tutu explains, "The church exists primarily to worship and adore God. It must praise [God's] most Holy name. But it can never use this as a form of escapism. Precisely because it worships such a God it must take seriously the world [God] has created and . . . loved so much."[66] For Tutu, first, the church is always in the world, but never of the world. Within this tension, the church must always maintain a critical distance from political structures so that it can exercise its prophetic ministry.[67] The church is to be the mixture of diverse cultures made one in Christ so that it continually denounces all that is contrary to the divine will. Whatever the cost, the church has only one ultimate loyalty, and that is to Christ. The church knows, therefore, that it will always have to say to worldly rulers whose laws are at variance with the laws of God, "We had much rather obey God than [you]."[68]

Second, Tutu's church must ever be ready to wash feet; it is a serving church, not a triumphalist one. His church is biased in favor of the powerless. When in solidarity with the poor, the oppressed, and the marginalized, the church first displays justice in the world since there can be no reconciliation without justice. In this sense, Tutu's church does not favor the oppressed without identifying the oppressor. In order for one identity to change, the other must change as well. Tutu has faith that God, through the life of the church, will demonstrate that Jesus has broken down the wall of partition. In its common life, there will be no artificial barriers to any follower of Christ, who creates this sense of community. Tutu agrees with Hauerwas that the church is to be that particular community of faith that welcomes strangers and has enemies whom it will not kill.[69]

Third, Tutu's church not only assumes an environment in which racial divisions no longer exist, but it is the community where class distinctions dissolve. A church that is in solidarity with the poor can never be a wealthy church. It must sell all to follow its master. It must hold loosely to the things of this world, using its wealth and resources for the sake of the least of Christ's people. Such a church is a suffering church, one that takes up its cross to follow Jesus. Tutu explains this commitment through this interpretation of John 12:24–26: "A grain of wheat remains a solitary grain unless it falls into the ground and dies; but if it dies, it bears a rich harvest. One who loves self is lost, but the one who hates self in this world will be kept safe for eternal life. If anyone serves me, that person must follow me; where I am, my servant will be. Whoever serves me will be honoured by my Father."

From this vantage point, Tutu sought to discern proper Christian church stances from unfaithful ones. For example, Tutu prayed that, for the sake of South Africa, the Dutch Reformed Church (DRC) would be converted to its true vocation as the church of God:

> Because if that were to happen, if [the DRC] were to stop giving spurious biblical support to the most vicious system—apartheid—since nazism, if it were to become truly prophetic, if it were to be identified with the poor, the disadvantaged, the oppressed, if it were to work for the liberation of all God's children in this land, then, why, we would have the most wonderful country in the world.[70]

However, Tutu concludes that "if it does not do these things and do them soon, then when liberation comes it will be consigned to the outer darkness for having retarded the liberation struggle and for misleading the Afrikaner. . . . Woe betide all of us if the grace of God fails to move this great church and all churches to be agents of the great God of the exodus, the liberator God."[71]

A New Anglicanism

Tutu's model of the church is revolutionary for most of Anglicanism in his insistence that political authorities not interfere in church matters. As he notes, "No secular authority, not even the government of the land, has any authority to sit in judgment on the churches about how to be church, and how it is to fulfill its God-given mandate, to work for the extension of God's kingdom of justice, peace, reconciliation, compassion, laughter, joy and goodness."[72] At another time, he said:

> We the Church of God are meant to be the alternative Society, a different kind of society. We have not always lived up to our calling, but God calls us to become—and be seen to be—a sharing society. We are to love our brothers and sisters, and really begin to share the spiritual and material gifts God has given into our stewardship. We are to be a compassionate society, caring for the weak and the powerless, especially to empower them; caring for the downtrodden, the disadvantaged and the poor; becoming the voice of the voiceless because there is where we find Christ particularly; urging our more well-to-do to let God use them to do His miracles of love and compassion.[73]

Charles Villa-Vicencio, a senior lecturer in religious studies at the University of Cape Town, believes that black leaders in the English-speaking churches in South Africa found themselves controlled by predominantly white European structures. This set up conflicting needs of language and culture. In most instances, however, it seemed that the European church structures proved more powerful than the leaders.[74]

Deeply planted in such an ecclesial structure, Tutu's involvement in church affairs as well as pastoral and official duties inevitably led him into greater opposition to any oppressive structure that regarded one culture as inferior to another. For example, when visiting a predominantly white Anglican congregation, Tutu said:

> Many whites such as yourselves have protested saying [that] blacks would be the ones to suffer. . . . [Yet] you here have

taken the law into your own hands and have applied sanctions to the church because of my views. A lot of things can be said about that. (a) Logical inconsistency—you are opposed in principle to sanctions but apply them yourselves, and (b) you have not in fact, so far as I know, opposed your government in applying sanctions to Lesotho leading to a coup in that country. . . . It is odd that blacks who most suffer aren't opposed to me.[75]

Yet Tutu did not look negatively at white people who had consistently opposed his leadership. For example, he said, "I remember as if it were yesterday the wonderful nonracial services that happened on Synod Sunday in this great Church when you caught a flitting glimpse of what this beautiful land could become."[76] Because of this reconciliatory disposition, Tutu was often described as compromising.

When Tutu was general secretary of the South African Council of Churches, his role brought scrutiny from the conservative as well as the more radical sectors of the church. These pressures heightened his awareness of the formidable challenge of establishing a context in which black and white Christians could flourish together in the same church. Despite severe criticisms from within the Anglican Church, Tutu maintained a keen vision of the church as "an icon of the community of the saints for the world."

Tutu's theology of the church was informed also by a rule of Anglicanism that insists that prayer, worship, and life itself are grounded in the everyday religious experience of affirming creation. God transforms our rituals of worship and our rituals of life into a witness of God's faithfulness and God's presence. God takes the cultural logic of the world—the underlying reason for the way things are done in a particular place—and uses it as an opportunity to disclose humanity's holy destiny. Tutu assumes that praise of

God creates the means by which cultural boundaries may merge. He believes:

> We are set to be the Church of God, to declare that despite all appearances to the contrary, this is God's world and that God, our God, is in charge. . . . In a setting that claims we are made for alienation, separation, dividedness, hostility and war; we must as the church of God proclaim that we are made for togetherness, for fellowship, for community, for oneness, for friendship, and peace.[77]

A Model of the Divine Life

Much moral theology revolves around attaining unselfishness. Tutu, however, changed the focal point to the individual's awareness of God, thus concentrating on the way of worship rather than on morality. Worship lifts the soul out of its preoccupation with itself and centers aspirations solely on God. The effort to conform to moral codes and standards falls into its proper place in worship through the liturgy. Communion with God reveals the rules we need, and nothing else can serve that purpose. For the Christian, worship is the paramount duty. Following the Anglican emphasis on worship as defining the Christian life, Tutu states, "We are constrained by the incarnational implications of our worship. We would say if you don't want to be involved in mundane secular affairs, then don't worship our God."[78]

Tutu's combination of morality and worship challenged those who assume a separation between religion and politics. He defended his position in the Anglican tradition through such examples as the radical monks of the Community of the Resurrection.[79] Instead of teaching a quietistic spirituality, Tutu extended worship to engage a South African context in great need of reconciliation.

Tutu's Anglicanism proved successful in this endeavor by enabling him to pray and act privately, on the one hand, and to pray and act through the church, on the other. That which was disparate and defined by the world as alien, Tutu defined sacramentally as reconciled. Tutu states:

> Christianity contained the seed that destroyed slavery ultimately. The effects could already be seen in Paul's letter to Philemon about Onesimus, the runaway slave whom Paul urged Philemon to receive back, not any longer as a slave but as a brother in Christ. What people were seeing in the early days of the church was a veritable miracle unfolding before their very eyes. It would have been remarkable for erstwhile slave owners to accept their slaves as equals. But what Christianity demanded was to receive them, not as equals whom you can acknowledge and thereafter safely ignore, but as sisters and brothers, children of the same heavenly Father, members of the same family.[80]

The visible sign of invisible grace is ultimately love, as demonstrated by a verse often recited by Tutu: "A new commandment I give to you, that you love one another; even as I have loved you, that you also love one another. By this all will know that you are my disciples, if you have love for one another" (John 13:34–35). Tutu continues:

> This kind of family is demonstrated by how it treats its weakest. . . . That is the wonder of family. Family members are not alike—they have a wonderful diversity. They don't agree about everything. In most families the parents are forever stopping battles between their children. Of course mother and father don't always agree about everything. . . . The important thing is that [family members] have confidence in each other. You don't impute unworthy witness to each other. You re-

spect each other's point of view. What makes a family have deep unity is its nice diversity.[81]

The marks of the church as one, holy, catholic, and apostolic are found in the Nicene Creed. Tutu adds another mark, liturgy, which denotes the work of the people and the rites of public worship. Thus, Tutu maintained that in order for true change to occur in South Africa, the church must be unashamedly itself through the particular nature and work of liturgy. But he cautioned, "God will not accept worship, however meticulously correctly performed unless it has affected the life of the people in their everyday concerns, particularly showing mercy and doing justice" (Isa. 1, 58).[82]

THEOLOGICAL ETHICS AND DOXOLOGY

For Tutu, the church is shaped by shared prayer that enables the transformation of individuals into a flourishing community. *An Anglican Prayer Book 1989*, used by the Anglican Church in South Africa, states, "A prayer book provides a shape and structure for the worship of the Church."[83]

The primary influence on *An Anglican Prayer Book* was the monastic movement's sevenfold office of prayer.[84] The general preface acknowledges the preceding twenty years of liturgical experiment and renewal. Tutu adhered to a doxological or worship system because it avoids both political quietism and political radicalism. Even if both sides are motivated by a noble cause, the concept of the church in its interaction with the world is unintelligible without an understanding of the church's purpose to gather and worship.

The liturgy forms the church into what Tutu describes as an "alternative society," enabling those operating in corrupt structures in the world to see and repent toward peaceful coexistence and respect for God's glorious creation. Such a church, according to Tutu, often runs the risk of breaking the law. Unfortunately, too many have been persuaded to think that legal right and moral right mean the same thing. For example, in much of South Africa's history, it has been illegal for church groups to meet for more than a day without the permission of the national government. But Tutu made it clear that it is not immoral to gather for the liturgy of the church. Worship, Tutu stated, must not be only for special occasions; it must be Christians' lifestyle because, as the general preface to the *Anglican Prayer Book* states, "Worship releases into the world, with its need and its pain, its sorrow and its hope, an influence for healing and wholeness which we shall never fully comprehend."[85]

The Eastern Orthodox understanding of theology is often described as doxology, in which two inseparable movements occur. One movement gathers the people of God together, and the other sends them into the world in a single rhythm of mission. Tutu sought to make this double movement representative of his theology as well as the theology in the Western church.[86] For theological empowerment to occur within a revolutionary culture, the church is obliged to rediscover the integration of both sacred and secular in worship, to relearn that worship (properly related to life) is the chief end of humankind. Little wonder that Tutu objected, "We are a Christian country where all enjoy freedom of worship, so they say despite the fact that white Christians would not be allowed to visit with black Christians to share Christian fellowship without official permission."[87]

Following from adoring God, whose movement of redemptive and gracious acts also pours the church into antagonistic political structures, how then does Tutu fit in his Anglican tradition? For example, what does a seventeenth-century country parson like George Herbert have to do with an alleged political activist like Tutu? Like Herbert, Tutu struggles with what is an appropriate response to God's grace. Tutu's conclusion, even in the midst of warring factions, is that Christians are to render authentic and relevant worship to God in their daily lives.

> If our worship is authentic and relevant, it prepares us for our combat with the forces of evil, the principalities and powers. It prepares us to be involved where God's children are hurt, where they spend most of their lives: at work, in the market place, in schools, on the factory floor, in Parliament, in the courts of law, everywhere they live and work and play. Jesus refused to remain on the mountain top of the transfiguration. He came down into the valley of human need and misunderstanding.[88]

A critique of Tutu's doxological method raises some troubling questions: To what extent does Tutu's model of community fit with an establishment ethos of Anglicanism? Can Tutu's methodology of worship successfully include the British, the Afrikaner, the Xhosa, and others in a way that promotes theological discourse by which all may cohabit peaceably? Tutu's answer is that such questions are faithless in their presumptions of impossibility in God's world. Instead he operates from a worshipful environment in which human identities may find unity without losing their particularity. A truly Afrikaner, Xhosa church may not exist until the eschaton, but that is no excuse to stop both praying for such an identity and acting to bring about its birth. In this hope, Tutu prays for the fulfillment of that tremendous vision in the Revelation of St. John the Divine (7:9–12).

Worship is at the very heart of Tutu's Anglicanism. Its styles vary from the simple to the elaborate, from evangelical to catholic, from charismatic to traditional, or any combination of these traditions. The *Anglican Prayer Book* gives expression to the comprehensiveness found within the whole church. Through it, the South African context can be a way of engaging God's presence through rites such as confirmation, holy orders, reconciliation, marriage, and anointing of the sick.

Tutu's understanding of the Anglican rite and the significance it attaches to worship and social engagement is crucial. It has shaped Tutu's thinking and provided the impetus for his public witness against apartheid. Thus, he has offered an ongoing alternative expression of liturgical protest against a corrupt state to the Anglican tradition's historic complicity with such oppression.

CHAPTER SIX

AN AFRICAN SPIRITUALITY OF PASSIONATE CONCERN

I am created by God [who] loves me for myself. It has nothing to do with anything extraneous to myself. No, it is intrinsic to who I am. It is given with who I am. . . . If I am so important, if I am so valuable, then it must mean then that every other human being is of equal worth, of equal value. . . . Every praying Christian, every person who has an encounter with this God, this triune God, must have a passionate concern for his or her brother or sister, his or her neighbour, because to treat any one of these as if they were less than the children of God is to deny the validity of one's spiritual experience. . . . Any policies that make it a matter of principle to separate God's children into mutually opposing groups is evil, immoral and unchristian. To oppose such a policy is an obligation placed on us by our faith, by our encounter with God.

—Desmond Tutu (sermon, 1987)

Until recently, African Christians have suffered from a form of religious schizophrenia. They have been compelled to pay lip service to Christianity as understood, expressed, and preached by whites. But what they have struggled to repress out of shame is that their Africanness was being violated. The mostly cerebral religion of the whites was hardly touching the depths of the African soul. Instead, Africans were being

123

redeemed from sins they did not believe they had committed; they were being given answers, and often splendid answers, to questions they had not asked.[1]

To counter this religious schizophrenia, Tutu's spirituality provided a crucial means to overcome the ambivalence of being black—the African encounter with European material culture, on the one hand, and their search for the spiritual side of "Africanness or African personality," on the other.[2] In this light, Tutu's distinctive ubuntu theology, formed out of his African culture and the Anglican theology of the church, emphasizes the discipline of Christian personality within the church community.

Tutu's spirituality does not, however, naively assume that its goal of Christian community has been achieved. When all African communities achieve full share in determining policies in South Africa, only then, believes Tutu, will the possibility exist for reconciliation among all races and cultures. Therefore, only by enacting this spirituality in the South African context can the correct relational complement of black and white liberation occur; no one is a person in South Africa until blacks attain the freedom to express their God-given personhood and humanity.

In *Hope in Crisis: South African Council of Churches National Conference Report 1986*, Tutu devised a relational approach to theology, rejecting the common either/or hermeneutic that sets contextual theologies against one another. For instance, Tutu opposed separating black, African, and liberation theologies. Instead he placed strong emphasis on the narrative of a catholic church in which all Christians are called to work toward a reconciled creation. Thus Tutu, an African and black theologian, is a liberation theologian who struggles with questions of how warring factions may live harmoniously in a violent world. He states, "I myself believe I am an exponent of Black Theology coming as I do from South Africa. I also believe I am an exponent of African theology coming as I do from Africa. I contend that Black Theology is like the inner and smaller circle in a series of concentric circles."[3] How does Tutu's spirituality allow him to be black, African, and Anglican—all successfully?

TROUBLING THE NORMAL

For Tutu, "the trouble with normal"[4] is that for too long Western theology has laid claim to a universality that he believes theology cannot so easily claim. For example, Christians in other parts of the world have found that they possessed answers—and splendid answers at that—but to questions that nobody in new contexts such as Africa were asking or likely to ask. New theologies need to arise in order to address the perplexities and issues in these new contexts; that is, Africans needed to grapple with their own grass-roots issues.[5] In South Africa, these issues are usually concerned in some way with racial identity, even to the point of claiming God's image is black or Afrikaner.

Rowan Williams has noted how the Christian response to racial questions can appear trite, often asserting little more than that all human beings share equally in God's image and therefore deserve equal treatment. Such a belief is banal because it has been embraced by those undertake all kinds of practical injustice, such as slavery and the oppression of women. The problem, as Williams notes, is not with this Christian view of human nature, but with its apparent impotence in the eruption of new power relations and the persistence of old ones. Theology needs to embrace the particularities of human history and yet to act as a point of judgment and hope within that history.[6]

To compensate for this inherited Western problem of racism, Tutu, following much of Anglican tradition, believes that the concept of imago Dei rests on a simple proposition: the will of God can be discerned in the observation of the way that we are made, namely, for ultimate fellowship in God. Race, then, cannot be a person's primary basis of identity because identity comes from the imago Dei, a spiritual reality possessed by every human being. Tutu states, "Race is not the most distinctive attribute of a human being. Our distinction stems from the fact that we are created in the divine image and are therefore of infinite worth."[7] Or again, "The Bible, as we have seen, asserts what seems the reasonable position—that all God's human creatures in some sense have a divine hunger referred to by St. Augustine in his famous dictum, 'Thou hast made us for thyself and our hearts are restless until they find their rest in thee.'"[8]

Thus, being created in the image of God explains why persons have moral freedom, why we can converse with God, and why we have an instinct to worship God. This instinct is a universal attribute of humanity. This instinct, however, is often corrupted in our efforts to gain power. Tutu explains his reasons for making this claim:

> Apartheid says that the most important fact about each of us is our ethnicity, some biological attribute which is really an irrelevance in determining our human worth. It exalts a particular biological characteristic to a universal principle determining what it means to be human. . . . skin colour and race assume an importance they never had in scriptures. . . . in many cases they determine which people can participate in Christian church services which are believed to be of salvific significance. It is not enough to be baptised after confessing that Jesus is Lord and Savior. One must possess yet another attribute which in the nature of the case must be reserved only for a select few.[9]

By implication, accepting the premise of the imago Dei demands a high view of the human capacity to know God, and it testifies to the essential goodness of creation. Tutu's ability to recognize God's image in others arises from two influences, namely, the ubuntu of his African context as well as the monastic tradition found both in the Community of the Resurrection,[10] in which Tutu was nurtured, and in Maggie Ross, an anchorite.

Tutu's view of the imago Dei presupposes a radical formation of human identity in the world. This identity detects the fluctuation of power both within the self and within the world. Tutu illustrates with his examples of Mother Teresa in India and Brother Roger of Taizé: "Mother Teresa epitomises the compassion at the heart of the universe and Brother Roger the attractiveness of Jesus for many young people who are in search of something more than the materialism which seems to be one of the few things a barren affluence has to offer."[11]

In order to discuss further Tutu's view of the imago Dei, it is necessary to understand the monastic influence on the Community of the Resurrection. As Rowan Williams explains, monastic influence dates back to the desert tradition, in which "early monks were profoundly concerned with the necessary and positive role of temptations. Certainly they conceived their vocation as the creation of God-reflecting communal life."[12] Williams goes on to define primitive monasticism as "a search for a context in which illusions and distortions of reality can be removed—individual reality, reality of other persons, social reality." To grow, one needs to strip away illusion, and monasticism's great contribution to Christianity, according to Williams, "is the acknowledgement that the believing community as a whole can save itself from seduction and deceit only if it allows for some who are prepared to undertake a drastic surgery upon the fantasizing and dominating self, and so remind the whole body of its vulnerability."[13]

Tutu's ascetic training, then, guards against a Christian ethic of love that retreats to the illusions of an ethic of personal and sentimental understanding. Tutu's theological model of ubuntu involves more than person-to-person interaction as the height of human attainment. His spirituality has been formed to include the view that prayer is not just an individual enterprise but a social one.

TUTU'S ASCETIC ROOTS

Tutu provides an alternative to the typical Western spirituality, with its focus on self-fulfillment. Specific forms of Christian spirituality, such as anchoritic and monastic, offer Tutu rich resources to show South Africa that God has created humanity to be defined by more than racial classification. Tutu may not operate self-consciously from the historical narrative of St. Antony—usually characterized as the leading figure of the desert tradition—but an account of how Antony contended against power and principalities is helpful in understanding the ecclesial and ascetic influences on Tutu's thought.[14] Characteristic of Tutu's ecclesial model, emphasis should not be placed so much on self-fulfillment as on the relational fulfillment of a person in God and neighbor.

The desert tradition represents the formation of a radical Christian witness against the corrupted forms of power in the world. This is not to say, however, that such power never found its form in the church. We learn from Christian asceticism that an unique understanding of theology developed in which one's theological convictions were contingent on how the imago Dei and society might be envisioned in the presence of God. In short, the desert tradition provides a resource of theological conviction on which Tutu draws to challenge the idolatry of privileging racial identity.

Several Western biases need to be identified so that the full import of the ascetic tradition can be seen. First, religious communities, while often seeming withdrawn from the world, nevertheless sought to redefine society radically through the convictions of Christian identity. Second, an ascetic's social identity was gained—and the religious community's larger goal enacted—through both contemplation of God and action against demonic principalities and powers; actual withdrawal from society did not take place. Third, the desert tradition was distinctive among the religious communities because, unlike the late Greco-Roman society of which Antony was a part, the desert barred no one on the basis of social pedigree, but encouraged all to strip away falseness. In this desert tradition, then, Tutu discovered a profound resource by which to counter racial classifications by oppressive regimes: The line was not clearly drawn between contemplation and action; prayer and social witness often became indistinguishable; and the stripping away of false identities left Tutu with a deep sense of the imago Dei.

St. Antony's Desert Tradition

Antony believed that formation through Christian *ascesis* ("to train the body") is vital to both individual and society. The imago Dei is not happenstance; it needs to be trained and disciplined. Therefore, the desert tradition from which the monastic movement originated focused primarily on the achievement of Christian character to enable participation in the salvation of the world—through prayer.

In the desert tradition, prayer is *anachoresis*, "the art of disengagement." This ascetic concept is applied both individually and socially. On an individual level, anachoresis is the art of solitude. Tutu explains:

> Prayer is the physical necessity to shut up. It is being in the presence of God which has to do with a relationship of love. . . . We often think of silence as a negative thing or the absence of noise. But it is a positive dynamic. You cannot do creative thinking if you are surrounded by distracting noise. . . . Jesus called His disciples to come away by themselves for a while.[15]

On a social level, anachoresis allows the individual to challenge the oppressive ways of the world. While at worship one day, Antony heard the Gospel story of Jesus telling the rich man to sell what he possessed and give to the poor in order to have treasure in heaven (Matt. 19:21). Upon hearing about this disengagement from possessions, Antony gained the courage to counter the oppressive society of late Roman Egypt; he sought a period of isolation in the desert.[16] The society of that day was filled with economic insecurity, severe tax burdens, and competition among village landowners. Antony disengaged from it even though he had been born an heir to a sizable amount of farm land on the left bank of the middle Nile. From this desert tradition, Christians— even fairly well-to-do ones—living in severe states of oppression saw by means of ascetic figures such as Antony that power and prestige could be redefined through acting out how one might truly live in freedom. The spiritual practices of anchorites and monks were not irrelevant to a social witness against corrupted forms of government; they helped to train persons in community to see a truer form of the imago Dei.

Tutu affirms this understanding: "As an African and as a Christian, I need to contribute to the emergence of a relevant spirituality. The spiritual, it goes without saying, is central to all that we do. The God we worship is an extraordinary God." But, Tutu continues, God does not allow worshipers "to remain in an exclusive spiritual ghetto. Our encounter with [God] launches us into the world, to work together with this God for the establishment of . . . a kingdom of justice, peace, righteousness, compassion, caring and sharing. We become agents of transfiguration, transformation and radical change."[17] This understanding is fully in line with St. Antony's model.

Tutu's Appropriation

The ascetic tradition is important in understanding Tutu as a political priest. Informed by such examples as St. Antony, the ascetic tradition sought to wrestle demons by breaking down false divisions between the sacred and the profane. Tutu's theological strategy also was to model the divine life to the corrupt society of apartheid.

Through the ascetic tradition persons are no longer identified by race but form a community, expressed in the particular witness of the Community of the Resurrection, able to contain and celebrate diversity. Here, Tutu's asceticism is highlighted by his ecclesiology and ubuntu. Not only did Tutu's African culture determine his ubuntu theology; his training in an Anglican religious community was also influential. Tutu states:

> I was greatly blessed to have been trained for the priesthood by a religious community, the Community of the Resurrection, sometimes called the Mirfield Fathers after the Yorkshire town in which their mother house is located. I learned much more from these wonderful C. R. Brethren by example than by precept. Life with them taught me that prayer, medi-

tation, retreat, devotional reading, and holy communion were all utterly central and indispensable to an authentic Christian existence. You could not but be impressed that they really lived by what they taught, when you regularly saw members of the Community on their knees in the chapel, outside of service times. We saw the same people deeply involved in the struggle for justice in South Africa.[18]

The Community of the Resurrection taught Tutu that what was required was not simply a political program of material improvement or the need to be black (or white or colored), but a whole new understanding of society based on religious community.[19] This spirituality made Tutu work from theological commitments derived on a deeper and more mystical level. On this deeper level, Tutu describes what he learned from Trevor Huddleston, perhaps the most famous monk of the community:

> I came to live in a hostel which the Fathers opened for young men who were working or at high school and had problems with accommodation. . . . I made my first real sacramental confession to [Trevor Huddleston]. . . . He was so un-English in many ways, being very fond of hugging people, embracing them, and in the way in which he laughed. He did not laugh like many white people, only with their teeth, he laughed with his whole body, his whole being, and that endeared him very much to black people. And if he wore a white cassock it did not remain clean for long, as he trudged the dusty streets of Sophiatown with the little urchins with grubby fingers always wanting to touch him and calling out "Fader" with obvious affection in their little voices.[20]

Through the Community of Resurrection, Huddleston realized that the command to love God involved more than the disciplines of democracy—there had to be an understanding of obedience.[21] But this would be a different kind of obedience. From the Community of Resurrection, Tutu learned to escape the identity offered by a corrupt society and to recognize the image of God in all persons. For both the Community of Resurrection and Tutu, however, it is an image of *kenosis* ("self-emptying") to which constant attention must be paid to destroy false identities that seek to replace God's image of fullness of relation.

Tutu explains the trouble with the normal perception of being defined as black:

> We are united willy nilly by our blackness (of all shades). Now some may feel squeamish about this apparently excessive awareness of our skin color. But are we not in fact so bound? If anyone of us assembled here today goes into a situation where racial discrimination is practiced, would we ever escape the humiliation and indignity that are heaped on us simply because we are black no matter whether we were native to that situation or not? Our blackness is an intractable ontological surd.[22]

SYNTHESIZING AFRICAN AND BLACK THEOLOGIES

The South African context presented political conquest and Christian faith side by side. Often the imago Dei was claimed by blacks and whites as something that one group possessed but the other lacked. In this context, Tutu sought a common theological understanding of humanity to which both black and white people could assent. This conciliatory perspective often made Tutu the object of criticism from black theologians who sought a break with white worldviews. In contrast, Tutu sought in his spirituality to take up the positive elements of black theology and African theology.

Awareness of the history of the black church and of African Christians is absolutely essential for understanding how Christianity was distorted in the West.[23] Black theology is demarked by the church's awareness of blackness as the single identification of the person. With racial identity comes the danger of oppressive definitions of personhood, especially as economic structures are established and controlled by the dominant group. Those who are the most powerful—white people—assume the all-encompassing identity by which all others are defined. Tutu illustrates:

> I was a Native who to many did not seem to count for much—as in newspaper accounts of, say, a road accident reading, "Three persons and a Native were injured." Then we became "non-whites," then "non-Europeans," negative entities who presumably came from somewhere called "non-Europe"; then we were Bantus, and wonder of wonders we even became "plurals" so that you probably might have a singular "plural," and urban "plural," or a rural "plural."[24]

Consciously and unconsciously, people use physical descriptions as though these were the ultimate characteristics by which to define persons. Through Tutu's view of the imago Dei, these false descriptions of human identity (that is, white and black) impede progress of the Christian life. In this respect, black theology becomes helpful for Tutu because like his ascetic training, black theology displayed a way of judging authentic Christianity. The historical configuration of the black Christian protest provided a ready critique of the dominant group's theology.

According to black theology, so-called traditional theology still assumes that blacks are called to believe in Christ, forgive the oppressor, and pray that the power structures stay the same. In this instance, the theological language of reconciliation lacks real meaning for the oppressed. Both the oppressed and those in power, according to Tutu, need to hope for a new culture of forgiveness. Otherwise, no one will be transformed, and the structures of power will remain the same until a new identity emerges in which both identities may be transfigured.[25]

Tutu illustrates the importance of this transfiguration in the following account of a colloquy between a Zambian and a South African: "In the course of the conversation the Zambian said, 'Well, our Minister of Naval Affairs did so and so. . . .' And the South African said, 'What? You are a land-locked country. How could you have a Minister of Naval Affairs?' The Zambian replied, 'But you have a Minister of Justice!'"[26] That is, an administrator of justice is needed only when all groups experience similar treatment or have common access.

The value of black theology for Tutu was in its sharp criticism of normative theology in the North Atlantic world. Such criticism, Tutu suggested, also occurred in antiquity when people were concerned about the fertility of their crops and herds. They wanted to be certain that the seasons would follow one another regularly and that there would be a proper amount of rain and sunshine. Their gods, Tutu noted, tended to be the forces of nature deified, such as the god of the rivers, the sun god, and so forth. The central purpose of these nature gods was to ensure that the steady round and rhythm of nature remainded undisturbed. Having such gods is really not surprising because they are the gods of the status quo. Black theology correctly located the modern white versions of these status-quo deities.

Tutu announced that something new needed to be proclaimed—the death and resurrection of Jesus Christ. God in Christ emptied the divine self in order to effect salvation, which is called *mercy*. God's very nature as related in three persons becomes the Christian paradigm, which can neither tolerate aggressive schemes of power nor allow deterministic cosmologies to fix human identity. This God is always procreating. This God saves fallen identities out of this bounty of relationship. Human identities, in the recognition of this loving God, are restored in the humility of knowing that they could not deserve salvation. It is here, in the state of wondering what to render back to God for God's unmerited mercy, that Tutu seems more like George Herbert, the seventeenth-century English country parson, than black theologians such as James Cone.[27]

Listening to what God said to the Israelites in Deutonomy 7, for example, was central for Tutu. For the Israelites, God is the God of liberation, the great Exodus God, who sides with the exploited. This God takes sides against the powerful on behalf of the widow, the orphan, and the alien—"those classes of people who were often at the back of the queue, at the bottom of the pile."[28] Tutu's theology, then, has a strong affinity with the prophets of the Old Testament in whom indignant theologians rebelled against the injustices both within and outside Hebrew society. For Tutu, early Jewish theologians also developed a theology that focused on worshiping God through an active relationship to the sociopolitical order.

Tutu sought for his theology to be fully determined by worship and the ancient traditions, and he held Western theology to do the same. Having worked for the World Council of Churches, Tutu was aware of the opposite extreme of theologizing, namely, where theology becomes merely a grammar to talk about universal morality. For Tutu, this is erroneous.[29] Western theology is no more universal than any other brand of theology. Theology can never properly claim a universality; this the church claims as belonging only to Jesus Christ. For Tutu, theologians must have the humility to accept the scandal of their particularity as well as its transience.[30] "Of course, the true insights of each theology must have universal relevance," Tutu believes, "but theology gets distorted if it sets out from the very beginning to speak, or attempt to speak, universally."[31] Christ is the universal human being only because he is, first and foremost, a real—and therefore, a particular—human being.

A diversity of theologies must therefore exist. Black theology rightly teaches that one can speak relevantly only when speaking to a particular Christian community. But unity arises because, ultimately, we all are reflecting on the one divine activity that sets us free from the slavery of sin. What is white cannot be excluded at the outset. We simply do not always apprehend the transcendent in exactly the same way, nor can we be expected to express our experience in the same way.

African and black theologies, according to Tutu, are rightly concerned with liberation because liberation often suffers casualties whenever identities are at war. Tutu's theology, however, seeks a different reality, one that avoids the realities of blackness or the domination of whiteness. Instead, the inescapable consequence of taking seriously the gospel of Jesus Christ is that black and white are already reconciled in Christ.

Herein was Tutu's impetus to synthesize the tenets of African and black theology. African theology emphasized the relationship between Christianity and African traditional religion and culture. Black theology, as black consciousness, emphasized that blackness is not to be negated as inferior, but affirmed as part of God's creation and its implications explored for the church. Black theology as liberation theology stressed that the gospel is one of liberation, a liberation of individuals from the oppressive social structures in which they live and the creation of a new society.[32]

Louise Kretzschmar believes that scholarly African theology developed slowly because its leadership in the churches and theological seminaries was largely in the hands of white men, who determined both the concerns and content of theological study and who generally had a low opinion of African culture and tradition. In such an environment, a distinctively African theology could not be propagated.[33] Opponents of Tutu often attempted to turn this against Tutu. For example, one asked, "Why does Tutu not wear tribal garb? Who paved the way for him to receive a western education different from his hereditary pattern?"[34]

For Tutu, then, African and black theology provided a sharp critique of Western theology, but from different angles. His object is clear: Westerners usually call for an ecumenical or universal theology, which they often identified with their own brand of theologizing. In the face of such presumption, Tutu sought an authentic and contextual theology:

> Let African theology enthuse about the awesomeness of the transcendent when others are embarrassed to speak about the King, high and lifted up, whose train fills the temple. It is only when African theology is true to itself that it will go on to speak relevantly to the contemporary African—surely its primary task—and also, incidentally, make its valuable contribution to the rich Christian heritage which belongs to all of us.[35]

Therefore, for Tutu, theology is a human activity possessing the limitations and the particularities of those who are theologizing. It can speak relevantly only when it speaks to a Christian community, particular in time and place. It also must have the humility to accept the scandal of its particularity as well as its transience.[36]

Christian unity will arise because ultimately believers are all reflecting on the one divine activity in which human identity is set free from all that enslaves it. There must be a plurality of theologies. Otherwise, some will claim that their apprehension of the divine life applies to all in exactly the same way. In South Africa, the promulgation of this notion was the sin of apartheid.[37] Yet Tutu was also able to explore and admit that this was a failing of his own liberation spirituality.

TUTU'S SELF-CRITIQUE

For Tutu, a liberation spirituality that does not include the unique characteristics of the particular people encourages a facile alliance between culture and Christ. True, Christ does come in fulfillment of all the best aspirations of African culture; but equally true, Christ stands in judgment over human identity. The weakness of creating too many Christs can be laid at the door of most theologies "unless they are constantly on the alert not to neutralize the scandal of the gospel."[38] Therefore, Tutu admits that his theology must always submit to the "scandal of the gospel." What does this scandal entail for Tutu?

A serious criticism of African theology is that attempts to make it particular for the people have been perhaps too concerned with historical continuities, thus giving the impression that the culture is static. African theology assumes the complicated task of taking the traditions seriously while holding faithfully to the truthfulness of its Christian convictions that Jesus died for the sins of the whole world. In the end, claims regarding both tradition and truthfulness must be made if the theology is to speak in a relevant way to any context. Tutu concludes, "It is perhaps in this area that African theology has performed least satisfactorily."[39]

Tutu found in J. C. Thomas[40] a model for African theologians to enable the process of Africanizing Christianity to occur through both the inheritance of African traditional religions and the doctrine of the Christian church. Both must be examined carefully and systematically so that the areas of agreement and conflict are made intelligible. Otherwise, African theology will fail to produce a sufficiently sharp cutting edge.[41]

African theology, for Tutu, performs well when addressing the split in the African soul. Yet it failed to speak meaningfully in the face of a plethora of contemporary problems that assail the modern African mind. For example, African theology advocated disengagement with the hectic business of life. Evidence of this is that little has been offered in African theology that is pertinent for a theology of power in the face of the epidemic of coups and military rule, poverty, disease, and other urgent African issues. Abrasive black theology taught Tutu the most at this point. Black theology helps African theology recall its vocation to be concerned for the poor and the oppressed, to be concerned for liberation from all bondage that threatens authentic personhood. Black theology also teaches that Christ's disciples are to be concerned about any political authority that constructs personal freedom in its own image:[42]

> We are still too much concerned to play the game according to the white man's rules when he often is the referee as well. Why should we feel that something is amiss if our theology is too dramatic for verbalization but can express itself adequately only in the joyous song and movement of Africa's dance in the liturgy? Let us develop our insights about the corporateness of human existence in the face of excessive Western individualism, about the wholeness of the person when others are concerned for Hellenistic dichotomies of souls and body, about the reality of the spiritual when others are made desolate with the poverty of the material.[43]

Yet Tutu's theological model viewed African theology as more inclusive than its counterpart, Western black theology. Tutu explains:

> By and large, it was legitimate to generalize and speak of African as an inclusive term. This anthropolitical concern of African theology has been an important achievement to chalk up. It was vital for the African's self-respect that this kind of rehabilitation of his religious heritage should take place. It is the theological counterpart of what has happened in, say, the study of African history. It has helped to give the lie to the supercilious but tacit assumption that religion and history in Africa date from the advent in that continent of the white man. It is reassuring to know that we have had a genuine knowledge of God and that we have had our own ways of communion with deity, ways which meant that we were able to speak authentically as ourselves and not as pale imitations of others. It means that we have a great store from which we can fashion new ways of speaking to and about God, and new styles of worship consistent with our new faith.[44]

The main achievements of African theology are its attention to "religious schizophrenia" (the conflict between Western and African views) and its attempt to remedy that malady by rehabilitating Africa's rich cultural heritage and religious consciousness. But this attempt alone is not sufficient.

The major criticism leveled against African theology is its claim that ethnic identity is the primary form of knowledge of God. Tutu describes the complaint further: "There is only one faith and, therefore, it is a serious aberration to try to nurture a particularistic theology instead of holding out for an ecumenical and universal one."[45] This criticism is often made as well by Africans who are apprehensive that a peculiar theology will lend itself to ready use by politicians desiring a supernatural sanction for their secular mindset.

For Tutu, African theology must both reflect the experience of a particular Christian community and relate this experience to what God has done in Christ. Thus theology must necessarily be limited by the characteristics—ethnic, temporal, cultural, and personal—of those who are theologizing. But it must also be mindful that this particularity is not fully descriptive of God. Tutu comments that theology "must glory in its in-built obsolescence because it must be ready to change if [change] will speak meaningfully to the situation which it addresses."[46] "Theology is a risky, albeit exhilarating business of reflecting on the experience of a particular Christian community in relation to what God has done, is doing and will do, and the ultimate reference point is the man, Jesus."[47] The root of racial identity in societies makes it naive to think that only economic or political oppression matter. Therefore, for Tutu, true liberation must be understood holistically as the removal of all that keeps human identity in bondage. Anything that makes human identity less than what God intends us to be is apartheid.

TUTU'S NEW LIBERATION SPIRITUALITY

Liberation theologians claim a new focus in theology through the question: Who takes part in the making of theology? The answer from liberation theologians is that theological reflection needs to be aligned with God's clear preference for the poor. Tutu states:

> Too many had thought that liberation theology was narrowly selective in the biblical paradigmatic passages that it used and that there seemed to be an inordinate obsession with the exodus motif. . . . Liberation theology is not just an aberra-

tion thought up by those who have a predilection for that sort of thing. It is biblical through and through, and utterly consistent with the God who is revealed to Moses. Jesus Christ has such a remarkable identification with those he came to save to the extent that for them and the world he was prepared to empty himself of his divine glory, to take on the form of a slave, and become obedient unto death, yes, even the death on the cross.[48]

Tutu's theology, however, is different in kind from liberation theologies in other contexts because Tutu does not need to construct, for example, a grammar for the existence of God. In Africa, questions of a-theism are simply nonsensical. Tutu states:

> We have always been a deeply religious people. This was so long before the advent of Christianity and the African worldview is at many points more consistent with the biblical worldview than that emanating from the West. There can never be only one theology, that of the West: the Bible itself presents us with a plethora of theologies. In the book of Genesis alone we find a mosaic of as many as three different theologies speaking about God. Theology that suffers from the limitations and imperfections of those theologising, and has relevance and validity only for a particular context, is simply inadequate.[49]

Tutu articulates a liberation from idolatrous submission to systems of oppression, such as apartheid or African cultural practices that deemphasize one's formation in the image of God. For him, idolatry is the deification of the ideology used to make holy the structures of oppression, allowing them to appear to reflect the will of God. Tutu believes that questions about God in the world of the oppressed are about knowing which side God is on. But to know which side God is on does not mean one can conclude that God desires a competition of human identities. For Tutu, spiritual training and formation in the church are required in order to discern what is and what is not of God.

The result of many liberation theologies is that they become a self-fulfilling prophecy. In the past, theological tools were borrowed from philosophy. Now liberation theologians and other theologians rummage through the social sciences tool kits. The result is that different truth claims regarding the poor are legitimated, perhaps too much so for Tutu, who is uneasy about being identified solely as a liberation theologian.[50]

According to Tutu's liberation spirituality, the formation of human identity is surely more complex than bantering back and forth about one's identity as Greco-Roman or American or South African or black or white. In Tutu's spirituality, human identity is primarily defined by God's image. Through prayer any abuses or negative determinations of identity are corrected. In contrast to retaliatory theologies, prayer also takes to heart the salvation of the oppressor.

Tutu's view of human identity is more than racial identity (even with an apartheid society in mind). Humans strive to become divine in character through the reality of the church. In this way, Tutu's theology constructs a holistic view of both individual and community, a community in which the identity of black and white become secondary to one's identity as Christian. Without recognizing this theological perspective, one cannot make sense of Tutu's agenda against apartheid.

Kretzschmar has summarized Tutu's theology in a helpful way. African theology's paramount concern is a holistic salvation that touches not only the soul, but "heals and changes all of life." The African worldview is predominantly (in Western terms) ontological, meaning that "relation is the essence of life" as a whole. Not only is this understanding characteristic of Tutu's theology, but it may be closer to the biblical view than that of a primary Western (Greek) dualism of the material and the spiritual.[51]

This does not mean, however, that Tutu romanticizes African community. He notes, "Of course this strong group feeling has the weaknesses of all communalism; it encourages conservatism and conformity. It needs to be corrected by the teaching about a human being's inalienable uniqueness as a person. We need both aspects to balance each other."[52] At the same time, he is keen to show how particularity is crucial to how communities form. Tutu states: "Religious people waste a great deal of time putting up barriers and boundaries as if they have sole rights to God, able to determine who may be God's children and who may not be."[53]

Tutu's theology and ecclesiology provide vital impetus in forging a society defined by more than race. Unlike many black theologians whose theological language prioritizes race as the sole criterion of particularity, Tutu's theology defines blackness as one identity among others in need of God's deliverance from oppressive forces. Tutu states:

> Our starting points are the Christian doctrines of creation, redemption, and sanctification. . . . Our worth, our dignity, all these are intrinsic to who we are, they come as a divine gift with our creation. They come with the whole package of being human. Our worth, our infinite worth does not depend on any extraneous attribute or achievement—it is an inalienable right which is a gift freely bestowed on us by God. . . . That doctrine is thoroughly and radically subversive of our discriminations, injustice, oppression and exploitation based on race, sex, culture, status, education and whatever else we might think up as giving worth and value to persons. That

was the basis thoroughly biblical for our structures against apartheid which said that the colour or race of a person was what made you important.[54]

Tutu's ubuntu theology tries to compensate for the narratives of disparate, racial identities. He seeks to display how diverse identities are, in fact, unintelligible in themselves without the recognition of the need to know God and one's neighbor. Tutu concludes that this recognition lies in understanding that we are children of God:

> For the oppressed the most vital part of the Christian gospel is its message of liberation from all that would make us less than the children of God—sin, political and economic deprivation, exploitation and injustice. It is also liberation to be people who enjoy the glorious liberty of the children of God, which must include political empowerment to determine the shape of one's destiny.[55]

Consequently, Tutu's theology cannot be categorized as radical in the sense of juxtaposing political identities of oppression as the hermeneutical key to theology. Being an archbishop, he has a much greater constituency of oppressed groups to defend. The following quote shows how Tutu sees his immense role as a theologian and an archbishop:

> Our theology is to become relevant and authentic. We should rehabilitate great Christian words such as reconciliation and peace which have fallen on bad days, being thoroughly devalued by those who have used them to justify evil. Christ is our peace, who bought at a great price His own death on the Cross. That is what real reconciliation has cost. We have been given the privilege of a share in Christ's ministry of reconciliation. We are serious about human liberation. It must be

total human liberation. That includes our attitude to the place of women in the church. I am myself fully in support of the ordination of women for I have not been persuaded by theological or non-theological argument that there are any compelling reasons why we should not ordain women. We impoverish ourselves in depriving them. Our language in theology and in society must be inclusive language. Language is not merely descriptive. It creates the reality it describes. . . . Theology is, in addition to all else, also ethics.[56]

For Tutu, it is inconsistent with the gospel to construct a method based on blackness by which to address all the categories of traditional theology. Instead of this approach, Tutu promotes the particularity of peoples through the catholic character of the baptized and faithful people of God, who find themselves constantly in awe of the mysteries of creation. In light of this qualification, Tutu states, "I thank God for black theology in the life of the church and in my own life."[57] He believes that black theology has caused its exponents to "Look to the rock from which you were hewn, to the quarry from which you were dug" (Isa. 51:1). Black theology throws us back on the Bible to discover therein just how theology is done. As Tutu believes, "The Bible has become paradigmatic for us in a way that I certainly did not experience when I thought to do theology, mainly in order to obtain a good divinity degree in one or other western institution of higher learning."[58] The Bible contains a diversity of theologies, underscoring the fact that it is difficult but necessary to form an ecumenical theology.

For Tutu, what must be communicated in this ecumenical theology is God's unchanging love for creation. God is immutable. Ultimately God's attitude toward the whole of creation is immutable, too. But how we apprehend and what we apprehend of God and the things of God will differ according to who we are and the circumstances that have shaped us into the persons we are. For example, Elijah, because of who and where he was, saw God as monarchical, and yet he so misunderstood God's love of creation that he believed God had decreed the massacre of the prophets of Baal (1 Kings 18:36–40). Thus, theology suffers from the limitations of those who are doing the theology and glories in the true insights of the same persons.

In a context such as South Africa, where concepts of universal theology served to justify racism, what merit can "traditional theology," the theology of the oppressor, have? Tutu defends traditional theology as a resource for spiritual, cultural, political, and socioeconomic renewal. When renewed by relevant questions, traditional theology complements liberation theology by causing epistemological preferences to confront the traditions of the church. Conversely, when theology is used as a basis for legitimizing an unjust order, such theologizing is the instrument of oppression.[59] Tutu recalls the subtlety of such theology:

> When I wanted to do my doctoral studies on a black theology topic, my likely promoter said he did not think that there was enough material in existence to provide a viable doctoral thesis. The black American theologian Gayraud Wilmore observed that whenever people ask "What is black theology?" they are really articulating an unspoken question, "Is black theology at all?"
>
> Others appear to be sympathetic to the concerns of blacks, and yet, while not being black themselves, want to determine the end for blacks.[60]

The price of adhering to theologies based on a context, however, is that they have little impetus to work for an ecumenical structure outside of privileging the particular identity. Tutu would agree that a plurality of theologies are jostling and competing with one another, but he would add that they can complement and challenge one another as well, because each theology seeks to address specific issues arising from the contexts of particular communities of faith. These particular theologies may become obsolete when their usefulness has passed, but this does not negate the mystery and gospel that our image of God has been restored in Christ:

> These are critical times, and we must respect the contextual differences between us, for the integrity of the gospel of Jesus Christ is at stake, and we cannot afford to be merely "nice" to each other. Our maturity must be tested by how well we can handle points of view which are not only at variance with our own but which may call in question whatever we have held to be dear and sacrosanct.[61]

Tutu takes the plurality of theologies seriously. Precisely because theology constantly answers a different set of questions, diverse theologies are needed. "So that we now find ourselves," Tutu concludes, "perhaps in a bewildering position of dealing with strange juxtapositions of different theologies, cheek by jowl with one another, complementing or contradicting one another."[62] For Tutu, the perplexity is— given that God is God and more—that blacks are so conspicuously singled out for suffering, at the hands not of pagans or other unbelievers but of white Christians who claim allegiance to the same God.[63]

Tutu's theology asks: on whose side are you, God? Is it possible to be black and Christian at the same time? Tutu's answer is that we must respect the autonomy of each context and that we must achieve the integrity that Christians in different parts of the world hold onto in order to know particular truths of the image of God. Yet the fit with other theologies is fairly loose because they do not seem pertinent to one's own context.

In the end, Tutu's theology does not readily fit into defined Western liberation hermeneutics of theology, many of which claim primary identities of race, economic class, gender, or culture as proper means to expose oppressive structures of thought.[64] For example, the rationale for an African liberation theology is that only Africans are in a proper hermeneutical position to give clarity. Therefore, theology from the position of dispossessed African people must make clear what theology looks like in order for God to be intelligible to them. The problem occurs when the need for dialogue with other dispossessed people is finally acknowledged. Liberation methodology seldom offers guidance on how interdependence is possible among persons who recognize that their dispossession is linked. Instead, liberation theologies often result in separate claims on God's providence by diverse communities. Therefore, solidarity is never realized. "We do not seem to realise," Tutu believes, "that we will not have dealt with the underlying causes of the unrest merely because we have bludgeoned people into sullen submission."[65]

In much current theological discourse, it is a false assumption to claim "Christian" or "the church" as one's primary identity. This is true because of the need to disclaim a Christian identity in the effort to expose structures of power and injustice. Tutu's theology claims otherwise, although he is mindful of oppressive structures. Tutu states:

> The government seems to be making concessions grudgingly and reluctantly responding to pressure but not as if they were serious about dismantling apartheid. We are really no longer interested in incremental, painfully slow evolution. We are

interested in the deployment of political power, that is the name of the game. So we have a serious crisis compounded by the fact that we have such different readings of what is actually ailing the country.[66]

Tutu's theology is based upon theological criteria that seek to reconcile the conflict between the African version of God's identification with their oppression and the Afrikaner's theology of election as the chosen race. Tutu's concept of ubuntu assumes a symbiotic construction of both the African and Afrikaner national identity that is formed only in relation to the other. From this assumption one might draw inferences of how Tutu's theological convictions are instrumental in the transformation of apartheid.

Real theology, according to Tutu, arises from cooperation between God and human beings. Consequently, the product of cooperation will be an amalgam of the claims of racial identity and the claims of the imago Dei. Therefore, Tutu's theology seeks to include oppressed groups while at the same time holding them accountable to the imago Dei, which transcends their particular claims. As Tutu would conclude, God became the God of the Exodus because of God's *hesed*, God's "covenant love," which always takes the initiative and is undeserved and unmerited. God is revealed in Jesus to be on the side of the sinner, the despised, the outcast, and the downtrodden.[67] But this God is not relative, because a relative God would make sin unintelligible and, most of all, would make impossible the spiritual exploration of the imago Dei.

In the South African context, Tutu not only thinks through racial and cultural categories but also thinks simultaneously through his theological convictions. In other words, culture and theology are not mutually exclusive for him. To think of what race means theologically includes the understanding of a particular people in a particular land. One's existence as a Christian ought to say something about who that person is in relation to where that person has come from. And yet this same theological understanding is sacramental, as the particular allows access to truth—namely, God.

God creates through judgment, out of grace; and through races and cultures the Word of God comes. The story of the tower of Babel (Gen. 11) illustrates this. It demonstrates a false unity based on disobedience. In such a context, unity is oppressive and gathers people together for the wrong reasons. This is the same as apartheid theology, in which a state's God blesses hegemonic tendencies to create economically viable republics. Equally caught up in a God of war, African theology stresses genealogy, which in the end displays the schizophrenic tendency to make culture and social history confine God to a homeland.

Tutu's ascetic training toward the imago Dei keeps him prayerful in this conflict. South Africa, like Jacob, is to adopt a new name of "struggling with God," so as to avoid the primary identity of race, which really assumes inborn strategies of power and dominance.

Tutu's theology offers a way out of apartheid. In his theology, what first appears to be compromise offers a new way for theory and practice to unite. God makes it possible to develop a different kind of history, in which "You must leave your kindred and your father's house" (Gen. 12:1). There is nothing particularly inherent in God's election other than the response of faith, the willingness to abandon one's identity.

Tutu's theological model is the living testimony of breaking with false forms of identity gained through a cultural history of apartheid. Instead of promoting warring human identities, Tutu's theological contribution is to move his society toward God's promise of a new creation. God promises a covenant with the church to restore the imago Dei as it makes human sin visible and human righteousness possible. In so doing, a self-emptying God is exposed to the risk of human failure to respond to new relationships.

CHAPTER SEVEN

CONCLUSION
God and a Political Priest

The evil of apartheid is perhaps not so much the untold misery and anguish it has caused its victims (great and traumatic as these must be), no, its pernicious nature, indeed its blasphemous character is revealed in its effect on God's children when it makes them doubt that they are God's children. This is why it has been of crucial importance that black consciousness should have succeeded—because it was of God—an almost evangelistic movement to awaken in the black person the realisation that [she or he] is a child of God.
—Desmond Tutu, "Jesus Christ, Life of World" (sermon, 1982)

You whites brought us the Bible; now we blacks are taking it seriously. We are involved with God to set us free from all that enslaves us and makes us less than what [God] intended us to be. I will demonstrate that apartheid, separate development, or whatever it is called is evil, totally and without remainder, that it is unchristian and unbiblical. If anyone were to show me otherwise, I would burn my Bible and cease to be a Christian.
—Desmond Tutu, *The Divine Intention* (1981)

Two major questions have been implied or raised in the previous chapters, but not addressed. First, how does Desmond

Tutu's theology of God compare with those of African or African American theologians? Second, in what sense can Tutu be called a political priest?

In answering both questions, the South African context in which political conquest and Christian faith have existed side by side again proves influential. And, again, Tutu's understanding of imago Dei is a consistent theological anthropology that Tutu applies to both black and white people. This emerges from Tutu's habitual recollection of God's presence in worship.

TWO CHALLENGES TO TUTU'S THEOLOGY OF GOD

The conciliatory character of Tutu's theological model invites criticisms by such black theologians as Itumeleng J. Mosala, who thinks that Tutu contradicts himself, and James Cone, who differs with Tutu's ecclesiology.

According to Simon Maimela's article in *Hammering Swords into Ploughshares*, Tutu naturally elicits contradictory perceptions.[1] Engaging Mosala's objections and Cone's disagreements with Tutu's liberation spirituality is to situate Tutu among African and black theologies. The extent to which Tutu's spirituality is one of either compromise or mediation should become obvious.

To anticipate the major lines of discussion: Tutu's theological model is a formulation directed against the ideology that laid the framework by which the majority of peoples in the Republic of South Africa were deprived of their human identity—that is, apartheid. Some, however, think that Tutu's theological model fails in its task to represent this majority of South Africans. For example, Mosala declares, "I contend that, unless black theologians break ideologically and theoretically with bourgeois biblical-hermeneutical assumptions, black theology cannot become an effective weapon of struggle for its oppressed people."[2] Mosala argues further that for an African Christian, the greatest difficulty in withstanding the oppression of apartheid is the fact that the oppression of black people was theologically justified. Therefore, African theologians like Mosala see the need for additional hermeneutical tools by which to combat European religion. As Takatso Mofokeng explains, "Black Christians, pastors and theologians were called upon to respond theologically to counteract and restrict the mental damage to black Christians. They had to join hands with black sociologists, economists, psychologists and other scientists."[3]

Because of the incompatible views of Christianity and apartheid, and secondarily influenced by the black theology of the United States, African theologians have given careful thought and voice to the task of empowering the oppressed majority in South Africa. The great resource for such African theologians is James Cone. Indeed, Tutu learned a great deal from Cone, especially from Cone's thesis that because Christianity had often been co-opted by white Christianity, the notion that God's image represented white identity was used to justify racism. To counter this implicit assumption of Western Christianity, there needed to be a more particular authorizing criterion by which to claim racial oppression as immoral. Therefore, Cone claims that God is black.

The problem regarding Mosala's response is that, in countering apartheid structures ordained by white theologians, African theologians increasingly have grown dependent on secular criteria to judge theological truth. Tutu's ascetic conviction of the imago Dei and his unique role and symbol as a Xhosa archbishop in a historically European church offer an important catalyst in the secularizing trend in black African theology. Mosala misunderstands Tutu because there is no space for the intelligibility of the desert tradition in Mosala's hermeneutic of Marxist struggle. And last, although Tutu is also deeply influenced by Cone, Cone's powerful voice of black theology is more effective in the United States than in Tutu's South Africa.

Tutu offers an uncharacteristic model of black theology that does not necessarily exclude the structures of the Anglican Church. Tutu explains that "most of what is subsumed under the heading 'African Theology' is the result of a reaction against cultural and ecclesiastical colonialism. Most of it certainly predates the agitation and struggle for Africa's liberation from colonial domination. But the two movements are very intimately linked."[4]

Instead of constructing a theology defined by Mosala's conflictual model, where the dominant ideas of every society are revealed as the dominant ideas of the dominant class, Tutu operates from a transformative, ascetic theological model. His model facilitates the movement of historically oppressive structures into supportive structures from which Christian identity (black and white) may be practiced in the South African context.[5] Therefore, for Tutu, the struggle for the church to be the church in South Africa is not necessarily defined by Mosala's criterion of Marxist struggle or Cone's view of the roots of racial oppression, but by *anachoresis*, the faithfulness of the peoples of God to practice the presence of God through an alternative community called the church in a naturally oppressive world.[6] This is true whether persons are identified as Xhosa, British, Afrikaner, Sotho, colored, Indian, or any other category.

Note, however, that Mosala (in particular) responds to Tutu rather than the converse. This discussion has been postponed until this concluding chapter because Tutu has not engaged in it directly. Indeed, Tutu is not threatened by the objections that others have raised because Tutu has seen himself in the

role of political priest rather than radical theologian or some
other role.

Does Tutu Contradict Himself?

In the 1970s, Steve Biko founded the black consciousness
movement in South Africa. Church leaders like Allan Boesak
became expert in the rhetoric of this movement by affirming
the language and conceptualization of blackness already developed in North America.[7] More recently, South African
thinkers such as Itumeleng Mosala have questioned the ef-
fectiveness of this inherited black theology in the South African context. Contending that black theology is not being
radical enough, Mosala has pointed out the inability of North
American black theology to become an autonomous weapon
in the hands of the oppressed and exploited black people of
South Africa.

Mosala thinks that black theologians, including Tutu, are
caught between espousing a black, revolutionary rhetoric
against white social discrimination, on the one hand, and,
on the other, adhering to a colonial Christian identity that
will always bring African identity into crisis because of the
privileges of white culture.[8] Mosala grants that this current
consciousness in South African black theology is inherited
from James Cone, whom Mosala sees in the same light as he
sees Tutu. What is acceptable about Cone's pioneering black
theology to Mosala is that Cone has exposed the cultural
assumptions of a dominant, white theology and has demonstrated the marriage between Christianity and the white
racial identity. In this way, Cone facilitated the demytholo-
gization of an idolatrous faith that had assumed no cultural
or ideological conditioning. Yet the Christian character of
Cone's theology remains troublesome for Mosala.

Even so, Mosala sees Tutu's theology as more problematic than Cone's in that Tutu perpetuates a contradiction in

his own goal of reconciling identity by conceding a political reading of the Bible to the power-holding sectors of society. Referring to Tutu's use of the comparison between Steve Biko's death and that of Jesus of Nazareth, Mosala states:

> The tradition that Tutu appropriates in the service of [the black South African liberation] is especially problematical. Having made the Jesus connection, he proceeds to collude with the oppressors in the Bible by describing Jesus—as do other black and liberation theologians—in terms of Isaiah 61:1–7. He ignores the class basis of the text, as it now stands, in the royal ruling-class ideology (the Hebrew term *masiah* is thoroughly royal).[9]

For Mosala, Tutu's theology colludes with a view of the Bible that reproduces the status quo. Thus, the essence of Mosala's critique is that black theologians—those who follow James Cone—have been unable to break ideologically and theoretically with bourgeois assumptions.

Besides his simplistic account of Tutu's thought, Mosala's biblical analysis is weak in its reworking of theological language to make Marxism the sole criterion by which to judge all other categories. One might ask, if a Western stance does not work in Africa, why would Marxism? If Mosala admits that black or African theology can only be done in particularity, it seems insufficient for his goal to use a Western hermeneutic of struggle to search for a correct method for African theology.[10]

Moreover, if Mosala thinks the South African context is unique, he seems to dismiss the profound insight of W. E. B. DuBois that the global problem of discrimination is that the darker-skinned peoples, regardless of race and nationality, are more likely to fall under the category of the oppressed in the world than lighter-skinned peoples.[11] Mosala's own secularizing criteria of Marxism seem unable to address this problem on a global scale apart from declaring war. That is, two ideologies can be seen as privileged when a Darwinian-type model of natural selection of the fitter racial character is employed: On the one hand, Mosala privileges the ideology of Marxist struggle, which otherwise would become relative; on the other hand, Tutu privileges the global Anglican Communion.

In sum, Tutu's theology is not about struggling against white identity so much as it is about becoming a stronger black person. Tutu's aim is the destruction of apartheid by being faithful to his daily prayers, which inform him to proclaim that people are more than black and white. Black people alone cannot destroy apartheid. For Tutu it is crucial to understand how black and white identities can coexist peacefully in order to undergird or reinforce black survival.

If Tutu were to respond formally to Mosala, he might ask to what theological criteria Mosala appeals in his answer of a hermeneutical struggle, other than a secular appeal to Marxist revolution. Is the meaning of life only the survival of the fittest? If so, white people have more to gain by perpetuating a Marxist ideology of human identity than black people do. After all, white people are winning—especially if life is about material (rather than spiritual) survival.

In view of the global scale of Western influence, Mosala's perception that Africans do not wish to be compromised by cultural assumptions of white theology seems miscalculated. As the world faces more catastrophes (in eastern and sub-Saharan Africa, India, the former Yugoslav republics, and China, for example), Mosala's biblical hermeneutic as "a tool of struggle" for cultural liberation seems hard pressed to articulate the what of Christian faith that is being passed on from one African generation to another. Instead of Mosala's antagonistic approach to theology, Tutu adopts a conciliatory model of theology, yet one that can envision its own demise:

> The Church must face up to the possibility that it may die in this struggle, but what of that? Did our Lord and Master not tell of a seed that will remain alone unless it falls to the ground and dies (John 12:24)? We can never have an Easter without a Good Friday; there can be no Resurrection without a Crucifixion and death.[12]

Without an articulated ecclesiology, Mosala fails to provide an apt articulation of why "the poor are always with us" (Matt. 26:6).

Peter Walshe offers two important insights. First, even though apartheid has been the focus of the struggle, the challenges facing the church are much larger. "The call for a more egalitarian, compassionate society in which racial, class[ist], and sexual exploitation is resisted will still be necessary as new political and economic systems are shaped."[13] Second, in the church's attempt to renew society in view of these larger challenges, "a constant, often conflict-ridden process" will need to be employed. "In the political arena, Christians who strive for their own empowerment, and that of their neighbors, will have to be watchful, working continually to maintain an open, participatory political system that fosters criticism."[14]

In view of this need to be ever vigilant to the South African context, Tutu is not ashamed of his European and African roots coming together. In fact, his theological model displays how each informs the other so as to encourage reflection on the image of God. Tutu's model of ubuntu claims that human identities are interdependent in such a way that any one person's survival is dependent on the survival of all others. And Tutu's ascetic training leads him to act through the church to encourage corrupted forms of human societies to see the truer image of God.

Therefore, Tutu rejects Mosala's conclusion that struggle is all there really is to life. Tutu seeks to move the discussion back to a normative language of Christian discourse so that prayer becomes intelligible and, most of all, the image of God comes back to light. This is also the movement and interdependence of ubuntu that, instead of perpetuating disparate viewpoints, allows a way for South African society to achieve the following insight:

> The evil of apartheid is perhaps not so much the untold misery and anguish it has caused its victims (great and traumatic as these must be), no, its pernicious nature, indeed its blasphemous character is revealed in its effect on God's children when it makes them doubt that they are God's children. This is why it has been of crucial importance that black consciousness should have succeeded—because it was of God—an almost evangelistic movement to awaken in the black person the realisation that [she or he] is a child of God. It has not been anti-white as its detractors have tried to make it out to be, but it has been pro-black, it has been affirmative of what God has done. It has said people must celebrate the fact of who they are and not accuse God of making a mistake in creating them black and looking forward to the time when they would celebrate their own culture and value system so that they could make their own distinctive contribution to the body politic. It is after all the glorious diversity among God's people which make us all interdependent because none can be self-sufficient.[15]

Black theologians such as Mosala locate primary identity in the racial structure of oppression with scant avowal of the Christian's vocation to participate in the transformation of the new identity in Christ. In Tutu's theological model, struggle for justice is not an end in itself; the meanings of justice constantly change, just as the identity of oppressor continues to change. This can be seen in the history of the Afrikaners, who overcame oppression by the British only to assume a new identity as oppressors. In addition, Afrikaners would see justification in Mosala's "tool of struggle," because their identity was determined on the basis of struggle and survival. Such a capricious context of struggle must be guarded against as Tutu qualifies those who may assume the identity of "oppressed":

> Oppressed peoples must hear that, according to the Bible, this God is always on the side of the downtrodden. [God] is so graciously on their side not because they are more virtuous and better than their oppressors, but solely and simply because they are oppressed, [God] is that kind of a God. . . . Those whom God has saved must become the servants of others, for they are saved ultimately not for their self-aggrandisment or self-glorification, but so that they may bring others to a saving knowledge of God.[16]

Mosala's criticism of Tutu's theology fails to acknowledge the structure by which black and white identity may reveal how to live together. This has been the exclusive focus of Tutu's theological model in which his ecclesiology and theology of ubuntu provide a way forward in the South African context. However, Tutu states, "We African theologians are quite as much to blame as anyone else, for we find it much easier to regurgitate what was fed into us, than to use our acquired skills for creative theological thinking."[17]

In summary, Tutu is an instrumental South African theologian who encourages common discourse between African and Western voices through a liberation spirituality emphasizing mutual identity. For him, it is necessary not to exclude "traditional" theology—even its European forms—because then theology would fail in its work of reflecting on God and creation. And, most pertinent to this discussion, Mosala fails to offer a critical theological voice against the vicious cycle of becoming the oppressor.

Influenced by the desert tradition, Tutu's theology proclaims that human identities become new through the creation of the church in the world. This newness is most clearly expressed in the death and resurrection of Jesus Christ when God broke the frantic cycle of death and effected salvation. The very nature of God related in three persons becomes the Christian paradigm of ubuntu. No longer can antagonistic schemes of power be tolerated, and no longer can deterministic ideologies fix human identity, because the Christian God is always creating anew.

James Cone and Desmond Tutu

James Cone is a Christian intellectual, contextualized by an African American ecclesiology; Desmond Tutu is a Xhosa archbishop, trained in the ascetic tradition of the Community of Resurrection. Their contexts, however, do not distinguish the two as much as their ecclesiologies do. In fact, Tutu has a strong affinity for African American culture. As he states:

> It is good to speak to you, my soul brothers and sisters. I address these words especially to you who are black. We have a solidarity, we here in South Africa and in Africa, with you in the USA. It is a solidarity that is like a threefold cord which is not easily snapped. First of all we have a solidarity that stems from the colour of our skins. . . . Secondly, the solidarity between yourselves and us blacks in South Africa, stems

from the fact that we are victims (in differing measure) of oppression, exploitation, and racism. . . . Thirdly, our solidarity as blacks in South Africa and the United States stems from our unity in Jesus Christ through our baptism.[18]

On the one hand, Cone's ecclesiology is estranged from Tutu's because Cone has difficulty understanding the preexistent ascetic strains in Tutu's theological model. This asceticism is a model of Christian spirituality in which individuals practice the discipline of God's image of kenosis, namely, learning to be vulnerable for the sake of the other. On the other hand, Tutu cannot accept Cone's notion that God's image is black or white. Tutu states, "I worry, however, about some of Cone's exclusiveness—that, for instance, only the oppressed can form a genuine Christian koinonia."[19]

But both Tutu and Cone agree on the meaning of black identity. Tutu continues, "Basically, Cone is concerned about how we do theology. . . . The black experience, he claims, provides the appropriate context for questions and answers concerning the divine."[20] Therefore, Tutu would agree that Cone's school of black theology—criticized by Mosala as not being radical enough—is correct in demonstrating how white and black identity may be reconciled.

Racial reconciliation involves personal and political relationships. In South Africa, Tutu is known to be one of the first theologians to see how this reconciliation may occur. Louise Kretzschmar reports that "the initial criticism from a South African black theologian was voiced by Bishop Desmond Tutu, who pointed out that in South Africa, the concerns of African, Black, and Liberation Theology come together."[21] Tutu states:

We cannot deny too that most of us have had an identical history of exploitation through colonialism and neo-colonialism, that when we were first evangelized often we came through the process having learned to despise things black and African because these were usually condemned by others. The worst crime that can be laid at the door of the white man (who, it must be said, has done many a worthwhile and praiseworthy thing for which we are always thankful) is not our economic, social, and political exploitation, however reprehensible that might be; no, it is that his policy succeeded in filling most of us with a self-disgust and self-hatred. This has been the most violent form of colonialism, our spiritual and mental enslavement, when we have suffered from what can only be called a religious or spiritual schizophrenia.[22]

Cone's theology is amicable to Tutu's in another sense as well. Both theologians assume an eschatological community in which a radical transformation takes place in people's identity. For Cone, however, this transformation seems to occur exclusively in the black church, where a janitor becomes chairperson of the deacon board, a maid becomes president of the steward board, everybody becomes Mr. and Mrs. or brother and sister. And everyone talks as if they know the truth about which they speak. The beauty of Cone's work lies in this experience of being radically transformed by the power of the Spirit, which defines Cone's primary view of the transformation of human identity.

For Cone, just as for Tutu, Christian identity is a spiritual vision through which the reconstruction of a new humanity can take place.[23] In such a vision, black people are no longer defined by oppression, but by freedom.[24] The problem in all this, however, is how Cone's preference for the black church could ever make sense of Tutu's Anglican Church. Indeed, it is difficult for black American Baptists to understand black Anglicans, even though there are more African Anglicans in the world than black National and Progressive Baptists combined.

Cone's hermeneutic (science of meaning) is from within this African American church, which implies a much different understanding of the nature of the church and salvation than Tutu's ecclesiological emphasis on sacraments and asceticism. In a sense, Cone understands the church as a prophetic voice to the world, a vibrant church centered in the prophetic call and response of singing and preaching. Although Cone is critical of his own church's witness in the world, his vision of the black church is like that of the prophets of the Old Testament, who stand and declare the judgment of God upon other kingdoms with little recourse to models of reconciliation.[25]

Based on Cone's question for the African American church—"How are we going to survive in a world in which black humanity is deemed an illegitimate form of human existence?"[26]—his work can be termed a *survivalist theology*. Tutu's theology, in contrast, could be named *cooperational*. For both Tutu and Cone, theology questions the premise of rational discourse about ultimate reality and aims higher in being a prophetic word of God's righteousness spoken in corrupted societal structures. More specifically, Tutu's and Cone's Christian theologies convey that what whites mean by *oppression* is what blacks mean by *liberation*. The difference between their theological approaches is that for Cone, blackness simultaneously symbolizes oppression and liberation in the black church, whereas for Tutu, black identity represents the imago Dei by which God redeems white identity.

Where Tutu agrees with Cone is in the definition of blackness. For both, all victims of oppression realize that the survival of their humanity is bound up with their liberation. The freedom they seek is from a whiteness that demonizes black human identity as criminal, subhuman, and anarchical.

Where Cone differs from Tutu is in ecclesiastical preference. Cone sees the existence of the church, especially the black church, in fundamental opposition to a dominant society that sometimes likes to call itself Christian. Cone states:

> We cannot solve the ethical question of the twentieth century by looking at what Jesus did in the first. Our choices are not the same as his. Being Christian does not mean following "in his steps" (remember that book?). His steps are not ours; and thus we are placed in an existential situation in which we are forced to decide without knowing what Jesus would do. The Christian does not ask what Jesus would do as if Jesus were confined to the first century. He asks, "What is he doing? Where is he at work?" And even though these are the right questions, they cannot be answered once and for all. Each situation has its own problematic circumstances which force the believers to think through each act of obedience without an absolute ethical guide from Jesus.[27]

While Tutu would not disagree with this view of black identity, he would contend that the church is prophetic by being the people of God among the nations of the world through both a sacramental and a prophetic witness. Sacramentally, the church is to model redeemed identities. Thus, the church is already "involved" in transforming a profane world.

For Cone's black church, the nature of the church's involvement has a different form than Tutu's Anglicanism. The black church gains its definition historically by being in opposition to white identity and, therefore, lacks the ability to model the imago Dei. What this really means for Cone is that the black church is better able to attend to the nature of the fragile existence of human identity in the United States than the white church because the life of African Americans in the United States remains a very dangerous reality. And as Cone later came to see, this danger can be international in the sense that one is under constant threat in black identity.[28] Tutu agrees that there are definite dangers involved in being black and voices these sentiments in the context of the U.S. involvement in South Africa in the 1980s:

> We have been deeply hurt. We have seen that when it comes to the matter of black freedom then we blacks are really expendable in the view of the mighty US. It is a case of blood being thicker than water. You can't really trust whites. When it comes to the crunch, whatever the morality involved, whites will stick by their fellow whites.[29]

Tutu's ecclesial vision serves as an important lens for organizing people for the transformation of society. Through the church, black people as oppressed people can know that they have more worth than those in power have attributed to them. This knowledge inspires oppressed people to struggle for freedom in society by practicing the church's life of worship. From this worship life, the church—not just the black church—forms persons whose grasp of salvation is no longer bound by the definitions of a corrupt society.

If the oppressed, while living in corrupt economic structures, can see a future beyond such oppression, then "the sigh of the oppressed creature" (to use Karl Marx's phrase) becomes a revolutionary cry of rebellion against the established order. This revolutionary cry is the one granted in the resurrection of Jesus. Salvation, then, is not simply freedom to be black and white societies; it is freedom to affirm a future that is beyond segregated identities. This is how the sacramental church transforms the world.

God does not take the church out of the struggle of racial identities. Instead, the church is to be firmly rooted in this world's cultures of death to show that death is not the goal of history. The transcendent factor in salvation helps us to realize that our fight for justice is God's fight. Cone states, "The power to be somebody in a world that had defined Blacks as nobody is what God meant to me and many other Black people."[30]

This knowledge of being somebody enabled black slaves to survive despite having their identity defined by others. These slaves escaped defeat and ultimate dehumanization because the church worshiped the eternal God of three persons in one nature, who acts in the world in such a way as to favor the oppressed. The slaves believed that death had been conquered in Jesus' resurrection. They also could transcend death and interpret salvation as a heavenly, eschatological reality.

Thus for Cone and Tutu, the church works for salvation, which is first reflected in the restoration of God's creation within economic, political, and social configurations. Cone emphasizes displaying the nature of salvation first through God's movement toward addressing unjust realities.[31] Although Tutu does not dispute the importance of addressing these realities, for him the church as a redeemed community must be the locus in which both God's movement becomes intelligible and these realities are first addressed.

For Cone, Tutu's locus would be too narrow and idealistic in a structured society such as the United States, where a black person must assume a certain identity that the American church has long defined as inferior. Doubtless, Cone would critique Tutu's kenotic God in the following way: "By emphasizing the complete self-giving of God in Christ without seeing also the content of righteousness, oppressors could then demand that the oppressed do likewise."[32] From this critique, Cone would surely state that Tutu's church presupposes a social configuration that is indeed different from his own. Perhaps Cone's distinctive voice contrasts most sharply with Tutu's with respect to God: "There is no place in black theology for a colorless God in a society where human be-ings suffer precisely because of their color. The black theolo-gian must reject any conception of God which stifles black self-determination by picturing God as a god of all peoples."[33]

Cone is provocative in his display of a God rooted in the experience of the black church, where one gains access to the work of God to save the oppressed.[34] Cone's fundamen-tal problem, however, is in his assumption that the church is subject to the same economic, political, and social realities as other realms and yet remains distinctive and prophetic as the church.

Cone's strength is iconoclastic; his black theology under-scores the ways in which different racial identities bring unexamined contents to their views of theology and vari-ous ecclesiologies naturally assume the church to be the people of God who can circumvent profane realities. But, in the end, these contents need to be examined and the pro-fane realities negotiated. (Indeed, perhaps this double stan-dard of profane reality is Cone's greatest criticism against Tutu's Anglican Church.) Yet Cone's weakness is in failing to acknowledge the positive ability of the church when it is able to pool resources or use Christian identity to interro-gate the world.

Cone teaches that a surreptitious dominant identity can longer define theology for other human identities. In this respect, Cone's theology is unparalleled in importance as it facilitates an onrush of those who were previously voiceless to speak and reflect in a public forum. This is Cone's invalu-able contribution to theological discourse.

In many ways, however, Cone's necessary black church continues to promulgate profane structures of racism. No doubt Tutu would agree that black identity is victimized by white identity, but he would still advocate that the church needs to strive to be the kind of community that can contain disparate identities made one in the triune God. That is, effort needs to made to put clapping and shouting in the same context as incense and sung liturgy.

For Tutu, the church as the locus of salvation is embodied by its way of life, its celebration of the presence of God through the Eucharist, and its demand that those perpetuating political injustice repent. For Cone, the church is the involvement of a rescued, oppressed community in the interrogation and questioning of the economic, political, and social configuration of nations. If white people responded to such interrogation, then salvation would be near, if not already upon them. But how does Cone's church exemplify a society in which racial classifications do not identify persons? And from Cone, is theological reflection about grace ever provided to account for the transformation of broken human identities that may be healed by participating in the sacraments of the church? In short, Cone's ecclesial vision precludes the possibility that the church can play a significant part in the restoration of society.

Both Tutu's and Cone's strength is in their vision to see that, ironically, no ecclesiology is particular enough. That is, given their notions of reconciliation, the relation of God to the church remains problematic in the reality of a divided church. They both have inherited the problems of being African thinkers in European theological discourse. Their genius is in their attempts to think aloud about what the relation of the church to the world should be. Specifically, Tutu's splaying out the implications of the incarnation and the Trinity in an apartheid society models how black and white identities depend on each other.

Both Cone and Tutu admit a dynamic relationship between the church and the state, although Cone seems less concerned about being able to specify its nature. Both advocate direct action to create not only a responsible society but also a church that is defined beyond its whiteness. Tutu's theology, however, is better able than Cone's to employ such theological notions as the form of the kenotic Christ. Instead, Cone employs the nature of a new power group seeking self-determination in terms of its particular conception of a good society. Cone's justification for such a move is that the new power group is God's manifestation of being on the side of the poor and black.

Cone might claim that the black church is the better working symbol of the dimensions of divine activity in a North American context. Therefore, black theology must exemplify contextual language because no uninterpreted fact is available. Cone might go on to say that theology can neither be written out of nothing nor written for all times, places, and peoples. For Tutu, in contrast, the church need not be focused on antagonistic debate, but may see itself as a community of disciples trained in the politics of Jesus to be agents in the world to birth a different dominion. In sum, Tutu's theology seeks the interdependent determination of the church to form a good society, whereas Cone's theology seeks a more autonomous means to bring about a good society through an exclusively black hermeneutic.

Tutu's ascetic formation is important in establishing how black theology may negotiate the transformation of the profane structures of the earth into the sacred realities of the church. Tutu's asceticism continually questions how the nature of the church is formed by the what from which we are being saved. Tutu and Cone both seem to agree that the task of theological ethics is to specify theological language in such a way that a person may view salvation through God's particular witness amidst the diverse communities that comprise the church. Such a view accentuates the belief that at Pentecost, the Holy Spirit displays how persons are dependent on others for their personhood.

A POLITICAL PRIEST

Desmond Tutu's ecclesiology is shaped by worship, the habitual recollection of God's presence through which he finds theological categories for his politics against apartheid. As an internationally renowned archbishop who is able to draw support against apartheid from diverse public sectors, the primary source from which Tutu can publicly protest apartheid has been the church's liturgy.[35] The question is raised how Tutu can maintain a distinct Christian spirituality of worship while also campaigning publicly against apartheid. For some, this question is in what sense, if any, Tutu can be called a political priest.

Tutu is a political priest in two ways. First, he resolved to work through the church to fight apartheid. Second, he sought to anchor the political struggle theologically. Thus, Tutu inspired the church in South Africa to dismantle apartheid in order to bring about a new model of how communities may negotiate with one another in a new South Africa. This commitment, shaped by his ubuntu theology and ecclesiology, put him at the center of a political storm. The white establishment viewed him as failing to separate religion from politics and confine his ministry to proper spiritual business. In contrast, black South African scholars have claimed that he has betrayed the struggle of the oppressed by being aligned too closely with European theology and church structures.

Tutu's theological model rejects the ideological premise of any black theology predicated on the idea that blackness can be one's primary identity. For Tutu, one's baptism into the church is one's primary identity.

One should not infer from this that race does not matter for Tutu. On the contrary, racial classifications are vital to the South African context because they determine how people relate to one another. In apartheid, however, those in power established the oppressive system of racial classifications, "and that," Tutu pointed out, "is totally contrary to what Jesus says about neighbours."[36]

As an archbishop who participates daily in the Anglican rite of the Holy Eucharist, Tutu rejects the lessening of human identity and is compelled to lead his society, even politically, to the recovery of human identity. In that sense, then, Tutu was a political priest because he actively opposed a civil religion that justified a corrupt state. He did not wish to imply any lack of political identity. In fact he stated, "I am an unabashed egalitarian and libertarian because God has created us freely for freedom. People in this new South Africa will matter and be seen to be of infinite value because they are human beings created in the image of God."[37]

Shaped by both church and African tradition, Tutu's theological model provides insight into how he achieves his identity as political priest. He is political precisely because he is a priest in the South African context. Tutu states:

> You whites brought us the Bible; now we blacks are taking it seriously. We are involved with God to set us free from all that enslaves us and makes us less than what [God] intended us to be. I will demonstrate that apartheid, separate development, or whatever it is called is evil, totally and without remainder, that it is unchristian and unbiblical. If anyone were to show me otherwise, I would burn my Bible and cease to be a Christian.[38]

When he spoke these words, Tutu was not yet archbishop of Southern Africa, not yet a Nobel Peace Prize winner, and not yet the international figure he is today. Yet the following statement indicates the character of the man who has sought to maintain an integrity of Christian faith in the midst of apartheid. When an interviewer asked, "How do you balance the spiritual and the political aspects of your life?" Tutu responded:

> I do not have a sense of tension between the two. I have come to learn that spirituality is absolutely essential to an authentic Christian life. That is how it was with almost all God's servants. Their encounters with God were not for their own self-aggrandizement but for the sake of others. You meet God as a burning bush in order to be sent to Pharaoh to redeem captives.[39]

Tutu's early leadership was in the South African Council of Churches (SACC), an ecumenical church organization that defended political prisoners, supported families, educated children, and assisted refugees. From the 1970s onward, the council became the center of theological and political assault on the ideology and practice of apartheid. In 1981, the Eloff Commission of the South African government sought to analyze the council's interpretation of Christian mission, its foreign connections, and its financial records to determine whether or not the council was a subversive organization. Tutu responded:

> I have told the South African government, who have consistently attacked us and placed us and the SACC under sharp and long scrutiny, that in fact to be attacked by them ensured that our credibility shot up several points in the rest of the world, and conversely, to be praised by them was the kiss of death. The award of the Nobel Peace Prize is not just a personal vindication, but is also a vindication of the SACC. We have been accused by the South African authorities of really being revolutionary, meaning thereby that we were in fact in favour of violence despite all our disclaimers to the contrary. . . . This award says we in the SACC and others are

peaceloving ones, agents of reconciliation, and that it is the perpetrators of apartheid who are carrying out a fundamentally violent policy and not against an external aggressor but against unarmed civilians. . . . This award . . . confirms that blacks are peaceloving to a fault and remain nonviolent despite the greatest provocation imaginable.[40]

For Tutu, this governmental inquiry was extremely frustrating. He stated, "I would want to state categorically for myself that I believe the South African State lacks legitimacy because the socio-political and economic dispensation is one that has not been developed after normal democratic processes of decision-making."[41]

From his SACC days, the drama of Tutu's political priestcraft continued to unfold into his days as archbishop of the Anglican Church of South Africa in March 1988. Then President Botha made this accusation against Tutu:

> You love and praise the ANC/SACP [African National Conference/South African Communist Party] with its Marxist and atheistic ideology, landmines, bombs and necklaces perpetrating the most horrendous atrocities imaginable; and you embrace and participate in their call for violence, hatred, sanctions, insurrection and revolution. The question must be posed whether you are acting on behalf of the kingdom of God, or the kingdom promised by the ANC and the SACP? If it is the latter, say so, but do not then hide behind the structures of the cloth and the Christian Church, because Christianity and Marxism are irreconcilable opposites.[42]

In his response, Tutu denounced Botha's accusation in an explicitly theological manner:

> I want to state quite categorically that I stand by all that I have done and said in the past concerning the application of the

Gospel of Jesus Christ to the situation of injustice and oppression and exploitation which are of the very essence of apartheid, a policy which your government has carried out with ruthless efficiency. My position in this matter is not one of which I am ashamed or for which I would ever want to apologise. I know that I stand in the mainline Christian tradition.[43]

Tutu defended himself further by saying that his theological position is derived from the church, which predates Marxism and the African National Congress. The church teaches that each person is invested with infinite value, made in the image of God, instead of being valued through arbitrary biological attributes which apartheid claims as defining criteria for personhood.

Using this reasoning also to defend himself when he was general secretary of the SACC, Tutu insisted that the secular commission had no authority to judge the SACC's theological credentials. He did this in such a way, as Allister Sparks describes, that those seated on the public benches in the room applauded with delight:

He sat bouncing and twisting in an upright chair, his hands shaping the outline of his ideas with vivid gestures. . . . His voice was the other instrument in this virtuoso performance, sometimes sonorous, playing with the cadences of his African accent, and sometimes breaking into a high-pitched chuckle as he hit on a pertinent new insight. His delivery was somber, joyful, impatient, humourous, reflective, switching rapidly through all these registers in response to a quicksilver spirit. And all the while the white commissioners watched expressionlessly.[44]

Tutu's vibrant response to apartheid offers a vivid description of an active Christian leader involved in the political activities of the world. Yet Tutu's struggle was not just against political forces. He also had to convince white Christians and black Christians that they are part of each other's family. It is from his extraordinary character of faith and humor that he was able to critique the interpretations of theological justification for apartheid so often drawn from the stories of Genesis and the tower of Babel:

> At the tower of Babel, human community became impossible because the languages were confused. At the first Christian Pentecost, all who were gathered there could understand each other's language and could understand what the apostles were saying. At Babel there was a dispersal, a separation. At Pentecost there was an ingathering of all the nations as provided in the catalogue of those who were present. Apartheid comprehensively contradicts the Bible and Christian teaching.[45]

Both black liberation theologians and Afrikaner theologians had used the narrative of the Exodus as a paradigm for their own saga of the liberation of an oppressed people. Tutu, however, interpreted these scriptural passages so as not to allow destructive conclusions that might be used to justify the separation of peoples on the basis of racial classification. Instead, in the book of Genesis he found a narrative of God's intention for a universe of shalom:

> This is the ultimate consequence of sin according to the Bible—separation, alienation, apartness. It is a perverse exegesis that would hold that the story of the Tower of Babel is a justification for racial separation, a divine sanction for the diversity of nations. It is to declare that the divine punishment for sin had become the divine intention for mankind.[46]

Tutu's ecclesiology is a demonstration of God's mission to restore the world into a primal flourishing through the enigmatic suffering of the incarnation of God and humanity. An important theological movement occurred in the church when the Afrikaner and African versions of God's election were resolved—namely, apartheid was deemed heretical.[47]

Tutu's opposition to apartheid caused him to be criticized as a "political" priest, unable to separate the spiritual from the political. In this light, the story of the Exodus becomes all the more crucial for Tutu, who seeks the liberation of all who are oppressed from such sin. Is the church subversive to the government by reckoning apartheid as sin? Yes, Tutu believes, because God is subversive of all situations of injustice. Therefore, with such an ally as God, Tutu concluded, the Eloff Commission would "fail because they are ranging themselves on the side of evil and injustice against the Church of God. Like others who have done that in the past, the Neros, the Hitlers, the Amins of this world, they will end up as the flotsam and jetsam of history."[48]

During the heightened governmental intimidation of the 1980s, Tutu's interaction with President Botha provided the example of Christian and political leadership. He and other church leaders filled political roles by promoting the essential tenet of the political creed of the ANC, namely, a nonracial government. Ironically, unlike many prominent African Christian leaders in the 1980s,[49] Tutu has been reluctant to join any political organization. The only exception was his patronage of the National Forum Committee, which was made up of a wide spectrum of perspectives.[50] Despite Tutu's reluctance to be characterized as a political leader, the government found itself having to deal with him as such.

In sum, Tutu's ecclesiology includes politics because he believes that God calls the church to be a dynamic witness against apartheid or any other form of oppression. Tutu's mission is to set forth how God has made people to depend on one another, even for their identity. Egil Aarvi, chair of the Norwegian Nobel Committee, describes the irony in the realization that D. F. Malan and Tutu are interdependent:

> The man who, more than anyone else was responsible for the implementation of the apartheid system—the National Party's first Prime Minister, Dr. Daniel Malan—was a churchman, an ordained priest in the Dutch Reformed Church. And Tutu has become the most dynamic opponent of the apartheid system, also a churchman—in fact, a bishop. In this way history corrects its own mistakes. It is even more ironic to consider that the apartheid system is the indirect reason for the fact that Tutu became a churchman. . . . His first wish was to become a doctor, but this was impossible with his parent's financial situation.[51]

NOTES

PREFACE

1. Desmond Tutu, "Some African Insights and the Old Testament," in *Relevant Theology for Africa: Report on a Consultation of the Missiological Institute at Lutheran Theological College* (Mapumulo, Natal, September 12–21, 1972), ed. Hans-Jurgen Becken (Durban: Lutheran Publishing House, 1973), 42.

2. Ibid., 43. For a similar conclusion also see Tutu, "Whither African Theology?" in *Christianity in Independent Africa*, by Edward Fasholé-Luke et al. (London: Rex Collings, 1978).

3. Tutu, "Some African Insights and the Old Testament," 44.

4. Desmond Tutu, "Black and African Theologies: Soul-Mates or Antagonists?" in *Black Theology: A Documentary History, 1966–1979*, ed. G. Wilmore and J. Cone (New York: Orbis Books, 1981), 388–89. (Originally published in *The Journal of Religious Thought* 32, no. 2 [1975].)

5. Ibid., 392.

6. Desmond Tutu, *Crying in the Wilderness: The Struggle for Justice in South Africa* (Grand Rapids, Mich.: Eerdmans, 1982), 7.

7. Desmond Tutu, *Hope and Suffering: Sermons and Speeches* (Grand Rapids, Mich.: Eerdmans, 1984), 33.

8. Desmond Tutu, *The Rainbow People of God: The Making of a Peaceful Revolution*, ed. John Allen (New York: Doubleday, 1994).

9. Ibid., "Editor's Preface," xxi. It is also noted that Nelson Mandela wrote the foreword.

10. For evidence of my argument, the reader is directed to two formal works by Tutu: "Church and Prophecy in South Africa To-

day" (Center for the Study of Theology in the University of Essex, Essex Papers in Theology and Society, 1991) and "The Theologian and the Gospel of Freedom," in *The Trial of Faith: Theology and the Church Today*, ed. Peter Eaton (West Essex: Churchman Publishers, 1988).

11. Desmond Tutu, "Foreword," in Mary Benson, *Nelson Mandela: The Man and the Movement* (New York: W. W. Norton, 1986).

1. INTRODUCTION: Holding Back a Tide of Violence

1. See T. Dunbar Moodie, *The Rise of Afrikanerdom: Power, Apartheid, and the Afrikaner Civil Religion* (Berkeley: University of California Press, 1975). Moodie points out that South Africa is largely defined by an interpretation of Calvinism that makes the Afrikaner's civil religion a doctrine for a New Israel. Many Afrikaners think of themselves as descendants of seventeenth-century Calvinist rebels who fled religious persecution in Europe. To them, God created the Afrikaner people with a unique language, a unique philosophy of life, and their own history and traditions. This theological narrative was explicit in the moral appeal of Afrikaner nationalists in 1944. Four years later, the theological term of "apartheid" (i.e., holy, set apart) developed.

2. Desmond Tutu, "Some Memories of My Life," June 28, 1990, draft.

3. Mike Green, "Close-Up: Desmond Tutu, Archbishop," *Runner's World* 1, no. 1 (May/June 1993), 29.

4. Judith Bentley, *Archbishop Tutu of South Africa* (Hillside, N.J.: Enslow, 1988), 11–12.

5. Desmond Tutu, handwritten address, "Pinelands Parish Meeting," February 18, 1988. Tutu recounts his letter to Vorster. Also see Tutu, *Hope and Suffering*, 28–36.

6. Beyers Naudé, as quoted in Winner, *Desmond Tutu: Brave and Eloquent*, 41.

7. Desmond Tutu, undated sermon, "Passiontide Addresses: Maundy Thursday."

8. Desmond Tutu, "Persecution of Christians under Apartheid,"

in *Concilium Revue Internationale de Théologie* (1982). In this article, Tutu names many Christians persecuted under the South African government.

9. Desmond Tutu, "Apartheid and Christianity" (speech), Rand Afrikaans University, March 1984, 2.

10. Charles Villa-Vicencio, "The Church in Africa: Interview with Archbishop Desmond Tutu," *Challenge: Church & People*, no. 12 (February 1993): 6.

11. Michael Schluter, "A Passion for Justice," *Third Way* 17, no. 4 (May 1994): 16.

12. Racial classification was explicitly embedded in South Africa's legal and legislative structure. See Appendix for a chronology of the progression of apartheid laws.

13. Rowan Williams, "Nobody Knows Who I Am till the Judgement Morning," in *Trevor Huddleston: Essays on His Life and Work*," ed. Deborah Duncan Honoré (Oxford: Oxford University Press, 1988), 141.

14. Desmond Tutu, "Awkward Questions" (commencement address), University of Western Cape, February 13, 1987.

15. Quoted in David Winner, *Desmond Tutu: Brave and Eloquent Archbishop Struggling against Apartheid in South Africa* (Dublin: Wolfhound Press, 1989), 26. Verwoerd is a major political figure in establishing "Bantustans," or independent homelands on which such separate development could take place.

16. Desmond Tutu, "Nobel Lecture, December 11, 1984," *Les Prix Nobel 1984* (Stockholm: Almqvist & Wiksell International, 1985), 243.

17. Desmond Tutu, "South African Violence: Ours Are Birthing Pains—Tutu," *Daily Nation* (Nairobi), October 9, 1993, 16.

18. Desmond Tutu, "General Secretary's Report to National Conference of SACC," June 25–29, 1984.

19. Desmond Tutu, "Response at Graduation of Columbia University's Honorary Doctorate" (address), University of the Witwatersrand, August 2, 1982. (The president and trustees of Columbia University presented the degree in South Africa because the South African government prevented Tutu from flying to New York.)

20. Williams, "Nobody Knows," 140. Williams here refers to Ann Dummett, *A Portrait of English Racism* (London: CARAF Publications, 1984), 150.

21. Tutu, "Nobel Lecture," 246.

22. "The Archbishop, the Church and the Nation," in *Monitor: The Journal of the Human Rights Trust*, June 1991 (Port Elizabeth: Monitor Publications), 7.

23. Desmond Tutu, "Where Is Now Thy God?" (address), Trinity Institute, New York, January 8, 1989.

24. Desmond Tutu, "God Who Is There" (handwritten address), National Christian Youth Convention, Australia, 1987.

25. Tutu, "The Theologian and the Gospel of Freedom," 65.

26. Tutu, "Where Is Now Thy God?"

27. Ibid.

28. Tutu, "The Theologian and the Gospel of Freedom."

29. Allister Sparks, *The Observer* (August 8, 1982). At this time, Tutu demonstrated his vital leadership on the threshold of the lifting of the ban on black political organizations.

30. Quoted in Winner, *Desmond Tutu: Brave and Eloquent*, 55.

31. Jim Wallis, ed., *The Rise of Christian Conscience: The Emergence of a Dramatic Renewal Movement in the Church Today* (San Francisco: Harper & Row, 1987), 58.

32. Quoted in Villa-Vicencio, "The Church in Africa," 5–6. In a sermon in Nairobi, 1988, Tutu is on record as having warned the church in Africa that it was in no position to condemn apartheid while it failed to condemn human rights violations in other parts of Africa.

33. Desmond Tutu, undated handwritten sermon, SACC staff worship, 8:30 A.M.

34. Tutu in James S. Murray's interview, "Racism: We Need a Prophet," *The Australian*, May 10, 1984.

35. Quoted in Wallis, ed., *The Rise of Christian Conscience*, 60.

36. See Desmond Tutu, "Foreword," in *Turning Points in Religious Studies: Essays in Honour of Geoffrey Parrinder*, ed. Ursula King (Edinburgh: T. & T. Clark, 1990).

37. Tutu, "The Theologian and the Gospel of Freedom," 61.

38. Tutu, "Apartheid and Christianity," March 1984, 1.

2. A MILK-AND-HONEY LAND OF OPPRESSION

1. Charles Villa-Vicencio, "The Church in Africa: Interview with Archbishop Desmond Tutu," *Challenge: Church & People*, no. 12 (February 1993): 6.

2. Ibid.

3. Desmond Tutu, "The Plight of the Resettled and Other Rural Poor: The Stand of the Church," in *Up Against the Fences: Poverty, Passes and Privilege in South Africa*, ed. Hermann Giliomee and Lawrence Schlemmer (Cape Town: David Philip, 1985), 277.

4. Trevor Huddleston, *Naught for Your Comfort* (London: Collins, 1956), 87, emphasis added.

5. Desmond Tutu, "A Black View of the Law" (address), Pretoria attorneys, March 25, 1983.

6. Desmond Tutu, sermon, Birmingham Cathedral, April 21, 1988, 4. Also see Desmond Tutu, "The Crisis We Face" (handwritten address), April 16, 1986, for showing disparities between black and white people and the ignorance between the two.

7. Currently, 87 percent of the total land area of South Africa (i.e., the most productive, arable, and fertile) is owned by white people. Of the remaining 13 percent, reserved for African ownership, 9 percent is state-owned. Though the Population Registration Act and the Group Areas Act were repealed, ownership of land was still on the basis of race. As the new black majority government begins, this is their major political issue. See the Institute for Contextual Theology's "Facts Sheet 5, Economy II." A growing urban crisis has resulted in "squatter settlements," which challenge legal access to land and housing, especially since blacks have never had legal recourse to own property until recently. See "New Squatter Act Allows Forced Removals" and "The Struggle for Land and Housing," in *Crisis News, Western Province Council of Churches Publication*, no. 27 (February 1989): 1, 6, 7.

8. Francis Wilson and Mamphela Ramphele, *Uprooting Poverty: The South African Challenge* (Cape Town: David Philip, 1989), 192.

9. Ibid., 191.

10. Wilson and Ramphele, *Uprooting Poverty*, 191.

11. See Orlando Patterson, *Slavery and Social Death* (Cambridge: Harvard University Press, 1982), which traces the development of slavery. Even in the referendum vote, states Tutu, we see the insidious nature of this control, "Coloured and Indians are thus being asked to maintain white domination and to help become co-oppressors of the blacks" (Desmond Tutu, "The State of the Nation" [address], Mirge, Cape Town, December 1, 1982).

12. Louis Leipoldt, quoted in Allister Sparks, *The Mind of South Africa* (New York: Ballantine Books, 1990), 28.

13. For more detail, see Odendaal, *Beyond the Barricades*, 30–39.

14. Moodie, *The Rise of Afrikanerdom*, 1–2.

15. See J. A. Lubser, *The Apartheid Bible: A Critical Review of Racial Theology in South Africa* (Cape Town: Maskew Miller Longman, 1987).

16. F. W. Reitz, *A Century of Wrong* (London: Review of Reviews, 1900); quoted in Moodie, *The Rise of Afrikanerdom*, 5.

17. Desmond Tutu, undated speech, 1985–1986, "The Evolution of Apartheid," 2.

18. D. F. Malan, "Apartheid: A Divine Calling," *The Anti-Apartheid Reader*, ed. David Mermelstein (New York: Grove Press, 1987), 97. For a more dynamic view of the tensions within the Dutch Reformed Church over racial matters, see John de Gruchy, *The Church Struggle in South Africa* (Grand Rapids, Mich.: Eerdmans, 1979), chap. 1.

19. See Templin, *Ideology on a Frontier*, 118.

20. John Calvin, *Institutes*, III, 8:1 and 8:7, quoted in Moodie, *The Rise of Afrikanerdom*, 12–13.

21. The special forces, part of the military forces, are officially known as "Soldiers of Jesus Christ," a name derived from the colloquial term for the disabled.

22. John Calvin, *Commentaries on the Epistle of Paul the Apostle to the Romans* (Grand Rapids, Mich.: Eerdmans, 1948), 469.

23. Villa-Vicencio, *Civil Disobedience and Beyond*, 71.

24. Karl Barth, *Church Dogmatics* II/I (Edinburgh: T. & T. Clark,

1957), 386. Barth also employed this methodology in rejecting Hitler's absolutist claims.

25. What I mean by the Enlightenment involves the following three ideological factors. First, there is in truth no authority other than the individual's ability to reason. Second, the concept of progress determines modernity through the growth of knowledge of self and environment; progress defines humanity. And third, science, on the basis of objectivity, determines reality. See David Bryan Davis, *Slavery and Human Progress* (New York: Oxford University Press, 1984).

26. This vision is examined in John B. Friedman's *The Monstrous Races in Medieval Art and Thought* (Cambridge: Harvard University Press, 1981). Friedman displays the complication of racial construction in antiquity through the modern description of "black," which weighs heavily in a history of slavery and oppression of Africans. Therefore, ancient African thinkers had different intentions from the usual European rhetoric of how black is associated with evil. See also Frank M. Snowden, *Blacks in Antiquity: Ethiopians in the Greco-Roman Experience* (Cambridge: Harvard University Press, 1970), especially the chapter titled "Early Christian Attitude toward Ethiopians—Creed and Conversion," 196–216.

27. V. Y. Mudimbe, *The Invention of Africa: Gnosis, Philosophy, and the Order of Knowledge* (Bloomington: Indiana University Press, 1988), 16.

28. See Steven Gould, *The Mismeasure of Man* (New York: Norton, 1981). Gould shows how early naturalists were informed by the Greek version of beauty: forehead, nose, and chin were at a 140-degree angle. The resulting contrast of beauty included Europeans with a 97-degree angle, and Africans with a 60- to 70-degree angle, closest to apes and dogs.

29. Desmond Tutu, undated speech, 1985–1986, "The Evolution of Apartheid," 2. Tutu goes on to add, "A Wag changed one of these to read somewhat harassingly: 'Drive carefully. Natives very cross here.'"

30. Biblical commentary was also used to support the primacy of race. See, for example, Everett Tilson, *Segregation and the Bible*

(Nashville: Abingdon Press, 1958), and Lewis Peavy, *The Cushite, or the Descendents of Ham* (Springfield, Mass.: Willey Press, 1843).

31. Desmond Tutu, "Postscript: To Be Human Is to Be Free," in *Christianity and Democracy in Global Context*, ed. John Witte Jr. (Boulder: Westview Press, 1993), 312.

32. *The Argus*, March 3, 1994.

33. Hannah Arendt, *Imperialism: Part Two of the Origins of Totalitarianism* (New York: Harcourt Brace Jovanovich, 1968), 63–64, quoted in Mudimbe, *The Invention of Africa*, 108.

34. Frank Snowden gives a different assessment of the chronology of racial definition prior to the thirteenth century in *Blacks in Antiquity*. However, Snowden's essential thesis remains aligned to the shift of racial criteria in the Enlightenment, when African history was documented not by Africans but by Europeans.

35. Cultural logic (e.g., language and customs) is the underlying reason for the way things are done in a particular place and how these things are seen as necessary (e.g., you marry a certain kind of person, you do not wear a hat in the house, and you do not wear shoes in the temple). African slavery permitted slaves to adopt their masters' cultural logic in order to become members of this culture.

36. Carolus Linnaeus (1753) classified humanity into four types: (1) homoeuropeanus (white, blue-eyed, gentle, covered with clothes, disciplined, flowing-haired, inventive, strong); (2) homoasiaticus; (3) homoamericanus (i.e., American Indians); (4) homoafer (black, relaxed, frizzy-haired, silky-skinned, flat-nosed, thick-lipped, large-breasted, negligent, indolent, crafty, oily, capricious). Frederick Blumenbach (1720) proposed a fifth variety: Caucasian, from Mt. Caucasus, because its environment supposedly produced the most beautiful race (featuring a beautiful skull, rosy cheeks, white skin, oval head and face, smooth forehead, narrow nose, slightly hooked jaw, and perpendicular teeth). Blumenbach's other racial classifications included Mongolian, Ethiopian, American, and Malay. Louis Agassiz (1804), a celebrated naturalist and devout Christian, believed that biological differences should be consistent with social and educational differences. Samuel George

Morton was concerned with the size of the cranium. His racial classifications included: (1) Germans, English, Americans; (2) Ancient Greeks, Semitics; (3) Asians; (4) Mexicans, Indians; and (5) Negroes, Native Africans, American Negroes. In the late nineteenth century, E. D. Cope, a paleontologist, identified as evolutionary lineages: (1) Northern Europeans, (2) Southern Europeans, (3) Blacks (not capable of resurrection). I am indebted to Willie Jennings for this genealogy. Also, for analysis of race and social theory, see Cornel West, *Keeping Faith: Philosophy and Race in America* (New York: Routledge, 1994), 251–70.

37. Gerhart, *Black Power in South Africa*, 24.

38. See Robert M. Price, *The Apartheid State in Crisis: Political Transformation in South Africa, 1975–1990* (New York: Oxford University Press, 1991). This uniqueness has also been its vulnerablity. Official racism has bedeviled South Africa's international relations, as efforts by the state to maintain its internal order place a strain on its external relationships. Many modern states oppress their populations without adversely affecting their global relations, but the incompatibility between South African white supremacy and global norms has denied the South African state this luxury. In sum, Price's evaluation for change in South Africa is materialistic in that fundamental political change occurs through economic decline and political unrest.

39. Michael Worsnip, *Between the Two Fires: The Anglican Church and Apartheid 1948–1957* (Pietermaritzburg: University of Natal Press, 1991), 38.

40. Quoted in Moodie, *The Rise of Afrikanerdom*, 1.

41. Translation from W. A. de Klerk, *The Puritans in Africa: A Story of Afrikandom* (Durban: Bok Books, 1975), 259.

42. Worsnip, *Between the Two Fires*, 38.

43. Desmond Tutu, "The South African Press: The Esau Complex" (undated speeches), 7.

44. Desmond Tutu, "A Vision for Humanity" (undated address).

45. Ibid., 8

46. Previous to this quote, he tells a story of two *oomies* (old men). "The one oom says he's put burglar bars on all his windows,

but he's still so scared of the blacks he can't sleep at night. 'That's nothing,' says the other. 'I'm so scared I have to sleep with the maid." Farmer Schalk Vorster interviewed in *The Argus*, March 24, 1994.

47. Desmond Tutu, "Christianity and Apartheid" (speech), 1982, 9.

48. Gail Gerhart, *Black Power in South Africa: The Evolution of an Ideology* (Berkeley and Los Angeles: University of California Press, 1978), 111.

49. Desmond Tutu, "Stop the Rot Everybody," *City Press* (Johannesburg), March 14, 1993.

50. See W. E. B. DuBois, "The Conservation of Races," American Negro Academy Occasional Papers, no. 2 (1897), in *W. E. B. DuBois Speaks: Speeches and Addresses 1890–1919*, ed. P. S. Foner (New York: Pathfinders Press), 1970; Rufus Lewis Perry, *The Cushite or the Descendants of Ham* (Springfield, Mass.: Willey Press, 1893), and *Sketch of Philosophical Systems, Suffrage* (Hartford: American Publication Company), 1895; and Leopold Senghor, "Negritude," *Optima* (1966), 16:1–8.

51. Although with more benign intention, to a large extent this is still the case, as Western organizations predict that sub-Saharan Africa is on a downward spiral that will bring half the continent's population—three hundred million people—below the poverty line by the beginning of the twenty-first century. This demise of Africa is documented by the World Bank, Oxfam, and the International Monetary Fund (IMF). Ironically, owing to enormous African debt, the IMF has recently been criticized for draining resources out of Africa ($3 billion). See South African newspaper *The Weekly Mail*, May 7–13, 1993, 21.

52. Odendaal, *Beyond the Barricades*, 179. On June 23, 1909, Mahatma Gandhi also went to London on behalf of the Transvaal Indians, appealing for equality based on what the imperial government espouses as Christian. At this time some white constituencies formed protest movements through weighty petitions by leading church figures from various denominations to remove the color restrictions from the South African Draft Act. Such a peti-

tion was signed, for example, by Cape Town's Anglican archbishop, W. M. Carter, in his first public act since his enthronement. Other radical whites followed suit through other Christian denominations (Odendaal, *Beyond the Barricades*, 194).

53. Desmond Tutu, "Christianity and Apartheid" (speech), 1982, 10.

54. Theological and political justifications for race were closely related. See, for example, statements by the Dutch Reformed Churches of South Africa on racial policy, including the 1960 "Statements on Race Relations" (Johannesburg: Information Bureau of the Dutch Reformed Church, November 1960) and the October 1974 Statement *Ras, Volk, en Nasie* (Pretoria: N. G. Kerk-Vitgewers), 1975. For a discussion of the relationship between Nederduitse Gereformeerde Kerk (NGK) and the political policy of apartheid, see *Die NG Kerk en Apartheid* (Johannesburg: Macmillan Press, 1986). I am indebted to Robert K. Massie for these references.

55. Desmond Tutu, "South Africa on the Way to 2000 A.D." (address), March 31, 1980.

56. Desmond Tutu, "Preamble" (undated speech), Wit's University, 9.

57. Moodie, *The Rise of Afrikanerdom*, 11–12.

58. Desmond Tutu, "Christianity and Apartheid" (speech), Rand Afrikaans University, March 1984, 7.

59. Moodie relies on interpretations of civil-religion speeches published in the Afrikaans press between 1930–1940 and the *Ossewa Gedenkboek*, 1940. A reviewer of *Ossewa Gedenkboek* in the Afrikaans newspaper *Die Burger* writes, "In all reverence, I would call it the New Testament of Afrikanerdom. Again with the greatest reverence I would declare that it deserves a place on the household altar beside the family Bible. For if the Bible shaped the Afrikaner People, then the Gedenkboek reveals that product in its deepest being" (*Die Burger*, March 30, 1940, quoted in Moodie, *The Rise of Afrikanerdom*, 11).

60. From an unpublished paper by Robert Massie, I gather the following sources to support this tendency of civil religion in the Afrikaner church. See Willem Saayman, "A Few Aspects of the

Policy of Separate Churches, " *Journal of Theology for Southern Africa*, no. 26 (March 1979); "The Case of South Africa: Practice Context, and Ideology," in *Exploring Church Growth*, ed. W. R. Shenk (Grand Rapids, Mich.: Eerdmans, 1983). See also Saayman's discussion in "Christian Missions in South Africa: Achievements, Failures, and the Future," in Martin Prozesky, *Christianity amidst Apartheid* (London: Macmillan, 1990), 34ff.

61. Desmond Tutu, sermon, printed after October 7, 1989.

62. Quoted in Sparks, *The Mind of South Africa*, 67, and in Catherine Ingram, *In the Footsteps of Gandhi: Conversations with Spiritual Social Activists* (Berkeley, Calif.: Parallax Press, 1990), 277–78. In Ingram's account, Tutu adds at the end of his common anecdote, "But maybe we got the better end of the deal."

63. Tutu, sermon, printed after October 7, 1989.

64. Desmond Tutu, "Message on Behalf of the South African Council of Churches at Frikkie Conradie's Funeral" (address), March 6, 1982.

65. Peter Walshe, "The Evolution of Liberation Theology in South Africa," in *The Journal of Law and Religion* 5, no. 2 (1987): 299–300.

66. Tutu, "Whither African Theology?" 368.

67. In these early years of South Africa, W. Schreiner provides the example of a radical white who became a strong advocate of blacks, especially as he often became the rallying figure in opposition to the draft South Africa Act. See Andre Odendaal, *Beyond the Barricades* (New York: Aperture Press, 1989), 197.

3. DELICATE NETWORKS OF INTERDEPENDENCE

1. Desmond Tutu, "Grace upon Grace," *Journal for Preachers* 15, no. 1 (Advent 1991): 20.

2. Augustine Shutte, "Philosophy for Africa" (paper presented at the University of Cape Town, South Africa), 31–32.

3. Some European historians counter this claim by painting a picture of South Africa before the arrival of the missionary as filled with tribal wars and famine. However, African scholars such as Gabriel Setiloane state that such accounts leave out three elements that may have contributed to such war and famine 150 years (1652)

before missionaries arrived in South Africa (i.e., "White man, the horse and the gun, and ammunition"). See Gabriel Setiloane, *The Image of God among the Sotho-Tswana* (Rotterdam: A. A. Balkema, 1976), 123.

4. Ifeanyi A. Menkiti, "Person and Community in African Traditional Thought," in *African Philosophy*, ed. R. A. Wright (New York: University Press of America, 1971), 158.

5. Desmond Tutu, address to South African Institute of Race Relations, quoted in Winner, *Desmond Tutu: Brave and Eloquent*, 26.

6. This description of sub-Saharan African people is now considered derogatory, especially through its use as a tool of social and racial division in South Africa.

7. D. A. Masolo, *African Philosophy in Search of Identity* (Bloomington: Indiana University Press, 1994), 87.

8. Mudimbe, *The Invention of Africa*, 149.

9. Shutte, "Philosophy for Africa," 5.

10. Desmond Tutu, "Viability," in *Relevant Theology for Africa: Report on a Consultation of the Missiological Institute at Lutheran Theological College, Mapumulo, Natal, September 12–21, 1972*, ed. Hans-Jurgen Becken (Durban: Lutheran Publishing House, 1973), 38.

11. A similar conceptualization of ubuntu may found in the doctrines of African socialism especially expounded by Julius K. Nyerere's *ujamaa*. See J. K. Nyerere, *Ujamaa: Essays on Socialism* (London: Oxford University Press, 1968); *Freedom and Development* (Oxford: Oxford University Press, 1973); and "The Rational Choice," in *African Socialism in Practice: The Tanzanian Experience*, ed. A. Coulson (Nottingham, U.K.: Spokesman Publishers, 1979), 19–26. Masolo, *Some Aspects and Prospectives of African Philosophy Today* (Rome: Institutio Italo-Africano, 1981), provides a critique of Nyerere's socialism as providing a poor sociological assessment of the causes and effects of communalistic attitudes.

12. Desmond Tutu, sermon, Birmingham Cathedral, April 21, 1988, 3.

13. Desmond Tutu, "A Christian Vision of the Future of South Africa," in *Christianity in South Africa*, ed. Martin Prozesky (Bergvlei, South Africa: Southern Book Publishers, 1990).

14. Desmond Tutu, "The Nature and Value of Theology" (undated address).

15. Desmond Tutu, "Human Rights in South Africa" (undated address), in *Monitor*, SACC Library Resource Center.

16. Tutu, sermon, printed after October 7, 1989.

17. Desmond Tutu, sermon, Birmingham Cathedral, April 21, 1988, 3.

18. Desmond Tutu, "Genesis Chapter 3" (handwritten sermon), St. Mary's, Blechingly, Surrey, October 6, 1985.

19. See Desmond Tutu, "Apartheid and Christianity" (September 24, 1982), for a discussion of this paradox.

20. Desmond Tutu, "Response at Graduation of Columbia University's Honorary Doctorate" (address), the University of Witwatersrand, August 2, 1982. The degree was presented by Columbia's president, who came to South Africa with university trustees because the South African government prevented Tutu from flying to New York.

21. Desmond Tutu, quoted in *Prayers for Peace, An Anthology of Readings and Prayers*, comp. Archbishop Robert Runcie and Cardinal Basil Hume (London: SPCK, 1987), 41.

22. Desmond Tutu, handwritten sermon, Sunday School Teachers' Eucharist, St. George's Cathedral, February 2, 1987.

23. Desmond Tutu, handwritten sermon, St. Philip's, Washington DC, Christmas 3, 1984.

24. Desmond Tutu, "Genesis Chapter 3" (handwritten sermon), St. Mary's, Blechingly, Surrey, October 6, 1985.

25. Shutte, "Philosophy for Africa," 90. Shutte outlines a philosophical conception of humanity that "incorporates and systematises the African insights." His methodology is a product of his particular training in European philosophical tradition (i.e., using "classical" figures like Aristotle).

26. Desmond Tutu, "God's Dream," in *Waging Peace II: Vision and Hope for the 21st Century*, ed. David Krieger and Frank Kelly (Chicago: Noble Press, 1992), 37.

27. Wilson and Ramphele, *Uprooting Poverty*, 269.

28. Desmond Tutu, "Apartheid and Confession" (undated hand-

written address), Pretoria University.

29. Tutu, "Where Is Now Thy God?"

30. Desmond Tutu, "My Credo," in *Living Philosophies: The Reflections of Some Eminent Men and Women of Our Time*, ed. Clifton Fadiman (New York: Doubleday, 1990), 235.

31. Desmond Tutu, transcript of sermon, Birmingham Cathedral, April 21, 1988, published by Committee for Black Affairs, Birmingham, Diocesan Office, 3.

32. Desmond Tutu, foreword in *World Winds: Meditations from the Blessed of the Earth*, ed. Earl and Pat Hostetter Martin (Scottdale, Pa.: Herald Press, 1990), 9.

33. Desmond Tutu, "Love Reveals My Neighbour, My Responsibility" (address), December 16, 1981.

34. Setiloane, *The Image of God*, 43.

35. Saliva and perspiration are also important elements of *seriti* that play an important part in African ritual: "A boy, pining for his long-absent father, is made to sleep in his father's bedding or smell the sweat from his clothes left at home. An article of clothing, belonging to a bedridden patient, may be sufficient for a diviner to diagnose the disease." Setiloane, *The Image of God*, 43.

36. Ibid., 40–43.

37. Ibid., 42.

38. Shutte, "Philosophy for Africa," 47.

39. Ibid, 48.

40. See K. Wiredu, "Philosophy and Our Culture," Proceedings of the Ghana Academy of Arts and Sciences, 1977.

41. Ibid, 86.

42. Desmond Tutu, "Alternatives to Apartheid," The Gilbert Murray Memorial Lecture (Oxford: Oxfam, 1990), 15.

43. Tutu, "Postscript: To Be Human Is to Be Free," 317.

4. FILLED WITH THE FULLNESS OF GOD

1. Masolo, *African Philosophy*, 92. For other studies of the African concept of God, see E. W. Smith, *African Ideas of God* (London: Edinburgh House, 1950); A. Kagame, *La Philosophie bantu-rwandaise*

de l'être, Académie Royale des Sciences Coloniales (Classes des Sciences morales et politique. Memoires in 8 Nouv. Serie 12, no. 1 [1956]); Mudimbe's exposition on Kagame in *The Invention of Africa,* 145–53; John S. Mbiti, *African Concepts of God* (London: The Society for Promoting Christian Knowledge, 1970), and John S. Mbiti, *New Testament Eschatology in an African Background: A Study of the Encounter between New Testament Theology and African Traditional Concepts* (Oxford: Oxford University Press, 1971).

2. Masolo, *African Philosophy,* 92.

3. Masolo provides extensive criticism of Kagame's work, pointing out that Kagame tries to do "too much and consequently also formulates too many concepts that are unknown to the Bantu, not because they cannot formulate them, but rather because such notions as unity, causality, categories of being, etc., lie outside the focus and interests of ordinary experience." The result of Kagame's work is therefore simply "a scholarly exercise in Aristotelian philosophy" (Masolo, *African Philosophy,* 93).

4. Tutu, *World Winds,* 9.

5. Masolo, *African Philosophy,* 88.

6. A. Kagame, "L'Ethno-Philosophie des Bantu," in *La Philosophie contemporaine,* ed. R. Klibansky (Florence: La Nuova Italia, 1971), 602–3.

7. See ibid., 603, and A. Kagame, "La Place de Dieu et de l'homme dans Bantu," *Cahiers des religions africaines* 4 (1968): 215; V. Mulago, *Un Visage africain du christianisme* (Paris: Presence Africaine, 1965), 152, quoted in Mudimbe, *The Invention of Africa,* 149.

8. John Mbiti, *African Religions and Philosophy* (New York: Doubleday, 1970), 42–43.

9. Desmond Tutu, "The Challenges of God's Mission" (address), United Methodists, Louisville, Kentucky, March 12, 1987.

10. Mbiti, *African Religions,* 37.

11. Desmond Tutu, "God's Strength—In Human Weakness," in *Your Kingdom Come: Papers and Resolutions of the Twelfth National Conference of the South African Council of Churches,* Hammanskraal, May 5–8, 1980, ed. M. Nash (Braamfontein: South African Council of Churches), 11.

12. Masolo, *African Philosophy*, 106; Mbiti, *African Religions*, 50ff.

13. John Mbiti, *Concepts of God in Africa* (London: SPCK, 1970), 161–77.

14. Ibid., 73.

15. A. Kagame, "La Philosophie bantu-rwandaise de l'etre," quoted in Masolo, *African Philosophy*, 92.

16. Tutu, "Postscript: To Be Human Is to Be Free," 318.

17. Kagame, "La Philosophie bantu-rwandaise," quoted in Masolo, *African Philosophy*, 92. This is an important philosophical point as well, because the problem of how African ancestors survive based solely on the living person's memory of them is no longer dependent on the caprice of human memory.

18. Desmond Tutu, "The Spirit of the Lord Is upon Me" (address), Trinity Institute, New York, 1989. Tutu quotes from Austin Farrer, *A Celebration of Faith* (London: Hodder & Stoughton, 1970), 72–73, and Maggie Ross, *The Fountain and the Furnace: The Way of Tears and Fire* (New York: Paulist Press, 1987), 200–201.

19. Desmond Tutu, "Ninth Sunday before Christmas" (handwritten sermon), St. George's Cathedral, 1986.

20. Masolo, *African Philosophy*, 122.

21. Ibid., 123.

22. Ibid., 122.

23. Desmond Tutu, "Suffering and Witness" (undated address).

24. Tutu, "The Challenges of God's Mission."

25. Desmond Tutu, "What Jesus Means to Me" (address), Durban University, August 6–7, 1981.

26. Desmond Tutu, "The Angels" (handwritten sermon), St. Michael's Observatory, 1986.

27. Ibid.

28. Shutte, "Philosophy for Africa," 52.

29. Desmond Tutu, sermon, Birmingham Cathedral, April 21, 1988, 4–5.

30. Quoted in Makhudu, "Cultivating a Climate."

31. Tutu, "The Challenges of God's Mission."

32. Desmond Tutu, handwritten speech, Morehouse Medical School Commencement, May 15, 1993.

33. Desmond Tutu, "Faith," in *The New World Order*, ed. Sundeep Waslekar (New Delhi: Konark Publishers, 1991), 177–78.

34. Desmond Tutu, sermon, Birmingham Cathedral, April 21, 1988, 4.

35. Ibid. Also see Desmond Tutu, "The Crisis We Face" (handwritten address), April 16, 1986, for showing disparities between black and white people and the lack of knowledge regarding each other.

36. Desmond Tutu, "My Search for God," St. Mary's Jubilee Lenten Talks—St. Alban's, Ferreirarstown. April 5, 1979.

37. Desmond Tutu, sermon, Birmingham Cathedral, April 21, 1988, 4.

38. Desmond Tutu, *The Meaning of Life: Reflections in Words and Pictures on Why We Are Here*, ed. David Friend et al. (Boston: Little, Brown, 1991), emphasis in original.

39. Tutu, "The Challenges of God's Mission."

40. Tutu, "Postscript: To Be Human Is to Be Free," 319.

41. Desmond Tutu, "Reply, November 7, 1991, to Publication Request," in *Fondest Hopes/Deepest Concerns: Lessons from the 20th Century*, ed. Neal Sperling.

42. Desmond Tutu, handwritten sermon, Ninth Sunday before Christmas, St. George's Cathedral, 1986.

43. Ibid.

44. Desmond Tutu, "The Role of the Church in South Africa" (address), Pretoria University, February 3, 1981.

45. Ibid.

46. Ibid.

47. Tutu, "The Church and Human Need," New York, 16–17.

48. Tutu, "My Search for God."

49. Tutu, sermon, printed after October 7, 1989.

50. Desmond Tutu, "The Centrality of the Spiritual" (address), South African Council of Churches National Conference Public Meeting on May 7, 1981.

51. For an example of Ross's influence, Tutu states: "I recall on one occasion speaking to an Anchorite and she spoke to me of her life of prayer and I said, 'Please just tell me a little about yourself' and she

said, 'Well, yes, Bishop Tutu, I live in the woods in California. My day starts at 2:30 in the morning and I pray for you.' I am prayed for in the woods in California at 2:30 in the morning and then you are able to say, what chance does the government of Mr. Botha stand?" (Tutu, sermon, Birmingham Cathedral, April 21, 1988, 2).

52. Ross, *The Fountain and the Furnace*, 79.

53. Tutu, "Where Is Now Thy God?"

54. Tutu, "The Spirit of the Lord Is upon Me."

55. Tutu, sermon, printed after October 7, 1989.

56. Desmond Tutu, "Statement of Bishop Desmond Tutu South African Council of Churches General Conference on the Death of Jenny Curtis and Her Daughter" (speech), June 29, 1984.

57. Desmond Tutu, "The Holy Spirit and South Africa Today" (sermon), St. Alban's Cathedral, October 29, 1983.

58. Desmond Tutu, undated handwritten sermon, during archbishopric.

59. Desmond Tutu, "The Styne Commission on the Media" (address), February 2, 1982.

60. See the Freedom Charter of the African National Conference (ANC), drafted by three thousand delegates in June 1955. Christian leaders such as Albert Luthuli were instrumental in proclaiming this nonracial theme, still the theme of the ANC.

61. In South Africa approximately 70 percent of the African population are Christian, and of these almost one-third are members of independent churches.

62. Desmond Tutu, "Apartheid and Christianity" (address), September 24, 1982.

5. INSPIRED BY WORSHIP AND ADORATION

1. Church of the Province of Southern Africa, *An Anglican Prayer Book* (Cape Town: David Philip, 1989; London: Collins Liturgical Publications, 1989), 432.

2. For an assessment of the renewal movement in the CPSA as being significant in awareness of the Holy Spirit and yet weak in

addressing societal renewal and the breakdown of structural sin, see Winston Ndungane, "An Evaluation of Charismatic Renewal within the Church of the Province of Southern Africa," in *Open to the Spirit: Anglicans and the Experience of Renewal*, ed. Colin Craston (London: Anglican Consultative Council, 1987).

3. Bishop Winston Njongonkulu Ndungane, in *We Are Anglicans: An Introduction to the Church of the Province of Southern Africa* (Marshalltown, South Africa: CPSA Publishing Committee, 1993). Tutu provides the introduction, anticipating the upcoming Primates and Anglican Consultative Council meeting held in January 1993. He welcomes George Carey, Archbishop of Canterbury, visiting the province for the first time.

4. Anglican Communion Secretariat, "The Anglican Communion: A Guide" (London).

5. Ibid.

6. See Peter Hinchliff, *The Anglican Church in South Africa: An Account of the History and Development of the Church of the Province of South Africa* (London: Darton, Longman & Todd, 1963), 100–106; Worsnip, *Between the Two Fires*, 7–8; and the following sources on the significance of Colenso: *Consecration and Trial etc. of Right Reverend Doctor Colenso*, vols. I and II (London: Rivingtons, Waterloo Place, 1867); Jeff Guy, *The Heretic: A Study of the Life of John William Colenso, 1814–1883* (Johannesburg: Ravan Press, 1983); Peter Hinchliff, *John William Colenso: Bishop of Natal* (London: Thomas Nelson & Sons, 1964). The result of the Colenso controversy was a split in the Anglican Church in South Africa between the Church of England and the CPSA, to which Tutu belongs. It is interesting that Colenso started the "Church of England" (vis-à-vis the CPSA) in South Africa, though the former became apolitical and, by and large, uninterested in any explicit challenge to the apartheid regime. On July 25, 1993, the Church of England re-emerged in the South African public consciousness when eleven people were killed and fifty-four injured at St. James Church of the Church of England.

7. Odendaal, *Beyond the Barricades*, 70.

8. Worsnip, *Between the Two Fires*.

9. Ibid., 3–4. "Almost by accident the Anglican Church in South Africa discovered that it was not established" (Peter Hinchliff, quoted in Worsnip, *Between the Two Fires*, 7).

10. Background concerning the diocese of Cape Town is taken from Ndungane, *We Are Anglicans*, an introductory pamphlet of the CPSA. The diocese of Cape Town covers the Western Cape, from the southern tip of Africa to the Orange River; also the South Atlantic Ocean island of Tristan da Cunha. Tutu was bishop, with three regional bishops, over 116 parishes with 139 stipendiary clergy.

11. Quoted in Schluter, "A Passion for Justice," 19.

12. Tutu, "Spirituality: African and Christian," 163–64.

13. Tutu, "Whither African Theology?" 365.

14. Tutu, "The Church and Human Need."

15. Tutu, "Enthronement Charge," on Tutu's enthronement as bishop of Johannesburg, February 3, 1985.

16. Ibid.

17. Desmond Tutu, "Handwritten Address Text No. 2," undated.

18. John Suggit, *Celebration of Faith: An Explanation of the Eucharist According to an Anglican Prayer Book, 1989* (Cape Town: Blackshaws Press, n.d.), 15.

19. Desmond Tutu, "Church Leaders' Meeting, Koinonia" (address).

20. See my personal journal, "Life with Tutu," for more details of Tutu's habits of prayer.

21. See Simone Weil, "Reflections on the Right Use of School Studies with a View to the Love of God," in *Simone Weil Reader*, ed. George Panichas (Mt. Kisco, N.Y.: Moyer Bell, 1977), 44–52. I will refer more to Weil in my last chapter.

22. Tutu, sermon printed after October 7, 1989.

23. Tutu, "Where Is Now Thy God?"

24. Tutu, "Enthronement Charge," Johannesburg.

25. Suggit, *Celebration of Faith*, 19.

26. Tutu, "Towards Post-Apartheid South Africa."

27. Tutu, "The Challenges of God's Mission."

28. Desmond Tutu, "Biblical and Christian Position vis-à-vis Apartheid."

29. Desmond Tutu, "National Day of Prayer" (address), St. George's Cathedral, June 5, 1992.

30. Sermon text for Tutu, "Sunday Service 8422," St. John's, Camberwell, Australia, May 1984.

31. Desmond Tutu, "Jn 13" (handwritten undated sermon), in my Christology folder.

32. My view of Tutu here is accentuated through Catherine LaCugna, *God for Us: The Trinity and the Christian Life* (San Francisco: HarperSanFrancisco), 1991, 17. LaCugna states: "A unitarian, patriarchal, monarchical, hierarchical theism gradually replaced a trinitarian monotheism, with disastrous political results. Christian theologicans justified every kind of hierarchy, exclusion and pattern of domination, whether religious, sexual, political, clerical, racial, as 'natural' and divinely intended."

33. Tutu, "Enthronement Charge," Johannesburg.

34. For an Anglican example, see Kenneth Kirk's dilemma of self-forgetfulness and God-centeredness, which also seems the bane of Kant's natural law emphasis and historicism. Even though Kirk's basis of Christian morality surrounds the Christian conscience, he is ever seeking proper criteria for the church's authority to form the conscience. For other accounts dealing with Christian themes of the relationship between the individual and community, see Stanley Hauerwas, *A Community of Character: Toward a Christian Social Ethic* (Notre Dame, Ind.: University of Notre Dame Press, 1981). See Shutte, "Philosophy for Africa," 54–64, as he discusses European philosophical accounts of the individual and community through Aquinas, Descartes, Hegel, and Rahner. See Teilhard de Chardin's *The Phenomenon of Man.*

35. Desmond Tutu, "Matthew 5:48—Be Ye Perfect" (sermon), St. George's Cathedral, Pentecost 18, 1987.

36. Desmond Tutu, "The Marks of the Church" (undated sermon).

37. Desmond Tutu, "Trinity Sunday" (handwritten sermon), All Saints Church, Sommerset West, May 29, 1988.

38. Hopkins provides this apt description of Tutu's theology as relational black theology. See Dwight Hopkins, *Black Theology USA*

and South Africa: Politics, Culture, and Liberation (Maryknoll, N.Y.: Orbis Books, 1989), 138f.

39. Tutu, "The South African Press: The Esau Complex," 7.

40. Tutu, "Inauguration of the Diocese of St. Mark the Evangelist."

41. Desmond Tutu, address, April 12, 1991.

42. Tutu writes this in response to Thomas Carey's moving letter of 7 June 1991, in which Carey describes his white presence in a black, low-income neighborhood in Brooklyn. Carey requested that Tutu submit a lead article for their provincial publication. Tutu, "Franciscan Vocation," submitted with July 30, 1991, letter for the American Province of the Society of St. Francis Provincial Publication, *The Little Chronicle.*

43. Suggit, *Celebration of Faith,* 34–35.

44. I gained this insight through my June 11, 1993, interview of Tutu's spiritual director, Francis Cull.

45. Tutu, "Enthronement Charge," Johannesburg.

46. Suggit, *Celebration of Faith,* 30.

47. Ibid., 31.

48. Ibid., 32–33.

49. Tutu, "Inauguration of the Diocese of St. Mark the Evangelist."

50. Desmond Tutu, "The Holy Spirit and South Africa Today" (sermon), St. Alban's Cathedral, October 29, 1983.

51. Tutu, "The Challenges of God's Mission."

52. Tutu, "Called to Unity and Fellowship," 25.

53. See the third and fourth Eucharistic prayers, *APB.*

54. Tutu,"God Who Is There."

55. Ibid., 38.

56. Tutu, "Enthronement Charge as Archbishop of Cape Town," 1986.

57. Ibid., 39–40.

58. Tutu, "The Challenges of God's Mission."

59. Tutu, "Koinonia II."

60. 1 Cor. 10:16–17.

61. Suggit, *Celebration of Faith,* 40–41.

62. Tutu, "Enthronement Charge," Johannesburg.

63. Desmond Tutu, "St. George's Cathedral" (handwritten sermon), Christmas Day, 1986.

64. Desmond Tutu, "St. Simon of Cyrene" (handwritten sermon), New Rochelle, December 14, 1986.

65. Desmond Tutu, "Trinity Sunday" (handwritten sermon), All Saints Church, Sommerset West, May 29, 1988.

66. Tutu, "The Role of the Church in South Africa."

67. Ibid.

68. Ibid.

69. See Hauerwas, *A Community of Character*.

70. Tutu, "The Role of the Church in South Africa."

71. Ibid.

72. Desmond Tutu, quoted in "S.A. Government Hits Council of Churches Admin.," Australia, *Church & Nation*, May 2, 1984, 4.

73. Desmond Tutu, "Called to Unity and Fellowship," in *The Church and the Alternative Society: Papers and Resolutions of the Eleventh National Conference of the South African Council of Churches Hammanskraal, July 23–27, 1979*, ed. M. Nash (Johannesburg: South African Council of Churches, 1979), 24.

74. See Charles Villa-Vicencio in Barry Streek, Cape Town, *Natal Mercury*, December 11, 1984.

75. Desmond Tutu, "Pinelands Parish Meeting" (handwritten address), February 18, 1988.

76. Desmond Tutu, "St. Mary's Cathedral Celebrations" (handwritten sermon), St. Mary's Cathedral, Johannesburg, September 24, 1989.

77. Desmond Tutu, "Charge Delivered to the Special Synod of the Diocese of Cape Town," St. Thomas's Church, Rondebosch, October 3, 1987.

78. Desmond Tutu, "Christian Witness in South Africa" (handwritten address), Drawbridge Lecture, St. Paul's Cathedral, London, England, November 19, 1984.

79. See Trevor Huddleston, *Naught for Your Comfort* (London: Collins, 1956).

80. Tutu, "Postscript: To Be Human Is to Be Free," 313–14.

81. Desmond Tutu, "Inauguration of the Diocese of St. Mark the Evangelist" (handwritten sermon).

82. Desmond Tutu, "Church Leaders' Meeting, Koinonia" (address), Johannesburg, February 7–8, 1984.

83. General Preface, *APB*, 10.

84. Geoffrey Wainwright's theological work is helpful in its explication of Christian liturgies. For his insight on the effects of the Enlightenment on the prayer book and Anglican liturgical practice, see Wainwright, 332ff.; and for his insight on how liturgical language is contingent on the understanding of the worshiping community, see "The Language of Worship," in Wainwright et al., *The Study of Liturgy* (New York: Oxford University Press, 1978), 465–73.

85. *APB*, 10–11. For Desmond Tutu's description of the liturgy as forming an alternative society, see Desmond Tutu, "Called to Unity and Fellowship," in *The Church and the Alternative Society: Papers and Resolutions of the Eleventh Conference of the SACC*, ed. M. Nash (Johannesburg: SACC, 1979).

86. I. Bria, ed., *Martyria/Mission* (Geneva: WCC, 1980), 9.

87. Tutu, "The Church and Human Need."

88. Desmond Tutu, "Spirituality: Christian and African," in *Resistance and Hope: South African Essays in Honour of Beyers Naudé*, ed. Charles Villa-Vicencio and John de Gruchy (Cape Town: David Philips, 1985), 162.

6. AN AFRICAN SPIRITUALITY OF PASSIONATE CONCERN

1. Tutu, "Whither African Theology?" 366.

2. Gerhart, *Black Power in South Africa*, 201.

3. Tutu, "Black Theology/African Theology," in *Black Theology: A Documentary History, 1966–1979*, ed. G. Wilmore and J. Cone (New York: Orbis Books, 1981), 391.

4. This is an allusion to a Bruce Cockburn political protest song.

5. Tutu, "On Being the Church in the World."

6. Williams, "Nobody Knows," 144.

7. Desmond Tutu, "A Christian Vision of the Future of South Africa," *Christianity in South Africa*, July 31, 1989.

8. Desmond Tutu, "The Secular State and Religions" (address), Archbishop Stephen Naidoo Memorial Lecture, July 8, 1992.

9. Tutu, "Apartheid and Christianity," March 1984.

10. The Community of the Resurrection (COR) was founded by Charles Gore in England in 1892. It was the second men's community in the Church of England to emerge from the catholic revival of the later nineteenth century, the first being the Society of St. John the Evangelist at Cowley, founded in 1866 by Father Benson. Growing out of the tractarian movement of the 1830s, the COR was an attempt to reaffirm the identity of the Church of England with the one catholic and apostolic church of the past, and to show this identity by holiness. For an overview of the COR, see *Mirfield Essays in Christian Belief: The Community of the Resurrection* (New York: The Faith Press and Morehouse-Barlow, 1962) and Nicholas Mosley, *The Life of Raymond Raynes* (London: The Faith Press, 1961).

11. Desmond Tutu, "Review of Rex Brico, *Taizé, Brother Roger and His Community*," *Journal of Theology for Southern Africa*, no. 36 (September 1980): 80.

12. Rowan Williams, *The Wound of Knowledge: Christian Spirituality from the New Testament to St. John of the Cross* (Boston: Cowley, 1991), 52.

13. Ibid., 99–100.

14. Based on "*Athanasius: The Life of Antony and the Letter to Marcellinus,*" in *The Classics of Western Spirituality*, trans. and with introduction by Robert Gregg (New York: Paulist Press, 1980).

15. Quoted in Ross, *The Fountain and the Furnace*, 23.

16. "Athanasius: The Life of Antony and the Letter to Marcellinus," 31f.

17. Tutu, "Spirituality: Christian and African," 161.

18. Desmond Tutu, "Where Is Now Thy God?"

19. Mosley, *The Life of Raymond Raynes*, 37.

20. Desmond Tutu, "An Appreciation of the Rt. Revd Trevor Huddleston, CR," in *Trevor Huddleston: Essays on His Life and Work*, ed. Deborah Duncan Honoré (Oxford: Oxford University Press, 1988), 2.

21. Mosley, *The Life of Raymond Raynes*, 37.

22. Tutu, "Black Theology/African Theology," in *Black Theology*, 385. In this essay Tutu discusses three levels of unity for African and black theology: blackness, African soil (implying ravages of colonialism), and baptism. It is this last unitive factor, baptism, that shapes my view of Tutu's theology (see ibid., 387). Tutu goes on to compare and contrast black and African theology. One similarity is that both become reactionary to Western discourse, and one difference is that African theology reacts to a different kind of white racism (except in South Africa), causing it to be less abrasive and political than black theology arising out of intense political suffering in the United States.

23. See Albert Raboteau's *Slave Religion* (New York: Oxford University Press, 1980) for insights into the formation of black and white Christianity. Raboteau displays how the black church assumes the racial classification of black but overcomes the power of its representation.

24. Desmond Tutu, "Allard K. Lowenstein Symposium on International Human Rights Law," keynote address, April 17, 1982.

25. This problem was recognized by both blacks and whites throughout the history of South Africa. For example, in the mid-1950s, Philip Qipu Vundla (PQ), active in the African Mine Workers' Union, worked in the "moral rearmament movement" (MRA), a movement of blacks and whites endeavoring to bring justice to South Africa.

26. Tutu, sermon, printed after October 7, 1989.

27. See George Herbert, *The Country Parson; The Temple* (New York: Paulist Press, 1981). Herbert's common theme, throughout his poetic display of moving through the church space, is what to render back to God in light of God's rich mercies.

28. Desmond Tutu, "Bible Study" (sermon), Cathedral of Holy Nativity, Pietermaritzburg, November 23, 1983.

29. Tutu, "The Role of the Church in South Africa."

30. Ibid.

31. Ibid.

32. Louise Kretzschmar, *The Voice of Black Theology in South Africa* (Johannesburg: Ravan Press, 1986), xii.

33. Ibid., 15.

34. Letters to the editor, *Daily Dispatch*, December 11, 1984.

35. Tutu, "Whither African Theology?" 369.

36. Tutu, "Black Theology / African Theology," in *Black Theology*, 389–90.

37. Ibid.

38. Ibid., 368.

39. Ibid.

40. J. C. Thomas, "What Is African Theology?" *Ghana Bulletin of Theology* 4, no. 4 (June 1973): 15.

41. Tutu, "Whither African Theology?" 368.

42. Ibid., 369.

43. Tutu, "Black Theology / African Theology," in *Black Theology*, 391–92. In large measure, Tutu is reacting here to John Mbiti's conviction that "the concerns of Black Theology differ considerably from those of African Theology. The latter grows out of our joy and experience of the Christian faith, whereas Black Theology emerges from the pains of oppression." For Tutu, Mbiti seems to imply that black theology is perhaps not quite Christian: "One would hope that theology arises out of spontaneous joy in being a Christian responding to life and ideas as one redeemed. Black Theology, however, is full of sorrow, bitterness, anger and hatred." See John Mbiti, "An African Views American Black Theology," *Worldview* 17, no. 8 (August 1974): 43.

44. Tutu, "Whither African Theology?" 367.

45. Ibid.

46. Ibid.

47. Ibid.

48. Tutu, "The Role of the Church in South Africa."

49. Desmond Tutu, in *The Future of Liberation Theology: Essays in Honor of Gustavo Gutiérrez*, ed. Marc H. Ellis and Otto Maduro (Maryknoll, N.Y.: Orbis Books, 1989), 25.

50. See Per Frostin, *Liberation Theology in Tanzania and South Africa: A First World Interpretation* (Malmö, Sweden: Lund University Press, 1988), 9 n. 46.

51. Kretzschmar, *The Voice of Black Theology*, 26.

52. Ibid., 37.

53. Desmond Tutu, "Mark 2:13–17" (handwritten sermon), Durbanville, Christmas VI, 1987.

54. Desmond Tutu, "The Church and Human Rights in South Africa" (handwritten address), University of Cape Town, Centre for Human Rights, May 18, 1992.

55. Tutu, "Spirituality: Christian and African," 163.

56. Ibid., 164.

57. Tutu, "Doing Theology in a Divided Society."

58. Ibid.

59. Also see Villa-Vicencio, *Civil Disobedience and Beyond*, 2.

60. Tutu, "Spirituality: Christian and African," 160.

61. Ibid., 160–61.

62. Tutu, "On Being the Church in the World."

63. Ibid.

64. I distinguish race as different from culture in that the latter is a system of inherited concepts rooted in experiences, a way of thinking and acting, a kind of community grammar demonstrated through stories and histories that shape peoples in a particular location. What is fundamental to culture is the place, the land. Most contemporary definitions of culture lack the centrality of land and having a place.

65. Desmond Tutu, "Preamble" (undated speech), at University of Witwatersrand.

66. Tutu, "Koinonia II."

67. Tutu, "Doing Theology in a Divided Society."

7. CONCLUSION: God and a Political Priest

1. See Simon Maimela, "Archbishop Desmond Mpilo Tutu: A Revolutionary Political Priest or Man of Peace?" in *Hammering Swords into Ploughshares: Essays in Honor of Archbishop Mpilo Desmond Tutu*, ed. Buti Tlhagale and Itumeleng Mosala (Grand Rapids, Mich.: Eerdmans, 1986), 41–61.

2. Itumeleng Mosala, *Biblical Hermeneutics and Black Theology in South Africa* (Grand Rapids, Mich.: Eerdmans, 1989), 3.

3. Takatso Mofokeng, "Black Theology in South Africa: Achievements, Problems, and Prospects," in Prozesky, *Christianity amidst Apartheid*, 50.

4. Tutu, "Whither African Theology?" 364.

5. For a more analytical perception into a model like Mosala's by an Anglican theologian, see John Milbank, *Theology and Social Theory: Beyond Secular Reason* (Oxford: Basil Blackwell), 1991.

6. See Tutu, "Alternative Society."

7. See Boesak, *Black and Reformed*. Boesak dedicated this book: "For Desmond Tutu, Prophet of God, Shepherd of his people, Brother and Friend in whom God's gifts are seen and admired."

8. Mosala critiques, in addition to Tutu (*Biblical Hermeneutics*, 37f.), James Cone (ibid., 14f.) and Allan Boesak (ibid., 27f.).

9. Ibid., 38.

10. Mosala states, "We can clearly see a biblical hermeneutics of liberation for black theology as liberating neither because it is black nor on the grounds simply that it is biblical. Rather, it is a *tool of struggle* in the on going human project of liberation" (*Biblical Hermeneutics*, 9); emphasis in original.

11. W. E. B. DuBois, *The Souls of Black Folk* (Greenwich, Conn.: Fawcett Premier Book, 1968), 23; quoted in James Cone, *A Black Theology of Liberation*, 2d ed. (Maryknoll, N.Y.: Orbis Books, 1989), xv.

12. Tutu, "God's Strength—in Human Weakness," 23.

13. Walshe, "The Evolution of Liberation Theology," 310–11.

14. Ibid.

15. Desmond Tutu, "Jesus Christ Life of the World," keynote address for 48-Hour Women's Colloquium, June 17, 1982.

16. Desmond Tutu, "The Theology of Liberation in Africa," in *African Theology en Route*, ed. Kofi Appiah-Kubi and Sergio Torres, Pan African Conference of Third World Theologians, Accra, Ghana (Maryknoll, N.Y.: Orbis Books, 1979), 166.

17. Desmond Tutu, "God—Black or White?" *Ministry* 11, no. 4 (1971): 111; quoted in Kretzschmar, *The Voice of Black Theology*, 26.

18. Desmond Tutu, "Brothers and Sisters Together" (address), Trans Africa Forum, April 29, 1981.

19. Desmond Tutu, "Review of James Cone's *God of the Oppressed*," *Journal of Theology for Southern Africa*, no. 31 (June 1980): 74. As Cone's views have changed, so has Tutu's view of Cone. For example, in 1989, Cone became more inclusive in his definition of blackness, stating, "Blackness symbolizes oppression and liberation in any society." See Cone, *A Black Theology of Liberation*, vii.

20. Tutu, "Review of James Cone," 73.

21. See Tutu, "Black Theology / African Theology," in *Black Theology*, 18.

22. Ibid.

23. Cone, *A Black Theology of Liberation*, 94–95. Here Cone states that it will be necessary for whites to destroy their whiteness by becoming members of an oppressed community.

24. See James Cone, "Sanctification, Liberation, and Black Worship," *Theology Today* 35 (1978–79): 139–52.

25. See James Cone, *For My People* (Maryknoll, N.Y.: Orbis Press, 1984).

26. Cone, *A Black Theology of Liberation*, 11.

27. James Cone, *Black Theology and Black Power* (New York: Seabury Press, 1969), 140.

28. Cone admits his previous failure to incorporate an international analysis of oppression in *A Black Theology of Liberation*, xviii.

29. Desmond Tutu, "Black South African Perspectives and the Reagan Administration" (address), Trans Africa Forum, February 1982.

30. James Cone, "God Is Black," in *Lift Every Voice: Constructing Christian Theologies from the Underside*, ed. Susan Brooks Thistlewaite and Mary Potter Engel (San Francisco: HarperSanFrancisco, 1990), 84.

31. Ibid.

32. Ibid., 90.

33. Ibid., 84.

34. Ibid., 89.

35. The church's funeral rite especially has given Tutu profound public impact against apartheid (e.g., Steve Biko's funeral, September 25, 1977; and Chris Hani's funeral, April 19, 1993).

36. Tutu, interview: Michael Schluter, "A Passion for Justice," *Third Way* 17, no. 4 (May 1994): 18. To make the point more fully: In contrast to Tutu's theological strictures, other South African Christian leaders have put more emphasis on political leadership, and without theological underpinnings. Two examples can serve as illustration. Through the Independent Church, characterized as apolitical in South Africa, Frank Chikane arose to be a major Christian leader against apartheid and now occupies a more political position as a member of the Independent Electoral Council. Similarly, Allan Boesak's work through the Reformed Church made him an effective leader and major Christian voice against apartheid, but now he occupies solely a political position with the African National Conference (ANC).

37. Desmond Tutu, "R40?" (address), Rhoedean Symposium, July 25, 1981.

38. Desmond Tutu, *The Divine Intention: Presentation by Bishop D. Tutu General Secretary of the South African Council of Churches to the Eloff Commission of Enquiry on September 1, 1982* (Braamfontein: SACC Publications), 26. In 1981, Tutu gave the above quotation to a government commission formed to investigate Tutu's role as Secretary-General of the South African Council of Churches (SACC), an organization that received substantial financial support from the United States and Europe.

39. "A Prisoner of Hope," *Christianity Today*, October 5, 1992, 40.

40. Desmond Tutu, "The Church and Mission" (undated handwritten speeches and addresses).

41. Desmond Tutu, "Conscientious Objection, Conscription and the Constitution" (address), July 16, 1983.

42. Quoted in Sparks, *Mind of South Africa*, 279–80.

43. Desmond Tutu, letter to President P. W. Botha, April 8, 1988.

44. Sparks, *The Mind of South Africa*, 290.

45. Desmond Tutu, "Why We Must Oppose Apartheid" (undated handwritten speeches), Grahamstown.

46. Quoted in Sparks, *The Mind of South Africa*, 291.

47. More officially, this movement occurred through the revisions of the Kairos Document, first published September 25, 1985.

48. Quoted in Sparks, *The Mind of South Africa*, 292.

49. For example, Frank Chikane, no longer general secretary of the SACC, is now a government official of the Independent Electoral Commission, and Allan Boesak is an ANC member of Parliament.

50. Sheridan Johns et al., *Mandela, Tambo, and the African National Congress* (New York: Oxford University Press, 1991), 196.

51. Editorial, *Daily Dispatch*, December 13, 1984.

BIBLIOGRAPHY

SPEECHES AND ADDRESSES BY DESMOND TUTU

Undated

Address, "The Church and Human Need," New York.
Address notes, "Church Leaders' Meeting, Koinonia."
Speeches, "Christmas Message."
Speeches, "Christmas Letter."
Address, "Setting the Record Straight, Those in Authority," Cambria.
Address, "Suffering and Witness."
Address, "A Vision for Humanity."
Address, "The Nature and Value of Theology."
Address to SACC.
Speech, 1985–1986, "The Evolution of Apartheid."
Handwritten address, 1984–1985.
Handwritten address, "Why We Must Oppose Apartheid," Grahamstown.
Speech, "Preamble," at University of the Witwatersrand.
Address, "Strict Embargo," while General Secretary of SACC.
Handwritten address, "For Justice and Peace."
Handwritten address, "Robert Kennedy."
Handwritten address for congressional subcommittee on Africa.
Handwritten address, "Semantics and Politics."
Handwritten address, "Jubilee and the Call of Jesus."
Handwritten address, "The Gift of the Jews to the World," United States.

Handwritten address, "What Students Must Do."

Handwritten address, "Perspectives in Black and White."

Address, "Stewart Memorial Lecture."

Handwritten address, "Jubilee and the Call of Jesus."

Speeches, 1985–1986, "The Evolution of Apartheid."

Speeches, "The South African Press: The Esau Complex."

Handwritten address, "The Sanctity of Life," accepting the Albert Schweitzer Award, Riverside Church, New York.

Handwritten address, "Apartheid and Confession," Pretoria University.

Handwritten address, "Jesus and the Justice of the Kingdom of God," Ireland.

Handwritten speeches and address, "The Church and Mission."

Handwritten text for BBC broadcast, United Kingdom.

Handwritten keynote address, "Apartheid Is Unchristian," U.N. Conference, Atlanta, Georgia.

Handwritten address, "USA Policy towards South Africa: The Perplexities of a Black South African."

Handwritten address, "Disinvestment and All That."

Handwritten speeches and addresses, "Koinonia II."

Speeches, 1984–1985, "The Referendum, Apartheid and Mogopa."

Handwritten address notes, "God Who Acts," G. Ernest Wright Seminary.

Address, "The Centrality of the Spiritual," General Theological Seminary, New York.

Handwritten address no. 1, 1980s.

Handwritten address no. 2.

Handwritten address no. 3, post-1986.

Handwritten address no. 4, "Homosexuality."

Handwritten address no. 5.

Handwritten address no. 5 (appears to be a university address).

Handwritten address no. 6 (appears to be accepting an award from a society of journalists).

Handwritten address no. 6, for video to the youth of the Norwegian churches in Frondheim.

Handwritten address (1980s), after U.S. trip in which Harry Belafonte, Sidney Poitier, Bill Cosby, and Coretta Scott King met with Tutu.

Handwritten address (1984–1985), introducing Senator Edward Kennedy.
Handwritten address (1980s).

Dated

"Greetings from Bishop Tutu to the Soweto Students," June 16, 1977.
"Wits University, SRC Academic Freedom Committee," March 18, 1980.
"South Africa on the Way to 2000 A.D." March 31, 1980.
"Where I Stand," to the Pretoria Press Club, August 4, 1980.
"The Role of the Church in South Africa," Pretoria University, February 3, 1981.
"Liberation as a Biblical Theme," Fourth Anniversary of the AACC, March 1981.
"Brothers and Sisters Together," Trans Africa Forum, April 29, 1981.
"The Centrality of the Spiritual," at South African Council of Churches National Conference Public Meeting, May 7, 1981.
"A Little Crystal Ball Gazing," Cape Town Press Club, May 15, 1981.
"The Church and Reconciliation in South Africa," P. E. Synod, June 1981.
"Discipleship as Liberation," Student Federation Conference, Pietermaritzburg, July 4, 1981.
"The Scattered Church and the Cost of Discipleship," Anglican Students Federation Conference, Pietermaritzburg, July 4, 1981.
"R40?" Rhoedean Symposium, July 25, 1981.
"What Jesus Means to Me," Durban University, August 6–7, 1981.
"E.O.C. and All That," August 28, 1981.
"On Being the Church in the World," Cape Town, October 13, 1981.
"Love Reveals My Neighbour, My Responsibility," December 16, 1981.
"General Secretary's Report to National Conference of the SACC," 1982.
"Christianity and Apartheid," 1982.
"The Role of White Opposition in South Africa," PFP Youth, January 15, 1982.

"Black South African Perspectives and the Reagan Administration," Trans Africa Forum, February 1982.

"The Styne Commission on the Media," February 2, 1982.

"Academic Freedom Week—The University of Witswatersrand (Wits)," February 11, 1982. (This address was not given because of Dr. Aggetis's death in detention.)

"Message on Behalf of the South African Council of Churches at Frikkie Conradie's Funeral," March 6, 1982.

"Blacks and Liberation," SAIC, March 29, 1982.

"Allard K. Lowenstein Symposium on International Human Rights Law," keynote address, April 17, 1982.

"Jesus Christ Life of the World," keynote address for 48-Hour Women's Colloquium, June 17, 1982.

"Response at Graduation of Columbia University's Honorary Doctorate," presented by Columbia's President at the University of the Witwatersrand, August 2, 1982.

"Why the Church Should Be Involved in Politics and Social Matters," Diakonia, Durban, September 22, 1982.

"Apartheid and Christianity," September 24, 1982.

"Apartheid, Thirdworld and Peace" (handwritten), Dublin Peace Conference, October 1982.

"PFP Incorporation of Kangwanes Ingwauuma in Swaziland, City Hall," July 14, 1982.

"The State of the Nation," Mirge, Cape Town, December 1, 1982.

"General Secretary's Report to National Conference of the SACC," 1983.

"Greetings to the Sixth Assembly of the WCC Assembled in Vancouver Canada" (handwritten), 1983.

"The Problems Facing South Africa and the Role of Students" (handwritten), Natal University, Pietermaritzburg, February 14, 1983.

"Black View of the Constitutional Proposals," PFP Germiston, February 23, 1983.

"A Black View of the Law," Pretoria Attorneys, March 25, 1983.

"The Churches in the South African Crisis," Africa Report, May 1983.

"Doing Theology in a Divided Society," Contextual Theology, Hammanskraal, May 19, 1983.

"Conscientious Objection, Conscription and the Constitution," July 16, 1983.

"Conscientious Objection and Conscription" (handwritten), testimony before court martial, July 16, 1983.

"Continuing Education Seminar" (handwritten), Diocese of East Oregon, Ascension Scool, Cove, Oreg., August 15–18, 1983.

"To the Presidium Executive Committee of the 67th General Convention of the Episcopal Church" (handwritten), New Orleans, September 5–15, 1983.

"The Issues Facing the Third World in Meeting Basic Needs" (handwritten), Episcopal General Convention, USA, New Orleans, September 5–15, 1983.

"Liberating Truth and Questioning Minds," University of Cape Town, September 22, 1983.

"October 19th Commemoration," Donaldson Community Centre, Orlando East, Florida, 1983.

"World Religions for Human Dignity and World Peace" (handwritten), Nairobi, 1984?

"Church Leaders' Meeting, Koinonia," Johannesburg, February 7–8, 1984.

"Apartheid and Christianity," Rand Afrikaans University, March 1984.

"General Secretary's Report to National Conference of SACC," June 25–29, 1984.

"Statement to South African Council of Churches General Conference on the Death of Jenny Curtis and Her Daughter," June 29, 1984.

"Christian Witness in South Africa" (handwritten), Drawbridge Lecture, St. Paul's Cathedral, London, England, November 19, 1984.

"A Peculiar Nation" (handwritten), Jewish Theological Seminary, New York, November 26, 1984.

"Nobel Lecture, December 11, 1984," *Les Prix Nobel 1984*. Stockholm: Almqvist & Wiksell International, 1985.

"Whither South Africa," SAIRR Public Meeting, Woodstock, Town Hall, October 17, 1985.

"The Crisis We Face" (handwritten), April 16, 1986.

"The Quest for Peace" (handwritten), Johannesburg, August 1986.

"Quiet Day: Why Be Silent?" (handwritten), Durbanville, January 2, 1987.

"St. Luke's Hospice," February 1, 1987.

"Awkward Questions," University of Western Cape commencement, February 13, 1987.

"Installation of Michael Bands as Chaplain" (handwritten), February 15, 1987.

"Speaking within the South African Context," Natal Youth Congress, March [recorded as February] 30, 1987.

"The Challenges of God's Mission," United Methodists, Louisville, March 12, 1987.

"Scape-Goatism," Cape Press Club, March 17, 1987.

"God Who Is There" (handwritten), National Christian Youth Convention, Australia, 1987.

"Being There for God—Our Response" (handwritten), National Christian Youth Convention, Australia, 1987.

"Violence and the Church," June 1987.

"Memorial to Pakamile Mabija Who Died in Detention in Kimberley" (handwritten), AST Conference Bothos Hall, July 1987.

"Liaison Committee of Development of NGO's to European Communities, Opening of General Assembly," 1988.

"Pinelands Parish Meeting" (handwritten), February 18, 1988.

"United Nations" (handwritten), May 1988.

"Launch of Bishop Tutu Peace Concert" (Los Angeles Coliseum, September 10, 1988; New York, May 1988).

"Address on the Occasion of the Installation of the Archbishop as Chancellor of the University of the Western Cape," May 20, 1988.

"In Soweto upon Return from Moscow" (handwritten), June 1988.

"Installation of John Gardener as Principal of Bishops," October 21, 1988.

"Preachers Licensing" (handwritten), St. George's Cathedral, November 22, 1988.

"Where Is Now Thy God?" Trinity Institute, New York, January 8, 1989.

"The Spirit of the Lord Is upon Me," Trinity Institute, New York, 1989.

"Alternatives to Apartheid," The Gilbert Murray Memorial Lecture (Oxford: Oxfam), 1990.

Address, April 12, 1991.

"The Monster of Racism," Shippensburg University, December 14, 1991.

"Human Rights and Racial Discrimination" (handwritten address and notes), Lectures at Universidad Complutense Cursos de Verano, July 1991.

"The Bible and Human Rights" (handwritten), Madrid, 1991.

"The Church and Human Rights in South Africa" (handwritten), University of South Africa, Centre for Human Rights, May 18, 1992.

"National Day of Prayer," St. George's Cathedral, June 5, 1992.

"The Secular State and Religions," Archbishop Stephen Naidoo Memorial Lecture, July 8, 1992.

"Press Freedom Is Essential to Democracy," Willie Musarurwa Memorial Trust Fund, Harare, April 2, 1993.

"Morehouse Medical School Commencement" (handwritten), May 15, 1993.

"My Vision for South Africa" (handwritten notes), Albion College, July 16, 1993.

"Uppsala at Jubilee Year," August 1993.

"Oxford Union Address—South Africa: Why I Am Hopeful," February 23, 1994.

"1994 Darwin Lecture Series: Change in Southern Africa," Cambridge University, February 25, 1994.

SERMONS BY DESMOND TUTU

Undated

"Address to 100th Anniversary of the Methodist Conference, in South Africa" (handwritten).

"Biblical and Christian Position vis-à-vis Apartheid."

"Coventry Cathedral," England (handwritten).

"During Archbishopric" (handwritten).

"Eighth Sunday before Easter" (handwritten—probably 1987 because seventh Sunday before Easter was June 6 that year).

"Genesis 38:12" (handwritten notes).

"Gospel of St. Mark" (handwritten notes).

"Jn 13" (handwritten).

"The Marks of the Church."

"Matthew 5:13," United States?

"Matthew 5:13."

"1983?" (handwritten).

"Passiontide Addresses."

"Passiontide Addresses: Maundy Thursday."

"Re: William Wilberforce," during archbishopric (handwritten).

"SACC Staff Worship" (handwritten), 8:30 a.m.

"16" written at the top, 1983–1989 (handwritten).

Written at top of page, "6, 14ff."

Dated

"My Search for God," St. Mary's Jubilee Lenten Talks, St. Alban's, Ferreirarstown, April 5, 1979.

"St. Mary's Cathedral," September 4, 1980.

"The Vineyard of Naboth and Duncan Village," East London, October 31, 1981.

"Christmas 1982" (handwritten).

"The Preacher as Prophet," St. Luke's Orchards, January 27, 1983.

"Preaching in the Old Testament," St. Luke's Orchards, January 27, 1983.

"Text of Revelation 7:9–11" (handwritten), Khotso House, Johannesburg, March 21, 1983.

"Consecration Sermon for Sigqibo Dwane, Bishop of the Order of Ethiopia; Charles Albertyn, Bishop Suffragan Elect of Cape Town; John Ruston, Bishop Suffragan of Pretoria, St. Patrick's Church Bloemfontein, text Revelation 4:1–6," April 24, 1983.

"Bible Study," Cathedral of Holy Nativity, Pietermaritzburg, November 23, 1983.

"The Holy Spirit and South Africa Today," St. Alban's Cathedral, October 29, 1983.

"Symposium to Commemorate 50th Anniversary of the Barmen Declaration," University of Washington, Seattle, April 28, 1984.

"Sunday Service 8422," St. John's, Camberwell, Australia, May 1984.

"St. Philip's, Washington, D.C.," Christmas III (handwritten), 1984.

"Enthronement Charge," on Tutu's enthronement as bishop of Johannesburg, February 3, 1985.

"Genesis Chapter 3" (handwritten), St. Mary's, Blechingly, Surrey, October 6, 1985.

"Enthronement Charge as Archbishop of Cape Town," 1986.

"The Angels" (handwritten), St. Michael's, Observatory, 1986.

"Love" (handwritten), St. George's Parktown, February 9, 1986.

"St. Catherine's Silver Jubilee" (handwritten), St. Catherine's Church, February 16, 1986.

"Maundy Thursday Address to the Clergy" (handwritten), 1986.

"St. Luke's" (handwritten), June 15, 1986.

"St. George's Cathedral, Commemorating Student Uprising" (handwritten), June 16, 1986.

"St. Mary's Cathedral, Ascension Day" (handwritten), 1986.

"Emergency Service" (handwritten), St. Mary's Cathedral, July 5, 1986.

"1 Corinthians 4:7" (handwritten), St. George's Cathedral, September 21, 1986.

"Ninth Sunday before Christmas" (handwritten), St. George's Cathedral, 1986.

"St. Simon of Cyrene," New Rochelle (handwritten), December 14, 1986.

"St. George's Cathedral" (handwritten), Christmas Day, 1986.

"Disciples" (handwritten), Chrismas III, January 18, 1987.

"Christmas 7" (handwritten), St. George's Cathedral, Grahamstown, 1987.

"Sunday School Teacher's Eucharist" (handwritten), St. George's Cathedral, February 2, 1987.

"St. Mark's Centenary" (handwritten), March 15, 1987.

"Service for Detainees," St. George's Cathedral, April 13, 1987.

"Easter Vigil" (handwritten), St. George's Cathedral, 1987.

"Pentecost" (handwritten), Mitchell's Plain, St. George's Kuils River, 1987.

"Centenary Celebration of SSJD" (handwritten), Cathedral of the Holy Nativity, May 10, 1987.

"Inauguration of the Diocese of St. Mark the Evangelist" (handwritten), Seshego, May 16, 1987.

"Seventh Sunday after Easter, Christ the Healer" (handwritten), June 6, 1987.

"Matthew 5:48—Be Ye Perfect," St. George's Cathedral, Pentecost 18, 1987.

"Charge Delivered to the Special Synod of the Diocese of Cape Town," St. Thomas's Church, Rondebosch, October 3, 1987.

"Washington National Cathedral, Washington, D.C.," December 2, 1987, published in *The Rise of Christian Conscience: The Emergence of a Dramatic Renewal Movement in the Church Today*, ed. Jim Wallis (San Francisco: Harper & Row), 1987.

"Mark 2:13–17" (handwritten), Durbanville, Chrismas VI, 1987.

"Bible Study for St. Alban's Clergy," Lambeth, 1988.

"Blessed Are the Meek for They Shall Inherit the Earth," BBC Lenten Series, February 16, 1988.

"St. Savior's Lentegeur" (handwritten), Ash Wednesday, 1988.

"Transcript of Sermon in Birmingham Cathedral," April 21, 1988. Published by Committee for Black Affairs, Birmingham, Diocesan Office.

"Trinity Sunday" (handwritten), All Saints Church, Sommerset West, May 29, 1988.

"St. Chad's, Tableview," Pentecost V, 1988 (handwritten).

"Harry Frieslaar's Silver Jubilee of the Priesthood" (handwritten), June 30, 1988.

"Easter Vigil, St. George's Cathedral" (handwritten), 1989.

"St. Mary's Cathedral Celebrations" (handwritten), St. Mary's Cathedral, Johannesburg, September 24, 1989.

"Sermon," printed after October 7, 1989.

"Synod of the Diocese of Cape Town Charge," October 17–20, 1990.

"God's Love," in *Tradition and Unity: Sermons Published in Honour of Robert Runcie*, ed. Dan Cohn-Sherbok (London: Bellew Publishing, 1991).

"Bishop's Charge: The God Who Takes Risks," Diocese of Cape Town, Clergy Synod, St. Savior's Church, Claremont June 3–4, 1991.

"Cape Town Diocesan Council Charge," St. Oswald's Church, Milnerton, May 23, 1992.

"St. Aidan's Lansdowne," (handwritten), XIX[?] Sunday, 1993[?].

"Diocesan Synod Charge," Belhar, August 11, 1993.

"Transcript of Sermon at the Funeral of Chris Hani," Bishopscourt Update, April 19, 1993.

BOOK ENDORSEMENTS BY DESMOND TUTU

Cassidy, Michael. *The Politics of Love: Choosing the Christian Way in a Changing South Africa.* London: Hodder & Stoughton, 1991. "God grant that we may try out Michael Cassidy's suggestions in *The Politics of Love.* We have little time left."

Cole, Jim. *Filtering People: A View of Our Prejudices.* Mill Valley, Calif.: Growing Images, 1987. "Your little volume presents the truth about people in a most acceptable manner. It deserves a wide public and I wish you every success."

Diar, Prakash. *The Sharpeville Six.* Toronto: McClelland & Stewart, 1990. "The trial, conviction and sentencing to death of the Sharpeville Six became, justifiably, a cause célèbre. . . . Prakash Diar has done us a great service in highlighting how a miscarriage of justice has occurred. I lend my support unreservedly, and pray others will be equally moved by this shattering record."

Hochschild, Adam. *The Mirror at Midnight: A South African Journey.* New York: Viking Penguin, 1990. "When I saw *The Mirror at Midnight* I groaned and said 'Oh dear, not another instant 'American expert' on South Africa': but I was happily disabused of my disillusionment, because this is a good book for anyone who wants a succinct and precise account of how this fascinating country has got where it is. Adam Hochschild has a perceptive insight into the workings of the minds of black, white, coloured and Indian South Africans and has woven contemporary and historical events skillfully. This is a book I recommend warmly."

Magubane, Peter. Artwork depicting South Africa since the Soweto uprisings of 1976. "Peter Magubane is a consummate artist with the lens and he has quite rightly gained an outstanding international reputation. . . . Perhaps we can be moved to take what action we can to help dismantle apartheid and ensure that such scenes captured in Peter's lens would not be repeated again and again in our land, work for justice and so work for peace."

Norris, Gunilla. *Becoming Bread: Meditations on Loving and Transformation.* New York: Bell Tower, 1993.

Russell, Diana E. H. *Lives of Courage: Women for a New South Africa.* New York: Basic Books, 1989. "I fairly burst with pride and expectation—pride that South African soil has produced such indomitable women and not the least the author herself, and expectation at the contribution such women will continue to make in a post-apartheid South Africa. . . . This remarkable book is a manifesto of hope."

Thompson, Leonard. *A History of South Africa.* New Haven: Yale University Press, 1990. "I did not think it was possible for a white person to write a history of South Africa which a black South African would find to be a fair and accurate account of a beautiful land and its people. Leonard Thompson has disabused me of that notion. His is a history that is both accurate and authentic, written in a delightful literary style."

Wilson, Lois. *Turning the World Upside Down: A Memoir.* Toronto: Doubleday, 1989. "What a lively, amusing and touching account of a wonderful person. She makes Christianity seem exhilarating and great fun. Splendid reading altogether."

VIDEOS INVOLVING DESMOND TUTU

Desmond Tutu: Apartheid in South Africa, Nobel Prize Series Video and Curriculum Library, Teacher Resource Book and Student Notebook by Eleanor Greene. Distributed by Sunburst Communications, Pleasantville, N.Y.

Future Watch, no. 137, J. Neff, CNN America, Inc., 320 1st St., N.E., Washington, DC 20002.

General Assembly/Synod, St. Louis, Missouri, July 15–20, 1993. no. 28, Shared Service of Worship. July 15–20, 1993.

God's Word in Our Lives: The Archbishop Desmond M. Tutu, May 21, 1990, Media Services, Fuller Theological Seminary, Pasadena.

"The Great Nobel Debate." Trans World International Inc. 1991, 420 West 45th St., New York, N.Y. 10036, (212) 772-8900.

The Kennedy Center Honors, December 27, 1989. Complete Post, Inc., 6087 Sunset Blvd., Hollywood, Calif. 90028.

A Transforming Vision: Suffering and Gloria in God's World. A dramatic account of the historic joint meeting of the Primates of the Anglican Communion and the Anglican Consultative Council, January 1993.

"We Know We Are Going to Be Free": A Visit by Archbishop Desmond Tutu to the Diocese of Southern Ohio. Michael Barnwell.

Witness to Apartheid. San Francisco: Southern Africa Media Center, 1986.

GENERAL REFERENCES

Abraham, Willam. *The Mind of Africa.* Chicago: University of Chicago Press, 1962.

Abrams, Irwin. *The Nobel Peace Prize and the Laureates: An Illustrated Biographical History, 1901–1987.* Boston: G. K. Hall & Co., 1988.

"Africa's Turbulent Priest." *Varsity,* no. 406 (March 4, 1994).

Allen, John. "Female-Priests Issue Tests Synod." *Star Africa,* August 20, 1992.

————. "Re-entry of the 'Meddlesome Priest.'" *Sunday Tribune,* June 28, 1992.

Amnesty International Report. London: Amnesty International Publications, 1990, 1992, 1993.

Anglican Communion Secretariat. "The Anglican Communion: A Guide." London.

Appiah, Kwame Anthony. *In My Father's House: Africa in the Philosophy of Culture.* New York: Oxford University Press, 1992.

"Arch Is Up in Alms." *Living,* undated photocopy.

"The Archbishop, the Church and the Nation." *Monitor: The Journal of the Human Rights Trust,* June 1991. Port Elizabeth: Monitor Publications.

Arendt, Hannah. *Imperialism: Part Two of the Origins of Totalitarianism.* New York: Harcourt Brace Jovanovich, 1968.

"Athanasius: The Life of Antony and the Letter to Marcellinus." In *The Classics of Western Spirituality,* translated and with introduction by Robert Gregg. New York: Paulist Press, 1980.

Baldwin, Lewis., ed. *Toward the Beloved Community: Martin Luther King Jr. and South African Apartheid*. Draft of manuscript.

Barth, Karl. *Church Dogmatics* II/I. Edinburgh: T. & T. Clark, 1957.

Believers in Dialogue: Introducing the South African Chapter of the World Conference on Religion and Peace. Krugersdorp: WCRP, 1993.

Bent, Ans J. van der, ed. *Breaking Down the Walls: World Council of Churches Statements and Actions on Racism, 1948–1985*. Geneva: World Council of Churches Press—Programme to Combat Racism, 1986.

Bentley, Judith. *Archbishop Tutu of South Africa*. Hillside, N.J.: Enslow, 1988.

"Bishop Tutu: Person of the Year." *Christian Century*, no. 102 (January 2, 1985).

Boesak, Allan. *Black and Reformed: Apartheid, Liberation, and the Calvinist Tradition*. Johannesburg: Skotaville Publishers, 1984.

———. *Farewell to Innocence*. Maryknoll, N.Y.: Orbis Books, 1984.

———. *If This Is Treason, I Am Guilty*. Grand Rapids, Mich.: Eerdmans, 1987.

The Book of Common Prayer, According to the Use of the Episcopal Church, USA. New York: Seabury Press, 1979.

Bouyer, Louis. *Orthodox Spirituality and Protestant and Anglican Spirituality*. London: Burns & Oates, 1969.

Brown, Peter. *The Making of Late Antiquity*. Cambridge: Harvard University Press, 1978.

Buthelezi, Mangosuthu. "Memorandum for Discussion with the Archbishop of Canterbury," Cape Town, January 22, 1993.

———. "An Appeal to the Primates of the Anglican Communion," Cape Town, January 22, 1993.

"Buthelezi Critical of Church." In *Communion 93*, a publication of the CPSA on the occasion of the joint meeting of the Primates of the Anglican Communion and the Anglican Consultative Council, January 1993.

Calmen, Mel. *My God*. London: Methuen, 1985 (a book of cartoons frequently referred to by Tutu).

Calvin, John. *Commentaries on the Epistle of Paul the Apostle to the Romans*. Grand Rapids, Mich.: Eerdmans, 1948.

"Can Christians Vote for Communists?" In *Challenge: Church and People*, no. 22. Braamfontein: Contextual Publications, April 1994.

"Cape Slave Emancipation and Rural Labour in a Comparative Context." Cape Town: Centre for African Studies, University of Cape Town, 1983.

"Catholic Church Sees a Future in Apartheid's Sunset." *Natal Witness*, October 9, 1991.

Chikane, Frank. "God's Option for the Poor." In *Cry Justice*, edited by Charles Villa-Vicencio and John deGruchy. Grand Rapids, Mich.: Eerdmans, 1985.

Christianity in South Africa. Bergvlei, South Africa: Southern Book Publishers, 1990.

Church of the Province of Southern Africa. *An Anglican Prayer Book 1989*. Cape Town: David Philip, 1989; Collins Liturgical Publications, 1989.

———. *Outlines of a Christian Response to the Constitutional Debate for a New South Africa*. Prepared by the Southern African Anglican Theological Commission and Endorsed for Study by the Synod of Bishops, November 1991.

Coetzee, J. M. *Life and Times of Michael K*. New York: Viking Press, 1983.

Cohen, Robin. *Endgame in South Africa? The Changing Structures and Ideology of Apartheid*. London: James Currey, 1986.

Cone, James. *Black Theology and Black Power*. New York: Seabury Press, 1969.

———. *A Black Theology of Liberation*. 2d ed. Maryknoll, N.Y.: Orbis Books, 1989.

———. *For My People*. Maryknoll, N.Y.: Orbis Press, 1984.

———. "Sanctification, Liberation, and Black Worship." *Theology Today* 35 (1978–79).

Consecration and Trial etc. of the Right Reverend Doctor Colenso. Vols. I and II. London: Rivingtons, Waterloo Place, 1867.

CR Quarterly Review of the Community of the Resurrection, House of the Resurrection. West Yorkshire, Eng.: Mirfield.

Davenport, T. R. H. *The Afrikaner Bond: The History of a South African Political Party, 1880–1911*. Cape Town: Oxford University Press, 1966.

Davis, David Bryan. *Slavery and Human Progress*. New York: Oxford University Press, 1984.

Davis, Gaye. "Tutu Backs Church Ban on Priestly Politics." *The Weekly Mail*, July 17, 1990.

A Decade of Dialogue: The First Ten Desmond Tutu Peace Lectures. Krugersdorp: WCRP-SA, 1993/1994.

de Chardin, Teilhard. *Letters from a Traveler*. London: Collins, Fountain, 1967.

de Gruchy, John. *Theology and Ministry in Context and Crisis: A South African Perspective*. Grand Rapids, Mich.: Eerdmans, 1987.

———. *The Church Struggle in South Africa*. Grand Rapids, Mich.: Eerdmans, 1979.

de Klerk, W. A. *The Puritans in Africa: A Story of Afrikanerdom*. Durban: Bok Books, 1975.

Devisse, Jean. "From the Demonic Threat to the Incarnation of Sainthood." In *The Image of the Black in Western Art*. Vol. 2. Cambridge: Harvard University Press, 1979.

Dickson, Kwesi. *Theology in Africa*. Maryknoll, N.Y.: Orbis Books, 1984.

Die NG Kerk en Apartheid. Johannesburg: Macmillan Press, 1986.

"Disastrous Postpone Election, Warns Tutu." *The Argus*, March 30, 1994.

DuBois, W. E. B. "The Conservation of Races." American Negro Academy Occasional Papers, no. 2, 1897. In *W. E. B. DuBois Speaks: Speeches and Addresses 1890–1919*, edited by P. S. Foner. New York: Pathfinders Press, 1970.

———. *The Souls of Black Folk*. New York: Times Mirror, 1969.

Du Boulay, Shirley. *Tutu: Voice of the Voiceless*. London: Hodder & Stoughton, 1988.

Dulles, Avery. *Models of the Church*. Garden City, N.Y.: Image Books, 1987.

Dummett, Ann. *A Portrait of English Racism*. London: CARAF Publications, 1984.

Dunn, Ross. "A Loud, Strong Voice for Peace." *Age*. Melbourne, Australia, October 4, 1993.

Eliade, Mircea. *A History of Religious Ideas: From the Stone Age to the Eleusinian Mysteries*. Vol. 1. Chicago: University of Chicago Press, 1978.

"End Violence Now, Say Black Leaders." *The Argus*, December 1, 1993.

"The Equal Opportunity Foundation—A Beacon of Hope." *The Weekly Mail and Guardian*, October 22–28, 1993.

"Expert Finds Decline in Church Membership." *Daily Dispatch*, November 24, 1993.

Ezard, John. "A Cry for His Unloved Country" (interview with Trevor Huddleston). *Guardian Weekly*, July 9–15, 1993.

Farrer, Austin. *A Celebration of Faith*. London: Hodder & Stoughton, 1970.

Friedman, John B. *The Monstrous Races in Medieval Art and Thought*. Cambridge: Harvard University Press, 1981.

Frostin, Per. *Liberation Theology in Tanzania and South Africa: A First World Interpretation*. Malmo, Sweden: Lund University Press, 1988.

Gerhart, Gail. *Black Power in South Africa: The Evolution of an Ideology*. Berkeley and Los Angeles: University of California Press, 1978.

Gould, Steven. *The Mismeasure of Man*. New York: Norton, 1981.

Greene, Eleanor. *Bishop Desmond Tutu: Apartheid in South Africa*. New York: International Merchandising Corp., 1990.

Green, Mike. "Close-Up: Desmond Tutu, Archbishop." *Runner's World* 1, no. 1 (May / June 1993): 29.

Guy, Jeff. *The Heretic: A Study of the Life of John William Colenso 1814–1883*. Johannesburg: Ravan Press 1983.

"Happy Tutu Calls for Investment." *Evening Post*. South Africa, November 18, 1993.

Harber, Anton. "A Third Nobel Nudge (Will We Get the Hint?)." *The Weekly Mail & Guardian*, October 22–28, 1993.

Häring, Bernard. *The Law of Christ: Moral Theology for Priests and Laity*. Cork, Ire.: Mercier Press, 1967.

Hastings, Peter. "Bishop Tutu—Impatient and Angry, but Not Bitter." *The Sydney Morning Herald*, May 10, 1984.

Hauerwas, Stanley. *A Community of Character: Toward a Christian Social Ethic*. Notre Dame, Ind.: University of Notre Dame Press, 1981.

———. *The Peaceable Kingdom*. Notre Dame, Ind.: University of Notre Dame Press, 1983.

———. "The Sermon on the Mount: Just War and the Quest for Peace." In *A Council for Peace*, edited by Hans Küng and Jürgen Moltmann. Edinburgh: T. & T. Clark, 1988.

————. *Suffering Presence.* Notre Dame, Ind.: University of Notre Dame Press, 1986.

————. *Vision and Virtue: Essays in Christian Ethical Reflection.* Notre Dame, Ind.: University of Notre Dame Press, 1981.

Hauerwas, Stanley, and L. Gregory Jones, eds. *Why Narrative? Readings in Narrative Theology.* Grand Rapids, Mich.: Eerdmans, 1989.

Heron, John. "The Phenomenology of Social Encounter: The Gaze." *Philosophy and Phenomenological Research.*

Hinchliff, Peter. *The Anglican Church in South Africa: An Account of the History and Development of the Church of the Province South Africa.* London: Darton, Longman & Todd, 1963.

————. *John William Colenso: Bishop of Natal.* London: Thomas Nelson and Sons, 1964.

Hood, Robert. *Begrimed and Black: Christian Traditions on Blacks and Blackness.* Minneapolis: Fortress Press, 1994.

Hope, Margorie, and James Young. "Desmond Mpilo Tutu." *Christian Century*, no. 97 (December 31, 1980).

Hopkins, Dwight. *Black Theology USA and South Africa: Politics, Culture, and Liberation.* Maryknoll, N.Y.: Orbis Books, 1989.

Hrbek, I., ed. *General History of Africa. Vol. 3: Africa from the Seventh to the Eleventh Century.* Berkeley and Los Angeles: University of California Press, 1992.

Huddleston, Trevor. *Father Huddleston's Picture Book.* London: Kliptown Books, 1990.

————. *Naught for Your Comfort.* London: Collins, 1956.

————. *Return to South Africa: The Ecstasy and the Agony.* Grand Rapids, Mich.: Eerdmans, 1991.

Issues in Human Sexuality: A Statement by the House of Bishops of the General Synod of the Church of England. London: Church House Publishing, December 1991.

Ive, Anthony. *The Church of England in South Africa.* Cape Town: The Church of England Information Office, 1966.

"The Isolation of Chief Buthelezi." *Sunday Times*, September 22, 1991.

Jacob, Sol, ed. *Hope in Crisis.* Report of the Eighteenth Annual National Conference of the South African Council of Churches held at St. Barnabas College (Johannesburg), June 23–27, 1986.

Johns, Sheridan, et al. *Mandela, Tambo, and the African National Congress*. New York: Oxford University Press, 1991.

———. "Protest and Hope 1882–1934." In *From Protest to Challenge: A Documentary History of African Politics in South Africa 1882–1964*, edited by Thomas Karis and Gwendolen M. Carter. Stanford, Calif.: Hoover Institution Press, 1972.

Jones, Alan. *Soul Making: The Desert Way of Spirituality*. San Francisco: Harper & Row, 1985.

"Just Another Day of Township Horror." *The Argus*, May 25, 1993.

The Kairos Document, 2d ed. Braamfontein: Skotaville Publishers, 1986.

Keating, Thomas. *The Mystery of Christ: The Liturgy as Spiritual Experience*. New York: Amity House, 1987.

Keller, Bill. "A Surprising Silent Majority in South Africa." *New York Times Magazine*, April 17, 1994.

King, Martin Luther, Jr. "Suffering and Faith." *Christian Century* 77 (April 27, 1960).

Kirk, Kenneth. *Some Principles of Moral Theology*. London: Longmans, Green and Co., n.d.

———. *The Threshold of Ethics*. London: Skeffington & Son, n.d.

———. *The Vision of God: the Christian Doctrine of the Summum Bonum*. London: Longmans, Green & Co., 1932.

Kretzschmar, Louise. *The Voice of Black Theology in South Africa*. Johannesburg: Ravan Press, 1986.

Kuper, L. *An African Bourgeoisie: Race, Class and Politics in South Africa*. New Haven, Conn.: Yale University Press, 1965.

LaCugna, Catherine. *God for Us: The Trinity and the Christian Life*. San Francisco: HarperSanFrancisco, 1991.

Ledward, Sally-Ann. *The Constitutional Development of the Church of the Province of South Africa, 1848–1936*. Cape Town: University of Cape Town School of Librarianship, 1957.

Leas, Allan. *Questions of Today: South Africa*. London, B. T. Batsford, 1992.

Leech, Kenneth. *Eye of the Storm*. San Francisco: HarperSanFrancisco, 1992.

———. *The Social God*. London: Sheldon, 1981.

———. *True Prayer*. New York: Harper & Row, 1980.

The Legal Development of the Church of the Province of South Africa: Judgments of the English and South African Courts in the Cases of Bishopscourt 1934–1936. Judicial Committees, South African Courts, 1934–1936.

Legum, Colin. *The Battle Fronts of Southern Africa.* New York: Africana Publishing, 1988.

Lelyveld, Joseph. "South Africa's Bishop Tutu." *New York Times Magazine,* March 14, 1982.

Les Prix Nobel: Nobel Prizes, Presentations, Biographies, and Lectures. Stockholm: Almqvist & Wiksell International, 1985.

Lewis, Cecil, and G. E. Edwards. *Historical Records of the Church of the Province of South Africa.* London: SPCK, 1934.

"Liberating Our Nation from the Antichrist." *The Weekly Mail,* October 22–28, 1993.

Lodge, Tom. *Black Politics in South Africa since 1945.* New York: Longman Group, 1983.

Logan, Willis, ed. *The Kairos Covenant: Standing with South African Christians.* New York: Friendship Press, 1988.

Lossky, Vladimir. *Mystical Theology of the Eastern Church,* Crestwood, N.Y.: St. Vladimir's Press, 1976.

———. *Orthodox Theology.* Crestwood, N.Y.: St. Vladimir's Press, 1989.

Lubser, J. A. *The Apartheid Bible: A Critical Review of Racial Theology in South Africa.* Cape Town: Maskew Miller Longman, 1987.

Luther, Martin. "Secular Authority: To What Extent Should It Be Obeyed?" In *Works of Luther.* Philadelphia: Muhlenberg Press, 1959.

Lutuli, Albert. *Let My People Go.* New York: McGraw-Hill, 1962.

———. *The Road to Freedom Is Via the Cross.* Vol. 3 of *South African Studies.* London: The Publicity and Information Bureau of the ANC, 1970.

Mahamba, Muendanyi. "Ubuntu and Democracy." *Challenge,* no. 16 (June/July 1993).

Makhudu, Nono. "Cultivating a Climate of Co-operation through 'Ubuntu.'" *Enterprise,* August 1993.

Malan, D. F. "Apartheid: A Divine Calling." In *The Anti-Apartheid Reader,* edited by David Mermelstein. New York: Grove Press, 1987.

Marks, Shula. "The Ambiguities of Dependence: John L. Dube of Natal." *Journal of Southern African Studies* 1, no. 2 (1975).

————. "Khoisan Resistance to the Dutch in the Seventeenth and Eighteenth Centuries." *Journal of African History* 13, no. 1 (1972).

Marolen, Daniel. "Another Nobel Peace Award for South Africa?" In *Imagine a Land: A Collection of Black Anti-apartheid Protest Poems.* Owings Mills, Md.: Watermark Press, 1991.

Mason, J. "Slaveholder Resistance to the Amelioration of Slavery at the Cape." Paper read at a conference titled "The Western Cape: Roots and Realities."

Mbiti, John. *African Religions and Philosophies.* New York: Doubleday, 1970.

————. *Concepts of God in Africa.* London: The Society for Promoting Christian Knowledge, 1970.

————. *New Testament Eschatology in an African Background: A Study of the Encounter between New Testament Theology and African Traditional Concepts.* Oxford: Oxford University Press, 1971.

McClendon, James. *Biography as Theology: How Life Stories Can Remake Today's Theology.* Nashville: Abingdon Press, 1974.

McComb, M. Editorial,"Tutu's Stand on Violence Hypocritical." *Weekend Argus,* August 14–15, 1993.

McKie, Robin. "Underneath, We're All Still Africans." *The Observer* (London), August 22, 1993.

Mdluli, P. "Ubuntu-Botho: Inkatha's 'People's Education.'" *Transformation* 5, 1987.

Menkiti, Ifeanyi A. "Person and Community in African Traditional Thought." In *African Philosophy,* edited by R. A. Wright. New York: University Press of America, 1971.

Milbank, John. *Theology and Social Theory: Beyond Secular Reason.* Oxford: Basil Blackwell, 1991.

Mirfield Essays in Christian Belief. The Community of the Resurrection. New York: The Faith Press and Morehouse & Barlow, 1962.

Moodie, T. Dunbar. *The Rise of Afrikanerdom: Power, Apartheid, and the Afrikaner Civil Religion.* Berkeley and Los Angeles: University of California Press, 1975.

Mosala, Itumeleng J. *Biblical Hermeneutics and Black Theology in South Africa.* Grand Rapids, Mich.: Eerdmans, 1989.

Mosala, Itumeleng J., and Buti Tlhagale, eds. *The Unquestionable Right to Be Free: Essays in Black Theology*. Johannesburg: Skotaville Publishers, 1986.

Masolo, D. A. *African Philosophy in Search of Identity*. Bloomington: Indiana University Press, 1994.

———. *Some Aspects and Prospectives of African Philosophy Today*. Rome: Institutio Italo-Africano, 1981.

Mosley, Nicholas. *The Life of Raymond Raynes*. London: The Faith Press, 1961.

Mudimbe, V. Y. "African Gnosis, Philosophy, and the Order of Knowledge: An Introduction." *The African Studies Review* 28, nos. 2/3 (June/September 1985).

———. *The Invention of Africa: Gnosis, Philosophy, and the Order of Knowledge*. Bloomington: Indiana University Press, 1988.

Mugambi, J. N. K., and Laurenti Magesa, eds. *Jesus in African Christianity: Experimentation and Diversity in African Christology*. Nairobi: Initiatives Publishers, 1989.

Mulago, V. "Vital Participation." In *Biblical Revelation and African Beliefs*, edited by Dickson and Ellinworth. London: Butterworth, 1971.

Naudé, Beyers. "Report of the Genral Secretary—National Conference of the South African Council of Churches, June 24–28, 1985." *Ecunews*, News Service of the South African Council of Churches, August 1985.

Ndungane, Winston. "An Evaluation of Charismatic Renewal within the Church of the Province of Southern Africa." In *Open to the Spirit: Anglicans and the Experience of Renewal*, edited by Colin Craston. London: The Anglican Consultative Council, 1987.

———. *We Are Anglicans: An Introduction to the Church of the Province of Southern Africa*. Marshalltown, South Africa: CPSA Publishing Committee, 1993.

Neill, Stephen. *Anglicanism*. New York: Oxford University Press, 1978.

"New Squatter Act Allows Forced Removals." *Crisis News*, Western Province Council of Churches Publication no. 27, February 1989.

Ngcokavane, Cecil. *Demons of Apartheid: A Moral and Ethical Analysis of the N.G.K., N.P. and Broederbond's Justification of Apartheid*. Braamfontein: Skotaville Publishers, 1989.

we've carried on ourselves and are working to overcome. That struggle is intrinsic to desire, which is a product of mind. The mind isn't our enemy—mind is of Vital Force just like everything else; but the mind is not the place in ourselves from which we want to live. In a state of Self-realization, thoughts occur—the mind doesn't shut down when we are fully realized—but no thoughts are embraced. We're not detached from our thoughts because when we understand that everything is One Thing, we also understand that there is no issue of separation from our thoughts. Rather, we are connected to the fundamental power from which all Life flows, and we are fulfilled. We are overflowing. It's not even that we would say that difficult things don't bother us anymore. It's more that we see everything for what it is; we see right through the veils. We still dance to the music, but we do not identify with it.

So from this understanding that there is no other—that we do not have to be identified with our individual life—we can easily have good wishes and warm feelings toward all human beings. We may step on a few toes upon occasion—everyone does—but we wish everyone and everything well.

This is also why I say that we don't have to renounce anything in order to lead a spiritual life. If there is only One Thing, and that is our essence manifest in all the forms of this world, then what will we renounce exactly? The real issue is not renunciation; the real issue is desire, diversity, appearance, and we don't renounce that, we just don't live from it anymore because we know it's the illusion, and God, service, love, flow is the Reality.

We will not even open our hearts, let alone love our lives, if we can't get over living from our desires, from the world of "me, me, me, me." If we can't get over that, we will never understand the truth, which is Oneness. Once we've gotten over the me-thing and actually are loving our Life, we find the essence of what we are loving and giving our one-pointed attention to has nothing to do with any form of anything. It is no form, no color, no texture, no sound, no experience, no circumstance, no nothing like that at all. It is a vibrancy, a kind of pregnancy—this Creative Energy. And more and more, our attention is drawn inward to the Creative Energy field which is beyond even the subtlest experience of "I" and has no cognitive processes—no thought, no recognition, just pure awareness. That state is Infinite Uncertainty, and it is in that state that infinite potentiality unfolds. In that ego-less state, Divine Power manifests Itself on the plane of worldly experience as a Life of love, for the benefit of all, not of "me."

A person in that state does not think he or she needs anything in order to be full. Such a person simply is full—of flow—and desires are seen for what they really are: shadows, illusions. No thing can fill the vastness which exists inside your chest. No thing. No person. No condition. No nothing. Except joy. Except love.

But ultimately the quest for Self-realization is not about getting anything, including a sense of joy or well-being or happiness. It is also, interestingly enough, not about achieving individual Enlightenment. Mahayana

Buddhism speaks to the need of being considerate of the whole, even to the point of working for the Enlightenment of the whole, not just for your own Enlightenment. Working for your own Enlightenment can easily deteriorate into a kind of materialism which fast becomes no practice at all. In our practice of kundalini yoga, because we are aware from the outset that everything is One Thing, we continually work in such a way as to pay our respects, always, to the whole. When you really open your heart to the core of you and feel its complete connection to the whole, that is Enlightenment; it is the Truth.

In the last year of his life, Rudi talked a great deal about living from the Truth, about expressing God's will in our lives and surrendering everything. He talked about the magic and understanding that arose within people who have really made this commitment and surrendered. He discussed this in terms of the whole fabric of time and space unfolding itself and of our own infinite journey revealing itself to us.

When we live from the Truth, we come to understand deeply the stresses and strains in our lives, and as a result, we are able to let go continually on a deeper and deeper—completely profound and amazing—level, until there is nothing left at all—no tension at all—not by forcing anything but by continually opening our hearts and going beyond, again and again, wherever it is we think we are. When Creative Energy is no longer bound up by tension, a tremendous power is unleashed in us which establishes itself in us and us in it and puts an end to the whole issue of struggle.

> *Thinking about what we want in life and struggling for it is really the source of disease and death. It's the source of every sickness, and ultimately, it is the death of our Life. Thinking about what Life wants of us and really working to serve It is the Life of our life.*

To live from the Truth is the real thrust of the practice of yoga, whether we're talking about asana practice—

the various postures of yoga—or meditation, which includes the science of breath. True yoga is not what it has become in the United States—some amorphous, do-what-you-want-as-long-as-it-feels-good exercise. It is a methodology with a specific aim, and that aim is Enlightenment and its maturer state, Self-realization.

In America, there has been a movement to popularize yoga, and in the process, Americans have made yoga a bit saccharine. But it definitely is not saccharine. It is about one thing only: Vital Force, the awakening of kundalini; and there is nothing saccharine about kundalini and Vital Force. Vital Force is the essence of breath. It is the Creative Energy that actually causes the fluctuation of our breathing and the circulation of the electrical impulses, which move through our nervous systems in various dimensions, sustaining our physiological existence, our emotional and intellectual existence, and our cognitive capacity.

While Vital Force is the essence of our individuality in each of its aspects, Vital Force is in no way limited by any of it. As we cultivate the experience of Vital Force through yoga, we come to see that all of our experiences are nothing more than waves of energy, each wave having a unique and intrinsically beautiful form to it. These waves are nothing to become excited about or depressed over, nothing with which to become identified.

Asana practice is about purification of the body through facilitation of flow. It is about allowing for a flow which will release tensions and bring new vitality and flexibility to our physical bodies. Pranayama, which is breathing, is about purifying the mind in this endeavor; it is about the release of all worries—all mental anxieties and concerns of any kind—in order to continue to facilitate this flow on a subtler level. In this way, we come to the recognition of the fluctuation of Vital Force, which is different from flow. Prana is the energy of the body, the energy that moves through the different channels, the chakras. It is the individuated creative energy which sustains our physical existence.

In the quest for Self-realization, we make the shift in our awareness from prana to Spirit or Vital Force. Yoga is about making this shift.

So, contrary to what the magazines may tell us, yoga—because it *is* about Self-realization—has nothing to do with personal growth. Yoga is not about our awareness being stuck in prana; it is not about self-improvement. Yoga is about transcending the personal energy of this body to re-merge with the universal Creative Energy, which is Life Itself. This transcendence is the essence of spiritual growth. It begins where personal growth ends. That's why a person can be smart, stupid, rich, poor, young, old—any which thing on a personal level—and still do this work.

In order for us to be the healthiest, happiest people we can be, we have no other choice but to focus on the unfoldment of Vital Force. Only in the flow of the energy in a rhythmic balanced interchange with the deepest part of us will we express complete health and happiness. This is not, as we've said before, a material level of benefit, but something for which there are no words, something of a superb elegance and richness. Vital Force must express Itself though all the physical structures and chemical processes which sustain our individual lives in order for us to be fully, deeply, truly happy and well.

Clearly, then, the goal of Self-realization is not a life-denying choice, it is a Life-affirming one because through this choice, the power which is our Life, the part of us which is completely alive, can fully unfold and express itself. Liberation is liberating our Life from the constraints of the limited resources of our material existence and from the strain and trauma of our material and physical development.

In the Trika system of spiritual practice, there is something called the cycle of cognition, which discusses Reality as Oneness, and how our awareness expands to encompass It. Put simply, the cycle of cognition is the extension of cognition from pure awareness of the Self—such a pure awareness that the experience of "I" has not yet emerged or condensed—to objectified reality and back again. Objectified reality is the field of our experience—it is all the condensed icebergs, the seemingly separate "I's." The cycle of cognition also shows us that there are many levels of manifestation between pure subject and the world of objects.

In *shavasana*, a hatha yoga asana, we find a practical way to view the cycle of cognition. Most commonly practiced at the end of a yoga routine, shavasana is a posture in which you lie flat on your back in a completely still position, totally relaxed and aware of your breath. Many people fall asleep in shavasana, but if you practice for a little bit and don't fall asleep, you enter into a state of awareness which is between sleeping and waking; you're no longer aware of your body, and your thoughts are very far away. In this state, there is no notion of "me" or "I." There is, therefore, no notion of desire. Subject, object, means of perception or cognition are one, and all choices evaporate. In this state, the self and the Self re-merge, and this re-merging is what the Hindus call "Bliss" and we call Enlightenment and Self-realization.

Another way to talk about the cycle of cognition is to say that awareness extends itself from stillness to a recognition of the unity of stillness and motion—of all seeming opposites—back to stillness, over and over, again and again. The highest state of awareness is greater than the sum of its two parts: stillness and motion. When you have the experience of the cycle of cognition, of this exchange, back and forth, back and forth, between you, Self, and the source of Self, when your awareness and Awareness are one and you merge with the intrinsic fullness of that state, then the Creative Energy is fully expressing Itself through you.

This is what class with a teacher truly is—the exchange of energy, of real love, back and forth, back and forth. This is what the experience of your entire life can be—an experience of profound Oneness. When you are tuned into the Creative Energy continually, your life becomes simple; it becomes deeply free of tension and anxiety because you've made the choice that ends all choices. You are full and complete within your Self, established in the perfection of the ultimate Reality, which is the fundamental, most basic part of you. It is both a deeply personal and profoundly transcendent state.

So it is not a paradox, but it does seem paradoxical: To be happy, you must make a choice on a regular basis to choose to live a Life beyond choices, beyond the condensation of energy that is choices and limitations and every other kind of thing. To be happy, you must choose to see in all things Reality, Unity—Infinite Uncertainty, yes, but Infinite Potential as well.

Unhappy is just a state of ignorance.

Now that you have an inkling of the happiness available to you, do you really want to choose to live in a state of complexity, struggle and turmoil? Is any desire you can concoct worth that price? Think about it carefully. You have a choice.

To be happy, you can choose choiceless awareness. You—anyone—can choose and achieve the ultimate.

Nolan, Albert. *God in South Africa: The Challenge of the Gospel*. Cape Town: David Philip, 1988.

―――, ed. "Priests in Politics: Challenge Listens to the Debate." *Challenge: Church and People*, March 1994.

Nyerere, J. K. *African Socialism in Practice: The Tanzanian Experience*. Edited by A. Coulson. Nottingham, U.K.: Spokesman Publishers, 1979.

―――. *Freedom and Development*. Oxford: Oxford University Press, 1973.

―――. *Ujamaa: Essays on Socialism*. London: Oxford University Press, 1968.

Odendaal, Andre. *Beyond the Barricades*. New York: Aperture Press, 1989.

―――. *Black Protest Politics in South Africa to 1912*. Totowa, N.J.: Barnes & Noble, 1984.

O'Donovan, Oliver. *Resurrection and Moral Order: An Outline for Evangelical Ethics*. Grand Rapids, Mich.: Eerdmans, 1994.

Ofstad, Harold. *Our Contempt for Weakness: Nazi Norms and Values — and Our Own*, translated by Clas von Sydow. Stockholm: Almqvist & Wiksell International, 1989.

Omer-Cooper, J. D. *The Zulu Aftermath: A Nineteenth Century Revolution in Bantu Africa*. London: Longman Group, 1966.

The Option for Inclusive Democracy: A Theological-Ethical Study of Appropriate Social Values for South Africa. University of Stellenbosch: Center for Hermeneutics, 1987.

"The Ordination of Women." Report of the CPSA Conference at St. Francis of Assisi, Waterkloof, Pretoria, March 24–26, 1992.

Ouspensky, Leonid, and Vladimir Lossky. *The Meaning of Icons*. Crestwood, N.Y.: St. Vladimir's Press, 1989.

Paris, Peter. *The Spirituality of African Peoples: The Search for a Common Moral Discourse*. Minneapolis: Fortress Press, 1994.

Patterson, Orlando. *Slavery and Social Death*. Cambridge: Harvard University Press, 1982.

Peavy, Lewis. *The Cushite, or the Descendants of Ham*. Springfield, Mass.: Willey Press, 1843.

Peires, J. B. *The House of Phalo: A History of the Xhosa People in the Days of their Independence*. Johannesburg: Ravan Press, 1981.

"The Power of the Pulpit." *Time*, September 15, 1986.

Price, Robert M. *The Apartheid State in Crisis: Political Transformation in South Africa, 1975–1990*. New York: Oxford University Press, 1991.

"Priest 'Unrepentant.'" *Cape Times*, April 15, 1994.

"A Prisoner of Hope." *Christianity Today*, October 5, 1992.

Prozesky, Martin. *Christianity amidst Apartheid*. London: Macmillan, 1990.

Raboteau, Albert. *Slave Religion*. New York: Oxford University Press, 1980.

Ras, Volk, en Nasie. Pretoria: N. G. Kerk-Uitgewers, 1975.

Rawls, John. *A Theory of Justice*. Cambridge: Harvard University Press, 1971.

Rickard, Carmel. "Top ANC Candidates Face Church Censure." *Sunday Times* (London), January 30, 1994.

Roberson, Rachel. "Tutu Returns to Convention as a Citizen Bringing Thanks." *Episcopal Life*, November 1994.

Rochman, Hazel. *Against Borders: Promoting Books for a Multicultural World*. Chicago and London: ALA Books/Booklist Publications, 1993.

Ross, Maggie. *The Fountain and the Furnace: The Way of Tears and Fire*. New York: Paulist Press, 1987.

———. *The Pilar of Flame: Power, Priesthood, and Spiritual Maturity*. San Francisco: Harper & Row, 1988.

Ross, R. *Cape of Torments: Slavery and Resistance in South Africa*. London: Routledge & Kegan Paul, 1983.

Rowell, Geoffrey, ed. *The English Religious Tradition and the Genius of Anglicanism*. Wantage, U.K.: Ikon, 1993.

Rozzell, Liane. "A Gesture of Honor." *Sojourners*, December 1984.

Willem Saayman. "The Case of South Africa: Practice Context, and Ideology." In *Exploring Church Growth*, edited by W. R. Shenk. Grand Rapids, Mich.: Eerdmans, 1983.

———. "Christian Keysser Revisited." In *Tokum* [n.d.].

———. "A Few Aspects of the Policy of Separate Churches." *Journal of Theology for Southern Africa*, no. 26 (March 1979).

Sanneh, Lamin. *Translating the Message: The Missionary Impact on Culture*. Maryknoll, N.Y.: Orbis Books, 1990.

———. "Christian Mission in the Pluralist Milieu: The African Experience," *International Review of Mission* 74, 1985.

Santangelo, Enzo. *Desmond Tutu: Hombre de Paz*. (Ediciones Afroamerica, Cetro Cultural Afroecuatoriano) Quito, Coleccion: *Os Libertadores*, no. 11, *Ediciones*: Loyola—Saõ Paulo, 1986.

Sartre, Jean-Paul. *Being and Nothingness: An Essay on Phenomenological Ontology*, translated with an introduction by Hazel E. Barnes. New York: The Philosophical Library, 1956.

———. "Existentialism Is a Humanism." In *The Existentialism Tradition: Selected Writings*, edited by Nino Languilli, trans. by Philip Mairet. New York: Doubleday-Anchor Books, 1971.

Schnell, W. G. *Is the Negro a Beast; A Reply to Chas. Carroll's Book Entitled The Negro a Beast: Proving That the Negro Is Human from Biblical, Scientific, and Historical Standpoints*. Moundsville, W.V.: Gospel Trumpet Publishing Co., 1901.

Shutte, Augustine. *Philosophy for Africa*. Unpublished manuscript. University of Cape Town, South Africa.

Sedgwick, Jonathan. "An Approach to Natural Law." *CR: Quaterly Review of the Community of the Resurrection*, no. 354 (Michaelmas, 1991).

Seidman, A. *The Roots of Crisis in Southern Africa*. Trenton: Africa World Press, 1985:

Senghor, Leopold. "Negritude." *Optima* 16 (1966).

———. *Negritude and African Socialism*. In St. Anthony's Papers No. 15, edited by K. Kirkwood, 1963.

Serfontein, Hennie. "God Has a Plan." *Vryeweekblad*, September 4–10, 1992.

Setiloane, Gabriel. *African Theology*. Johannesburg: Skotaville, 1986.

———. *The Image of God among the Sotho-Tswana*. Rotterdam: A. A. Balkema, 1976.

Setiloane, Gabriel, et al. *Pangs of Growth: A Dialogue on Church Growth in Southern Africa*. Braamfontein: Skotaville, 1988.

Smith, E. W. *African Ideas of God*. London: Edinburgh House, 1950.

Snowden, Frank M. *Before Color Prejudice: The Ancient View of Blacks*. Cambridge: Harvard University Press, 1983.

———. *Blacks in Antiquity: Ethiopians in the Greco-Roman Experience*. Cambridge: Harvard University Press, 1970.

Soga, John Henderson. *The Ama-Xosa: Life and Customs*. Lovedale, South Africa: Lovedale Press, 1931.

South African Council of Churches. *Summary of the Aims, Objectives, Attitudes, and Divisions of the South African Council of Churches*. SACC, 1974.

"South African Government Hits Council of Churches Admin." Australia, *Church & Nation*, May 2, 1984.

Sparks, Allister. *The Mind of South Africa*. New York: Ballantine Books, 1990.

"Standing Ovation for Tutu at Union Society." *Cambridge Evening News*, February 26, 1994.

"Statement from the Bishops of the Church of the Province of Southern Africa," Synod of Bishops, Kempton Park, from February 28 to March 4, 1994.

Steele, Andrew, and Ulli Michel. *South African Portfolio: Public People . . . Private Views*. Cape Town: Struik Publishers, 1991.

Steward, Alexander. *You Are Wrong Father Huddleston*. London: The Bodley Head, 1956.

Storey, Peter. "Press Statement by SACC President." September 11, 1981.

Strangler. "I Will Give Myself Up to Tutu." *Cape Times*, February 28, 1994.

"The Struggle for Land and Housing." *Crisis News*. Western Province Council of Churches Publication no. 27, February 1989.

Suggit, John. *Celebration of Faith: An Explanation of the Eucharist according to an Anglican Prayer Book, 1989*. Cape Town: Blackshaws Press, n.d.

Surin, Kenneth. *Theology and the Problem of Evil*. Oxford: Blackwell, 1986.

Swan, Maureen. *Gandhi: The South African Experience*. Johannesburg: Ravan Press, 1985.

Taylor, J. V. *The Primal Vision*. London: S.C.M., 1963.

Tempels, Placide Frans. *Bantu Philosophy*. Paris: Presence Africaine, 1959.

Templin, J. Alton. *Ideology on a Frontier: The Theological Foundation of Afrikaner Nationalism, 1652–1910*. London: Greenwood Press, 1984.

Tesfai, Yacob, ed. *The Scandal of a Crucified World: Perspectives of the Cross and Suffering*. Maryknoll, N.Y.: Orbis, n.d.

Thistlewaite, Susan Brooks, and Mary Potter Engel, eds. *Lift Every Voice: Constructing Christian Theologies from the Underside*. San Francisco: HarperSanFrancisco, 1990.

Thomas, David. "Tutu Gets the VIP Treatment." *The Sydney Morning Herald*, May 2, 1984.

Thompson, Leonard. *A History of South Africa*. New Haven, Conn.: Yale University Press, 1990

Thompson, Richard H. *Theories of Ethnicity: A Critical Appraisal*. New York: Greenwood Press, 1989.

Thornton, Martin. *English Spirituality: An Outline of Ascetical Theology according to the English Pastoral Tradition*. Cowley Publications, 1986.

Tilson, Everett. *Segregation and the Bible*. Nashville: Abingdon Press, 1958.

Tlhagale, Buti, and Itumeleng Mosala, eds. *Hammering Swords into Ploughshares: Essays in Honor of Archbishop Mpilo Desmond Tutu*. Grand Rapids, Mich.: Eerdmans, 1986.

Trocmé, André. *Jesus and the Nonviolent Revolution*. Scottdale, Pa.: Herald Press, 1973.

"Turning Apartheid's Victims into Leaders." *The Christian Science Monitor*, October 1, 1986.

"Tutu, Desmond." *CB*, 1985.

Tutu, Desmond. "African Theology and Black Theology: The Quest for Authenticity and the Struggle for Liberation." In *African Challange*, edited by Kenneth Best. Nairobi: Trans Africa Publishers, 1973.

———. "Afterword." In *Christianity amidst Apartheid: Selected Perspectives on the Church in South Africa*, edited by Martin Prozesky. New York: St. Martin's Press, 1990.

———. "An Appreciation of the Rt. Revd Trevor Huddleston, CR." In *Trevor Huddleston: Essays on His Life and Work*, edited by Deborah Duncan Honoré. New York: Oxford University Press, 1988.

———. "Apartheid: An Evil System." In *The Anti-Apartheid Reader*, edited by David Mermelstein. New York: Grove Press, 1987.

———. Article to honour M. M. Thomas's 75th birthday, a collection of essays focusing on the reformulation of a new theological methodology from different perspectives shaped by James Cone, by Orbis Books, New York. Tutu was to write on spirituality. In Tutu's letter of June 2, 1988, he said he would do his best to send something by the end of 1988.

———. "Barmen and Apartheid." *Journal of Theology for Southern Africa*, no. 47, June 1984.

———. "The Basic Paradigm Must Be the Family." In *A Democrative Vision for South Africa: Political Realism and Christian Responsibility*, edited by Klaus Nürnberger. Pietermaritzburg: Encounter Publications, 1991.

———. "The Bias of God." *The Month: A Review of Christian Thought and World Affairs*, November 1989.

———. "Black and African Theologies: Soul-Mates or Antagonists?" In *Black Theology: A Documentary History, 1966–1979*, edited by G. Wilmore and J. Cone. New York: Orbis Books, 1981.

———. "Blacks and Liberation." SAIC, March 29, 1982.

———. "Black Theology / African Theology—Soul Mates or Antagonists?" *The Journal of Religious Thought* 32, no. 2 (1975).

———. "Burma as South Africa." *Far Eastern Economic Review* 156, no. 37 (September 1993).

———. "Called to Unity and Fellowship." In *The Church and the Alternative Society: Papers and Resolutions of the Eleventh Conference of the SACC*, edited by M. Nash. Johannesburg: SACC, 1979.

———. "A Christian Vision of the Future of South Africa." In *Christianity in South Africa*, edited by Martin Prozesky.

———. "Christmas Letter 1." 1985–1986.

———. "Church and Nation in the Perspective of Black Theology." *Journal of Theology for Southern Africa*, no. 15, 1976.

———. "Church and Prophecy in South Africa Today." Center for the Study of Theology in the University of Essex, Essex Papers in Theology and Society, 1991.

———. *Crying in the Wilderness: The Struggle for Justice in South Africa*. Grand Rapids, Mich.: Eerdmans, 1982.

———. "Clarifying the Word! A Sermon by Desmond Tutu." In *Crucible of Fire: The Church Confronts Apartheid*, edited by Jim Wallace and Joyce Hollyday. Maryknoll, N.Y.: Orbis Books, 1989.

———. "Deeper into God—Spirituality for the Struggle." In *Crucible of Fire: The Church Confronts Apartheid*, edited by Jim Wallace and Joyce Hollyday. Maryknoll, N.Y.: Orbis Books, 1989.

———. *The Divine Intention.* Presentation by Bishop D. Tutu, General Secretary of the South African Council of Churches, to the Eloff Commission of Enquiry on September 1, 1982. Braamfontein: SACC Publications.

———. Draft of article mailed to *Woord en Daad* (Word and Action), June 24, 1991.

———. "The Education of Free Men." In *Apartheid in Crisis*, edited by Mark A. Uhlig. New York: Vintage Books, 1986.

———. Essay on Justice. *The Living Pulpit*, forthcoming.

———. "Faith." In *The New World Order*, edited by Sundeep Waslekar. New Delhi: Konark Publishers, 1991.

———. "Foreword: A Gift of Peace." In *Imagine/Reader: Gift of Peace*, edited by John Hartom and Lisa Blackburn. Michigan Art Education Association, 1990.

———. Foreword. *1993 Children of War Peace Calendar*. War Resisters League, March 13, 1992.

———. Foreword. In *The Cape of Storms: A Personal History of the Crisis in South Africa*, by Anthony Heard. Fayetteville: University of Arkansas Press, 1990.

———. Foreword. In *The Politics of Peace*, by Brian Frost. London: Darton, Longman & Todd, 1991.

———. Foreword. In *South Africa the Cordoned Heart*, edited by Omar Badsha. Cape Town: The Gallery Press, 1986.

———. Foreword. In *World Winds: Meditations from the Blessed of the Earth*, by Earl and Pat Hosteller Martin. Scottdale, Pa.: Herald Press, 1990.

———. Foreword. In *I Was Lonelyness: The Complete Graphic Works of John Muafangejo*. Cape Town: Struik Winchester, 1992.

———. Foreword. In *Nelson Mandela: The Man and the Movement*, by Mary Benson. New York: W. W. Norton, 1986.

———. Foreword. In *The Politics of Love: Choosing the Christian Way in a Changing South Africa*, by Michael Cassidy. London: Hodder & Stoughton, 1991.

———. Foreword. In *Poor Man, Rich Man: The Priorities of Jesus and the Agenda of the Church*, by Peter Lee. London: Hodder & Stoughton, 1986.

———. Foreword. In *Sing Freedom! Songs of South African Life*, edited by Margaret Hamilton. London: Novello, 1993.

———. Foreword. In *Soweto: Portrait of a City*, photography by Peter Magubane, text by Avid Bristow and Stan Motjuwadi. Cape Town: Struik Publishers, 1990.

———. Foreword. In *Independent Churches and Movements in Southern Africa*, edited by G. C. Oosthuizen and H. J. Becken, forthcoming.

———. Foreword. In *I Will Meet You in Heaven Where Animals Don't Bite*, by Michael Seed. London: St. Paul Publications, n.d.

———. Foreword. In *Turning Points in Religious Studies: Essays in Honour of Geoffrey Parrinder*, edited by Ursula King. Edinburgh: T. & T. Clark, 1990.

———. Foreword. *Dramatic Play: The Life of Steve Biko.*

———. Foreword. In *The Worshipping Church in Africa*. A special issue of *Black Sacred Music: A Journal of Theomusicology* 7, no. 2 (fall 1993).

———. "Franciscan Vocation." *The Little Chronicle*, The American Province of the Society of St. Francis Provincial Publication, forthcoming.

———. "Freedom Fighters or Terrorists?" *Theology and Violence: The South African Debate*, edited by Charles Villa-Vicencio. Johannesburg: Skotaville Publishers, 1987.

———. Geen Vrede Met Apartheid, Nobelprijsrede 1984 en andere Texten. Uitverij Jan Mest, Werkgroep Kairos, Amsterdam, 1985.

———. "God—Black or White?" *Ministry* 11, no. 4 (1971).

———. "God-Given Dignity and the Quest for Liberation in the Light of the South African Dilemma." *Liberation: Papers and Resolutions for the Eighth National Conference of the SACC*, edited by D. Thomas. Johannesburg: SACC, 1976.

———. "God-Given Dignity and the Quest for Liberation" (paper to the National Conference of the SACC, July 1973). Reprinted from *Ecunews*, 4 August 1976, in *African Perspectives on South Africa: A Collection of Speeches, Articles, and Documents,"* edited by Hendrik W. van der Merwe, Nancy C. J. Charton, D. A. Kotzé, and Åke Magnusson. Cape Town: David Philip, 1978.

———. "God and Nation in the Perspective of Black Theology." *Journal for Theology for Southern Africa* 15 (1976).

———. "God Intervening in Human Affairs." *Missionalia* 5, no. 2 (1977).

———. "The God of Surprises." In *A Democratic Vision for South Africa: Political Realism and Christian Responsibility,* edited by Klaus Nürenberger. Pietermaritzburg: Encounter Publications, 1991.

———. "God's Dream." In *Waging Peace II: Vision and Hope for the 21st Century,* edited by David Krieger and Frank Kelly. Chicago: The Nobel Press, n.d.

———. "God's Love." *Tradition and Unity: Sermons Published in Honour of Robert Runcie,* edited by Dan Cohn-Sherbok. London: Bellew Publishing, 1991.

———. "God's Strength in Human Weakness." In *Your Kingdom Come.* Papers and Resolutions of the Twelfth National Conference of the South African Council of Churches, Hammanskraal, May 5–8, 1980, edited by M. Nash. Braamfontein: SACC Publications, n.d.

———. "Grace upon Grace." *Journal for Preachers* 15, no. 1 (Advent 1991).

———. "Greetings." In *The Future of Liberation Theology: Essays in Honor of Gustavo Gutiérrez,* edited by Marc H. Ellis and Otto Maduro. Maryknoll, N.Y.: Orbis Books, 1989.

———. "Greetings from Bishop Tutu to the Soweto Students, June 16, 1977." *Pro Veritate,* June 1977.

———. *Hope and Suffering: Sermons and Speeches.* Grand Rapids, Mich.: Eerdmans, 1984.

———. "Hope against Despair." In *A Book of Hope.* Cape Town: David Philip, 1992.

———. "Hope That South Africa May Be on Path to Reconciliation." *Chronicle Zimbabwe,* May 13, 1993.

———. "Human Rights in South Africa." *Monitor,* SACC Library Resource Center, undated.

———. Interview. In *Dispensations: The Future of South Africa as South Africans See It,* by Richard John Neuhaus. Grand Rapids, Mich.: Eerdmans, 1986.

———. Interview. "The Blood of the Lamb." In *Leadership: For Reconciliation and Reconstruction* 12, no. 3 (1993).

———. Interview. In *The Rise of Christian Conscience: The Emergence of a Dramatic Renewal Movement in the Church Today*, edited by Jim Wallis. San Francisco: Harper & Row, 1987.

———. Interview. Warick Beutler interviews Tutu for Parliament of the Commonwealth of Australia, Department of the Parliamentary Library, May 2, 1984.

———. Interview. In *In the Footsteps of Gandhi: Conversations with Spiritual Social Activists*, by Catherine Ingram. Berkeley, Calif.: Parallax Press, 1990.

———. Interview. *The Guardian* (London), August 11, 1986.

———. Interview. "A Conversation with Desmond Tutu." *St. Louis Post Dispatch*, July 25, 1993.

———. Interview. "Racism: We Need a Prophet." James S. Murray interview, *The Australian*, May 10, 1984.

———. Interview: Michael Schluter. "A Passion for Justice." *Third Way* 17, no. 4 (May 1994).

———. "Into a Glorious Future." *Sojourners*, February 1985.

———. "Introduction." *Icarus* 2, spring 1991.

———. "Introduction." *Marx-Money-Christ: An Illustrated Introduction into Capitalism, Marxism and African Socialism — Examined in the Light of the Gospel*, edited by O. Himer. Gweru, Zimbabwe: Mambo Press, 1982.

———. "Introduction." *We Are Anglicans: An Introduction to the Church of the Province of Southern Africa*, edited by Michael McCoy. Marshalltown: CPSA, 1993.

———. "It Has Happened at Last." *The Guardian* (London). Endpiece for book to mark election and end of apartheid.

———. "The Jesus I Love." In *Star Sun*, August 20, 1992.

———. "Lament from Africa." *Praying for Peace: Reflections on the Gulf Crisis*, edited by Michael Hare Duke. London: Fount Paperbacks, 1991.

———. Letter of March 8, 1982, to Helen Muller in response to teaching "The Old Testament" at the Academy for Christian Living.

———. Letter. Handwritten draft of letter to the Rev. Canon Malusi Mpumlwana.

———. "Mass Action—for a Better Sense of Values." *NCW News*, January 1993.

———. "Mission in the 1990s." *International Bulletin of Missionary Research* 14, no. 1.

———. "Momentous Choice, without Us." *Los Angeles Times*, March 20, 1992.

———. "My Credo." *Living Philosophies: The Reflections of Some Eminent Men and Women of Our Time,* edited by Clifton Fadiman. New York: Doubleday, 1990.

———. "The New World Order." Paper in absentia, the International Foundation for Socio-Economic and Political Studies, Moscow Conference, July 14–15, 1992.

———. "On Behalf of Millions: A Sermon of Thanksgiving." *Sojourners,* February 1985.

———. "Opening Worship." In *The Road to Rustenburg: The Church Looking Forward to a New South Africa,* edited by Louw Alberts and Frank Chikane. Cape Town: Struik Christian Books, 1991.

———. "The Options Which Face South Africa: Real Political Power Sharing or a Bloodbath." In *Divided or United Power: Views on the New Constitutional Dispensation by Prominent South African Political Leaders,* edited by J. A. du Pisani. Johannesburg: Lex Patria Publishers, 1986.

———. "Pastoral Letter to Anglicans in South Africa." Lent 1994.

———. "Persecution of Christians under Apartheid." In *Martyrdom Today,* edited by Johannes-Baptist Metz and Edward Schillebeeck. Edinburgh: T. & T. Clark and New York: The Seabury Press, 1983.

———. "The Plight of the Resettled and Other Rural Poor: The Stand of the Church." In *Up Against the Fences: Poverty, Passes, and Privilege in South Africa,* edited by Hermann Giliomee and Lawrence Schlemmer. Cape Town: David Philip, 1985.

———. "PostScript: To Be Human Is to Be Free." In *Christianity and Democracy in Global Context,* edited by John Witte Jr. Boulder, Colo.: Westview Press, 1993.

———. "Press Statement—for Khotso." November 26, 1981.

———. "Preface." Booklet in support of a Global Peace Service, published by the Swedish Ecumenical Council, August 30, 1991.

———. "Preface." In *Festo Kivengere: A Biography,* by Anne Coomes. Eastbourne, E. Sussex, U.K.: Monarch Publications, 1990.

————. *The Rainbow People of God: The Making of a Peaceful Revolution*, edited by John Allen. New York: Doubleday, 1994.

————. *The Rainbow People of God: The Ministry of Desmond Tutu as Anglican Archbishop of Cape Town.* First Manuscript: Speeches, sermons, writings, off-the-cuff remarks, and interviews reflecting South Africa's path from the depths of oppression to the euphoria and confusion of transition. Draft of John Allen, ed. *The Rainbow People of God.*

————. "The Religious Understanding of Peace." First Desmond Tutu Peace Lecture by Bishop Desmond Tutu. Krugersdorp: WCRP-SA, 1985.

————. "Reply, November 7, 1991, to Publication Request." Manuscript draft for *Fondest Hopes/Deepest Concerns: Lessons from the 20th Century*, edited by Neal Sperling.

————. "Review of James Cone's *God of the Oppressed.*" *Journal of Theology for Southern Africa*, no. 31 (June 1980).

————. "Review of *The Prayers of African Religion*, by J. Mbiti." *Journal of Theology for Southern Africa* 17, 1976.

————. "Review of Rex Brico, *Taizé, Brother Roger and His Community.*" *Journal of Theology for Southern Africa*, no. 36 (September 1980).

————. "Review of *Black Theology: A Documentary History, 1966–1979.* Wilmore and Cone, eds." *Journal of Theology for Southern Africa*, no. 46 (March 1984).

————. "Sanctions vs. Apartheid." *New York Times*, June 16, 1986. Adapted from commencement address at Hunter College, New York.

————. Selected prayers. In *Prayers for Peace: An Anthology of Readings and Prayers*, compiled by Archbishop Robert Runcie and Cardinal Basil Hume. London: SPCK, 1987.

————. Selected prayers. In *Prayers, Praises, and Thanksgivings*, compiled by Sandol Stoddard. New York: Dial Books, 1992.

————. Selected quotes. In *Freedom Is Coming: Songs of Protest and Praise from South Africa.* Uppsala: Utryk, 1984.

————. Selected quotes. In *The Meaning of Life: Reflections in Words and Pictures on Why We Are Here*, edited by David Friend. Chicago: Time Inc. Magazine, 1991.

———. Selected quotes. In *The Words of Peace: Selections from the Speeches of the Winners of the Nobel Peace Prize*, edited by Irwin Abrams. New York: Newmarket Press, 1990.

———. Selected quotes. In *Tips from the Top: Wise and Witty Words from Well-Known South African Personalities*, compiled by Oliver M. Souchan. Cape Town: Don Nelson, 1988.

———. Selected quotes. "Vision of the Future: An Anthology of Writings and Speeches by Nelson Mandela, Winnie Mandela, Allan Boesak, Desmond Tutu." *Third World Quarterly* 9, no. 2 (April 1987).

———. "Some Memories of My Life." June 28, 1990, draft to be published in King's College London's *In Touch Magazine* featuring famous alumni.

———. "South Africa—A World Apart: An Urgent Message from Bishop Desmond Tutu to Presbyterian Women." *Concern*, October 1984.

———. "The South African Elections." *Der Zeit*, May 1, 1994.

———. "South African Violence: Ours Are Birthing Pains—Tutu." *Daily Nation* (Nairobi), October 9, 1993, 16.

———. "Some African Insights and the Old Testament." In *Relevant Theology for Africa: Report on a Consultation of the Missiological Institute at Lutheran Theological College*, Mapumulo, Natal, September 12–21, 1972, edited by Hans-Jurgen Becken. Durban: Lutheran Publishing House, 1973.

———. "South African Insights and the Old Testament." *Journal of Theology for Southern Africa* 1 (December 1972).

———. "South Africa's Blacks: Aliens in Their Own Land." *Christianity and Crisis*, November 26, 1984.

———. "The State of South Africa." *Monitor: The Journal of the Human Rights Trust*, June 1991.

———. "Spirituality: Christian and African." In *Resistance and Hope: South African Essays in Honour of Beyers Naudé*, edited by Charles Villa-Vicencio and John de Gruchy. Cape Town: David Philip, 1985.

———. "The State of South Africa." *Africa Forum* 2, no 1 (1992).

———. "Stop the Rot Everybody." *City Press*, March 14, 1993.

———. "Tearing People Apart." *South African Outlook*, October 1980.

———. "The Theologian and the Gospel of Freedom." In *The Trial of Faith: Theology and the Church Today*, edited by Peter Eaton. West Essex: Churchman Publishers, 1988.

———. "The Theology of Liberation in Africa." In *African Theology en Route*, edited by Kofi Appiah-Kubi and Sergio Torres. Pan African Conference of Third World Theologians, Accra, Ghana. Maryknoll, N.Y.: Orbis Books, 1979.

———. "This Is Now My Country." *The Argus*, May 3, 1994.

———. "Towards Post-Apartheid South Africa." In *Religion and Politics in Southern Africa*, by Carl Fredrik Hallencreutz and Mai Palmberg. Uppsala: The Scandinavian Institute of African Studies, Seminar Proceedings no. 24, 1991.

———. "The United States and South Africa: Human Rights and American Policy." *Columbia Human Rights Law Review* 17, no. 1 (fall 1985).

———. "Viability." In *Relevant Theology for Africa: Report on a Consultation of the Missiological Institute at Lutheran Theological College, Mapumulo, Natal, September 12–21, 1972*, edited by Hans-Jurgen Becken. Durban: Lutheran Publishing House, 1973.

———. "A View from South Africa." In *Robert Runcie: A Portrait by his Friends*, edited by David L. Edwards. London: Fount Paperbacks, 1990.

———. "Violent Storm Will Lead to Calm." *Cape Times*, September 2, 1993.

———. "The WCC's Major Contributions—a Testimony." *Commemorating Amsterdam 1948: 40 Years of the World Council of Churches*. Geneva: WCC, 1988.

———. "Welcome and Introduction." Draft for WCC Central Committee Meeting in Johannesburg. *International Review of Mission*, January 1994.

———. "Whither African Theology?" In *Christianity in Independent Africa*, by Ed'oward Fasholé-Luke et al. London: Rex Collings, 1978.

———. "Whither Theological Education? An African Perspective." *Theological Education* (South Africa), summer 1973.

———. *The Words of Desmond Tutu*. Selected by Naomi Tutu, New York: Newmarket Press, 1989.

Tutu, Desmond, with Bishop Charles Albertyn, Bishop Geoffrey Quinlan, Bishop Edward Mackenzie and Bishop Merwyn Castle.

"The Christian and the X (flier)." Cape Town: Diocesan Organisers for Voters Education (DOVE), 1993.

"Tutu Arranges Watershed Talks." *The Argus*, 6-7-93.

"Tutu Condemns 'Racist Tactics.'" *Cape Times*, April 18, 1994.

"Tutu Pleads for Calm in Face of Attacks by 'Ghastly' Men." *The Argus*, April 25, 1994.

"Tutu: A Mandate from God." *Tribute*, September 1988.

"Tutu, Mandela Clash over Parliament's Pay." *News & Observer*, September 28, 1994.

"Tutu Says Local Press Is White-Oriented." *Weekend Argus*, May 8 / 9, 1993.

"Tutu Warns 'Political' Priests." *Cape Times*, April 14, 1994.

Villa-Vicencio, Charles. "The Church in Africa: Interview with Archbishop Desmond Tutu." *Challenge: Church and People*, no. 12, February 1993.

―――. *Civil Disobedience and Beyond*. Grand Rapids, Mich.: Eerdmans, 1990.

―――, ed. *The Spirit of Hope: Conversations on Politics, Religion, and Values*.

―――. *Trapped in Apartheid: A Socio-Theological History of the English-Speaking Churches*. Maryknoll, N.Y.: Orbis Books, 1988.

―――, ed. *The Theology of Violence: The South African Debate*. Johannesburg: Skotaville Press, 1987.

Villa-Vicencio, Charles, et al. *Doing Theology in Context, Doing Ethics in Context*. Maryknoll, N.Y.: Orbis Books, n.d.

―――. *When Prayer Makes News*. Philadelphia: Westminster, 1986.

Vorster, Farmer Schalk. Interview. "I'm So Scared I Have to Sleep with the Maid." *The Argus*, March 24, 1994.

Vorster, W. S., ed. *Church Unity and Diversity in the Southern African Context*. Pretoria: University of South Africa, 1979.

"Voters Go for Tutu in Survey." *Evening Post* (South Africa), November 26, 1993.

Wainwright, Geoffrey. *Dictionary of the Ecumenical Movement*. Grand Rapids, Mich.: Eerdmans, 1991.

―――. *Doxology: A Systematic Theology*. New York: Oxford University Press, 1980.

———. "Reconciliation in Ministry." *Ecumenical Perspectives on Baptism, Eucharist, and Ministry,* edited by Max Thurian. Faith and Order Paper 116, Geneva: World Council of Churches, 1983.

Wainwright, Geoffrey, et al. *The Study of Liturgy.* New York: Oxford University Press, 1978.

Walshe, Peter. *Church versus State in South Africa.* New York: Orbis, 1983.

———. "The Evolution of Liberation Theology in South Africa." *The Journal of Law and Religion* 5, no. 2 (1987).

———.*The Rise of African Nationalism in South Africa: The African National Congress, 1912–1952.* Berkeley and Los Angeles: University of California Press, 1971.

War and Conscience in South Africa: The Churches and Conscientious Objection. London: Catholic Institute for International Relations and Pax Christi, 1982.

Weil, Simone. *Gravity and Grace.* New York: Putnam, 1952.

———. *The Need for Roots.* Boston: Beacon Press, 1952.

———. "Reflections on the Right Use of School Studies with a View to the Love of God." In *Simone Weil Reader,* edited by George A. Panichas. Mt. Kisco, N.Y.: Moyer Bell Ltd., 1977.

———. *Waiting on God.* London: Routledge & Kegan Paul, 1979.

West, Cornel. *Keeping Faith: Philosophy and Race in America.* New York: Routledge, 1994.

———. *Prophesy Deliverance! An Afro-American Revolutionary Christianity.* Philadelphia: Westminster Press, 1982.

Wiles, Maurice. "Theology and Unity." In *Theology* 77, no. 643 (January 1974).

Wilkinson, Alan. *The Community of the Resurrection: A Centenary History.* London: SCM Press, 1992.

Williams, Harry. *The True Wilderness.* Harrisburg, Pa.: Morehouse, 1994.

Williams, Rowan. *The Wound of Knowledge: Christian Spirituality from the New Testament to St. John of the Cross.* Boston: Cowley, 1991.

———. "Nobody Knows Who I Am till the Judgement Morning." In *Trevor Huddleston: Essays on His Life and Work,* edited by Deborah Duncan Honoré. Oxford: Oxford University Press, 1988.

Wilson, Francis, and Mamphela Ramphele. *Uprooting Poverty: The South African Challenge.* Cape Town: David Philip, 1989.

Wink, Walter. *Jesus' Third Way*. Philadelphia: New Society Publishers, 1987.

Winner, David. *Desmond Tutu: Brave and Eloquent Archbishop Struggling against Apartheid in South Africa*. Dublin: Wolfhound Press, 1989.

———. *People Who Have Helped the World: Desmond Tutu*. New York: Morehouse-Barlow, 1989.

Wiredu, K. "Philosophy and Our Culture." Proceedings of the Ghana Academy of Arts and Sciences, 1977.

Wirgman, A. Theodore. *The History of the English Church and People in South Africa*. London: Longmans, Green & Co., 1985.

Worden, Nigel. *Slavery in Dutch South Africa*. Cambridge: Cambridge University Press, 1985.

Worsnip, Michael. *Between the Two Fires: The Anglican Church and Apartheid 1948–1957*. Pietermaritzburg: University of Natal Press, 1991.

Yoder, John Howard. *The Politics of Jesus*. Grand Rapids, Mich.: Eerdmans, 1972.

SO WHAT'S IT TO BE

A Cottage or a Raft?

*R*UDI USED TO tell a story which sums up the choice we all have in life; the story is about a cottage and a raft. It goes something like this: A woman—or man—came to the edge of a wide, vast river and realized that she had just enough material to build one of two things: a cottage in which to settle down or a raft from which to explore new worlds. It was pouring rain at the river's edge, and there was the immediate temptation to build a shelter and stay put. But beyond the storm of the river lay a distant horizon with a small line of unbroken light beneath the gray-black clouds.

The story has no definite end. So the question we all have to ask ourselves is: In life, is our goal to build a cottage or a raft? When we come to the river's edge, what's it to be—a cottage to stay snug in or a raft to take us to that unbroken line of light?

The choice is ours—and ours alone—to make.

Building the raft—transcending the waters of diversity to find the unbroken line of light, the light of ultimate Truth, which lies in the heart of each of us—is not an easy thing. For me, though, the prospect of living a life dragged around by desire has been so unappealing, I've done what it took to transcend the waters of diversity, to build the raft and use it well. But it really is up to each of us to choose what we will do.

Whether we build a cottage or a raft, the most important thing is not to deceive ourselves about the nature of what we're doing and to try, in either endeavor, to be the most productive people we can be. If we choose "doing" over "being," then we must "do" with as much integrity, grace, and good will as we can muster every moment of every single day, and "do" with our newfound recognition that any "other" person talking to us is much more "us" than we ever would have guessed before.

Having a seed planted in us and cultivating that seed to harvest are two different things. If we're serious about the harvest, then we have to stop every single day and become completely quiet, empty ourselves of everything we think we know and everything we think we're doing, and look carefully at the essence of the work we're doing. We need to let it explain itself to us more clearly, and we need to be a little skeptical of ourselves in the process. We need to ask ourselves again and again, "Am I doing what I say I'm doing? Am I really reaching for and connecting to and expressing the deepest and finest part of me?"

If our goal is to cross over the ocean of diversity, we will have to be intensely focused, completely empty of our self, totally surrendered and dedicated to that Power within us from which every goal arises and into which every goal subsides. When we have emptied ourselves of our self, which is the same as emptying ourselves of our propaganda, a deeper place inside us has the opportunity to assert itself. Then the Truth, which is within all of us, has the chance to speak.

In closing this book, I would like you to remember above all that happiness is your birthright. Remember that whatever state you are in will give the flavor to your life. It is from your state that you determine how to look at your experiences, and most states taste like road apples. So the point of your meditation practice is to change your state and discover that, no matter what, you can be happy.

What you discover by practicing being-happy-no-matter-what is that happiness has a profound effect on the effects of your actions and words and the feedback you get. So by being happy-no-matter-what, your life is transformed into a life you can really be happy about. Happiness breeds happiness breeds happiness. The real treasure is within you.

There is nothing you can have, nothing you can get, nothing more valuable than what you already have and who you already are.

All stages of activity are transitory. All stages are an effect of Vital Force. To reach within yourself, beyond all the effects to that fundamental source of Life Itself, allows you to find true happiness and be completely fulfilled irrespective of your material circumstances.

There is no external form that is the form for you to be;
the form for you to be is purely an internal form—the
form of total realization—and the internal form simply is
that you are completely your Self, that you are your deep-
est and purest Self, celebrating gain and loss, health and
sickness, aloneness and togetherness, celebrating all the
appearance of positive and negative everything, the same—
celebrating it all as the forms of the form of God.

Stabilize your mind in the fluctuation, the pulsation of Vital Force and its unfoldment as the essence of your Life's experience. Then you will understand completely: Everything is in God's hands, and you needn't worry. In all life, there are some fine moments and some lesser moments. Cultivate the capacity to connect to and sustain the finest within you.

Nobody gets only happy alternatives. "Good" has to do with your inner state, not with external circumstances. You create a good life by living from a happy state within yourself. You create an unpleasant life by being consumed by your suffering. You decide for yourself and I decide for myself. And on a daily basis. You may not choose your circumstances, but you can choose the quality of your life. You can choose consciously to cultivate openness and flow and calmness and virtue for yourself. You can cultivate within yourself the power to manifest a good life.

When events become exciting, don't get too excited. When things are depressing, don't get too depressed. Keep yourself on an even keel every day and recognize that some days, some months, some years are more compelling than others. And some days, some months, some years are just like marching through mud. Don't feel bummed out about marching through mud. And don't get too exhilarated when you experience an inner airlift. Because you *will* hit the mud again; that just is life, with a little "l."

We are earthbound here; our bodies are made of mud, and our feet are generally buried in it. This is our position in the world: We are infantry. But here is the wonderful thing: We can slog through the mud with love; we can slog through it with care; we can slog through it with genuine compassion and consideration for the people around us. We can slog through it having as much fun as possible within our Self and making an effort to stay cheerful. And then we can slog through it making an effort to cheer up those around us, making it as much fun as possible for them, too. This marks a person of real substance.

Be as deeply open and a part of this moment as you possibly can be, and when the next moment comes, meet it. It's only when you are in this moment that you begin to experience the transition from moment to moment, and after awhile, to know the future because you understand how everything unfolds, how one moment becomes another moment becomes another moment—and how it is all actually the same moment.

If we're honest with ourselves, we know that we don't really care what's going to happen tomorrow or the next day or the next day—we just want to know if we're going to like it. And the truth is, the only reason we ever like anything is because we choose to, because we reach inside and participate. Yes, it's easier to like some things more than others, but we've all had the experience of coming to like someone or something we previously didn't because we came to see them or it in a new light. So then like and dislike and issues generated from superficial chemistry are an illusion, and the reality is that we like because we choose to.

> *Our lives*—your *life becomes a temple of that which is sacred when you choose to live with love in this moment. You make your life sacred when you open yourself up and allow, create, an environment in which Spirit can exist and become powerful and strong in you. And then the reason you sit, the reason you meditate every day, is first to find the Spirit, the love in you that you live from every day, and then to find the love in every moment of every day.*

When you start struggling, breathe. The tensions with which you're wrestling are energy, too; just circulate it. Be as quiet as possible. Don't open your mouth too much at these points. Remember, expanding awareness has nothing to do with thought and everything to do with stillness. It is in stillness that you become aware; it is at the stillpoint at the top of the pendulum—it is in living from the still-point inside you—that you find peace. Trust it and wait, and as you are quiet, that place where you are waiting suddenly becomes filled with awareness. But you have to dump who you think you are, what you think you need, your fears, and your desires. In that stillness, old patterns, tensions, ego, fear, will assert themselves first, but if you stay quiet, they will dissolve.

The more love grows in you, the more you will see Vital Force as It is. You will see through all the forms of manifestation of Vital Force into the very ocean of love, and you will be at peace. Then it is love that will make the choices, it is love that will shine out from within you and light your way through this very confusing and chaotic world to a continual experience of total well-being, which you can live from within your Self and share with all the lives that your Life touches.

And in your endeavor, I sincerely wish you well.

ABOUT RUDRA PRESS

Rudra Press strives to publish the finest books, audios, and videos on health and healing, yoga, and self-mastery. Practical and powerful, our products are designed to support you in your quest for personal growth as you discover greater balance, harmony, and happiness.

ALSO FROM RUDRA PRESS

BOOKS

WILL I BE THE HERO OF MY OWN LIFE?
Swami Chetanananda
This book explores the process by which the hero in each of us is born. Although this journey may take you into the darkest places of your mind and force you to confront your deepest fears, it also promises the possibility of profound freedom and a life lived in the spirit of creativity, integration, and happiness.
$14.95 ★ 184 pages ★ 0-915801-38-8

THE BREATH OF GOD
Swami Chetanananda
A collection of essays penetrating to the core of a spiritual quest. These words offer powerful insights that deepen our experience, expression, and appreciation for what our life is today, right now. The author believes that our wish to grow propels us toward our highest creative potential and that spiritual fulfillment is expressed in the fabric of our everyday lives.
$15.95 ★ 310 pages ★ 0-915801-05-1

NITYANANDA: IN DIVINE PRESENCE
M.U. Hatengdi and Swami Chetanananda
Fascinating eyewitness stories and rare photographs offer an intimate portrait of the life and teachings of this Indian saint. Who was this man who millions around the world consider to be one of the greatest saints of this century? Previously titled *Nityananda: The Divine Presence.*
$14.95 ★ 176 pages ★ 0-915801-76-0

RUDI IN HIS OWN WORDS
Swami Rudrananda
One of the most beloved spiritual teachers in the West, Rudi
was fiercely committed to living a spiritual life. In this book,
Rudi shows us how to transform the energy inherent in the
stresses and tensions of everyday life into the energy needed
for spiritual growth.
$14.95 ★ 197 pages ★ 0-915801-20-5

YOGA FOR YOUR LIFE
A Practice Manual of Breath and Movement for Every Body
Margaret D. Pierce and Martin G. Pierce
Richly illustrated with over 400 full-color photographs, this
practical book is designed for every body, regardless of fitness
level, body type, or familiarity with yoga. Offered inside are
innovative ways to bring yoga into your life: to wake up, prepare
for sleep, calm anxiety, focus your mind, even work up a sweat.
$20.00 ★ 160 pages, over 400 photographs ★ 0-915801-60-4

YOGA FOR BODY, BREATH, AND MIND
A Guide to Personal Reintegration
A. G. Mohan
In this clearly illustrated, comprehensive book the author
explains how to modify each of the 20 major yoga poses for
every body type. The building blocks of a yoga program are
reviewed: proper preparation, correct sequencing, balancing postures, inversion poses, breathing techniques, and meditation.
$16.95 ★ 219 pages ★ 0-915801-51-5

QI GONG FOR BEGINNERS
Eight Easy Movements for Vibrant Health
Stanley D. Wilson, Ph.D.
If you want to exercise but just can't find the time, this book
provides the perfect solution: eight simple yet powerful no-
impact stretching exercises that take only six minutes a day.
When practiced regularly, they are a proven method for better
health and increased longevity. In 1981, Dr. Wilson was diag-
nosed with lymphoma and was told he had five years to live. He
attributes this full recovery to his twice-daily qi gong practice.
$16.95 ★ 148 pages ★ 0-915801-75-2

THE NATURAL HEALING COOKBOOK
A Wellness Program for Optimal Health
Bessie Jo Tillman, M.D.
This treasure of a cookbook has two parts. The first is an easy-to-follow eight-week program for getting vibrantly healthy. The second is a collection of mouth-watering recipes. Designed to spark your creativity, this fun and motivating cookbook includes worksheets, charts, and over 300 scrumptious vegetarian and non-vegetarian recipes.
$14.95 ★ 261 pages ★ 0-915801-55-8

AUDIOS

MEDITATION
A Guided Practice for Every Day
Swami Chetanananda
Be guided into stillness with this exceptional program. Designed to support a daily meditation practice, the first side leads the listener into an experience of meditation. The second side contains a talk on the purpose and benefits of meditation and a discussion of what may be your most important choice: the choice to be happy. Packaged with a 24-page booklet to help you establish a meditation practice.
$12.95 ★ 90-minute audio tape ★ 0-915801-57-4

HEALING, IMAGERY & MUSIC
Pathways to the Inner Self
Carol A. Bush
This breakthrough book with companion CD introduces the Bonny Method of Guided Imagery (GIM), a holistic therapy which uses the harmonies and melodies of classical music to unlock stresses deeply embedded within our psyches.
$22.95 ★ 220-page paperback with 60-minute companion CD
0-915801-50-7

LILIAS FOLAN YOGA VIDEOS
Four tapes, sold individually or in sets of 2, 3, or 4
Reduce stress and tension regardless of your age, current level of physical fitness, or knowledge of yoga with these dynamic, easy-to-follow workouts led by ex-PBS-TV yoga expert Lilias Folan. For over 25 years Lilias has helped millions of people stretch, strengthen, and relax with yoga. With these four home-practice videos, she remains the exercise and yoga teacher of choice.
$19.95 each or less if purchased in sets
Each tape is 60 minutes • 0-915801-06-X, 0-915801-12-4, 0-915801-21-3, 0-915801-40-X

ORDER INFORMATION

For more information on Rudra Press products, to place an order, or to request a free catalog, please call toll-free
1-800-876-7798
or write to
Rudra Press, P.O. Box 13390, Portland, Oregon 97213